THE AGE OF I

Sweden 1719

CW00548192

THE AGE OF LIBERTY

Sweden 1719–1772

MICHAEL ROBERTS

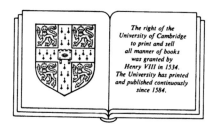

The right of the
University of Cambridge
to print and sell
all manner of books
was granted by
Henry VIII in 1534.
The University has printed
and published continuously
since 1584.

CAMBRIDGE UNIVERSITY PRESS

CAMBRIDGE

LONDON   NEW YORK   NEW ROCHELLE
MELBOURNE   SYDNEY

PUBLISHED BY THE PRESS SYNDICATE OF THE UNIVERSITY OF CAMBRIDGE
The Pitt Building, Trumpington Street, Cambridge, United Kingdom

CAMBRIDGE UNIVERSITY PRESS
The Edinburgh Building, Cambridge CB2 2RU, UK
40 West 20th Street, New York NY 10011–4211, USA
477 Williamstown Road, Port Melbourne, VIC 3207, Australia
Ruiz de Alarcón 13, 28014 Madrid, Spain
Dock House, The Waterfront, Cape Town 8001, South Africa

http://www.cambridge.org

First published 1986
First paperback edition 2002

A catalogue record for this book is available from the British Library

Library of Congress Cataloguing in Publication data
Roberts, Michael, 1908–
The age of liberty.
Bibliography: p.
Includes index.
1. Sweden – History – 1718–1814.   2. Sweden – Politics
and government – 1718–1772.   I. Title.
DL748.R63   1986   948.5'03   85-12745

ISBN 0 521 32092 5 hardback
ISBN 0 521 52707 4 paperback

for
Ian and Pepe

pro tanto quid

Contents

Preface

I acknowledge with gratitude two obligations incurred in regard to this book: first, to Margaret Shepherd and Renee Vroom, for their patience, care and expedition in typing it; and secondly to the editors of *L'età dei lumi: Studi storici sul Settecento europeo in onore di Franco Venturi* (Naples 1985), who graciously permitted me to borrow some paragraphs from my contribution to that *Festschrift*, for use in Chapter v.

Chapter ii is a revision and expansion of a James Ford Special Lecture, delivered in Oxford in 1973, and represents my second thoughts on some of the questions with which it is concerned.

Introduction

The Age of Liberty began and ended with a revolution. Neither movement was tumultuous or violent, and no Swedish blood was shed on either occasion. Nevertheless, each was a true revolution, for each effected a radical alteration in the political system. Historians have always been ready to perceive the revolutionary character of the *coup* of 19 August 1772, whereby Gustav III brought the Age of Liberty to a sudden end; but outside Sweden they have been less inclined to appreciate the true nature of the events of 1719–20. Yet those events resulted in shifts of power and constitutional changes so dramatic, so far-reaching, and so firmly maintained, that only another revolution could undo them.

For nearly forty years before 1718 Sweden had been an Absolutism: an Absolutism popular, and to some extent parliamentary, under Charles XI; unrestrained, ruthless, and at last odious, under his son. By 1718 the sufferings which a period of two decades of continuous war had brought with it had irretrievably alienated the Swedish people. Admiration of the king's heroic qualities and his personal virtues did indeed survive, and would never be extinguished, but the Absolutism, as a political system, was not merely discredited; it was hated. On that point, at least, there was unanimity. Whatever was to be done, and whoever was to do it, Sweden must be safeguarded against a repetition of that experience: this was basic to all the constitutional discussions that took place in the months after the king's death.

For Absolutism, apart altogether from the devastation for which it had been responsible,[1] was a type of government wholly alien to the traditions of Swedish history. In the Middle Ages monarchy had been elective: kings had been chosen under such conditions as the magnates might from time to time succeed in imposing upon a candidate; and Gustav Vasa himself had come to the throne in 1523 as an elected king. But in the course of the sixteenth century the monarchy had ceased to be purely elective: in 1544, by the so-called Succession Pact (*arvförening*) the Estates

---

[1] Ulrika Eleonora, in her Accession Charter of 1719, was made to declare that the Absolutism had 'damaged, diminished, mutilated and almost laid waste the land'; Axel Brusewitz, ed., *Frihetstidens Grundlagar och konstitutionella stadgar* (Stockholm 1916), p. 51.

I

had agreed that the Crown should be hereditary in the male line of the
Vasa family, or, to look at it in another way, they had extended their
election to all Gustav Vasa's male descendants. This decision could have
had the dangerous consequence of depriving the representatives of the
nation of their chance to impose conditions as the price of coronation, of
their right to 'take and break kings'; it could have equated hereditary
monarchy with unlimited monarchy. Though the high aristocracy,
traditionally the effective check upon the Crown, might insist upon the
essentially elective nature of the Succession Pact of 1544, Gustav Vasa's
successors contended that it had in fact been a free donation by a grateful
people, and that king might now succeed king without limitation of any
sort. But in the 1590s the accident that John III's successor, Sigismund,
was a Roman Catholic (and also King of Poland) offered an opportunity
to retrieve some of what had been given away in 1544. The device the Diet
hit upon was the Accession Charter (*konungaförsäkran*). In 1594 Sigismund was required to accept an Accession Charter as a precondition for
his coronation. No doubt the main concern of the Estates was to
safeguard Sweden from any attempt to undo the work of the Reformation; but for the great magnates of the Council of State it was a deliberate
effort to ensure that even though monarchy might now be hereditary, it
should not therefore be unlimited.

The precedent so established was faithfully followed. Every Swedish
king, from Sigismund to Gustav III, signed an Accession Charter before
he was crowned – with one single exception. That exception was Charles
XII, who upon his accession in 1697 neither gave one nor was asked to
give one, who swore no coronation oath, and who placed the crown on
his head with his own hands. It is true that after 1611, when the most
stringent Accession Charter of them all had been extorted from Gustav
Adolf, the Charters required of his three successors had tended to be less
restrictive; but even when the monarchy was most powerful and popular
men did not wholly lose sight of the elective principle. In 1633 Axel
Oxenstierna could write of Christina's being queen 'in virtue of the
unanimous *designation* of Council and Estates'; in 1634 his brother
remarked that 'the Estates have power to elect a king'; and as late as 1660
the Estate of Clergy, demanding the right to approve the great officers of
state during a minority, argued 'We have the power *eligendi Regem, quod
majus videtur*'.[2] The proceedings of Charles XII in 1697 were thus a violent
and deliberate breach of a constitutional custom, the visible sign that
henceforward the king would recognise no limitations of any sort, and
would be responsible only to God.

---

[2] *Axel Oxenstiernas skrifter och brevvexling* (Stockholm 1954) I. x. 12; *Svenska riksrådets protokoll*
IV (Stockholm 1886), p. 8; *Prästeståndets riksdagsprotokoll* II (Uppsala 1954), p. 93.

Throughout the sixteenth and much of the seventeenth centuries the function of law-bearer, watchdog of the constitution, custodian of the rights of the subject, was discharged by the high nobility, and especially by the Council of State. It had been so already in the fifteenth century, though then it had been mostly a question of protecting the interests of the great fief-holders; and it was so afterwards when the great fiefs had disappeared. Erik Sparre in the 1590s had maintained that the Council was an ephorate, in whom alone was vested the right of legal rebellion; Axel Oxenstierna in the 1630s declared that the Council were mediators between king and people, entrusted with the duty of holding a balance in the constitution. But the constitutional pretensions of the Council and the high aristocracy in the 1590s (and afterwards) had been based not only on the need to limit the Crown, but also – almost equally important – on the need for better governance and more effective administration than had been the case under the personal and paternal rule of the early Vasas, with their *ad hoc* devices and their tendency to rely on irresponsible low-born secretaries. The reforms which were needed came through piecemeal legislation in the time of Gustav Adolf, and achieved solidity in the Form of Government of 1634, which remained one of the basic documents of the constitution for many years to come. It set up a central government based on five *Collegia*, or Boards, each headed by one of the great officers of state;[3] it defined duties; it prescribed procedures; it fixed emoluments. Axel Oxenstierna, who was mainly responsible for its final drafting, thus fulfilled one of the aspirations of the aristocratic constitutionalists of the 1590s. And in 1660 it was supplemented by an *Additament* which modified or extended it in the light of experience, and in response to new developments.

Yet twenty years later the Council lost – and lost for ever – the ability to discharge the constitutional functions, or to exercise the authority, which they had enjoyed in Oxenstierna's day. And they lost it by reason of their participation, during Charles XI's minority, in the financial incompetence and irresponsibility of those who acted as Regents on his behalf, and by the flaccid discharge of their duties after he came of age. The 'retribution' (*räfst*) which, from 1680 onwards, Charles exacted of the former Regents, soon extended to the Council also. Their pretension to be mediators was explicitly rejected. Their right and duty to give advice, unsolicited, was repudiated. They ceased to be the Council of State: henceforward they would be the King's Council. Their participation in the work of government was curtailed; new, efficient, bureaucrats did much of the king's business, and were ennobled as a new aristocracy,

---

[3] The great officers of state were the High Steward, the Marshal, the Admiral, the Chancellor, and the Treasurer.

swamping the old historic families; and the transformation was accelerated by the economic ruin which overtook many of those families through the pitiless operations of Charles XI's *reduktion*.

By this time, however, the Council had long ceased to be the sole proponent of constitutional principles, or the only brake upon the actions of the king. Another champion of constitutionalism was already on the scene, in the shape of the Diet. The Diet, comprising the four Estates of Nobility, Clergy, Burghers and Peasants, had in the fifteenth century gradually attained sufficient consistency to be available as a political instrument to those who knew how to exploit it; and Sten Sture the younger had indeed exploited it in his struggle to break out of the Scandinavian Union which had been established in 1397. The example had not been lost on Gustav Vasa, who used the Diet with great skill to legitimate his plunder of the Church – and also, of course, to obtain the Succession Pact of 1544. Eric XIV, who followed him, enlisted its help against his personal and dynastic enemies. Charles IX found in it his most effective ally in his struggle against Sigismund, and in his usurpation of the throne. Gustav Adolf collaborated with it in order to spread the responsibility for his hazardous enterprises. Christina turned to it to defeat the Council's resistance to her installation of the future Charles X as her successor. And finally the Absolutism itself was – to begin with – essentially dependent upon the Diet's endorsement of Charles XI's drastic reforms and its acceptance of his constitutional principles.

But though for nearly two centuries the Diet had been the monarchy's ally, and at times its tool, that had not prevented it from putting forward constitutional claims of growing importance; and it had long had in its hands a potential restraint upon the Crown in virtue of its right to grant, or to withhold, new taxes, should the king find himself unable to live within his ordinary income. But after 1632 the Diet began to advance new pretensions. In 1634 the Estate of Nobility demanded that during the Regency for Christina the great officers of state be appointed with the Diet's agreement, and that they be responsible to it in the event of misconduct. In 1650 the three lower Estates, led by the Clergy and the Burghers, for the first time seized the parliamentary initiative. In 1660 the Diet secured acceptance of its position as the only body to make laws; in 1660 also it demanded triennial meetings. A development of far-reaching importance came in 1675, when Charles XI, disillusioned with the Regents who had governed for him since 1660, authorised the Estates to set up an investigating committee to examine their actions, and directed them to scrutinise the minutes of the Council and the *Collegia* in order to provide the evidence required. Here begins the method of securing ministerial responsibility to parliament which was to be a characteristic feature of the constitution during the Age of Liberty. And when the report of the committee in 1680 led to the Diet's being constrained by the king to undertake the prosecution and judgment of those whom the report pointed out as culprits, that too was an innovation which cast long shadows before.

These might seem to be notable advances; but the Estates soon found that their alliance with the king against the Regents and the Council, and their eagerness to endorse the Crown's resumption of lands alienated to the nobility, had in fact entailed the sacrifice of most of the gains they had made in the preceding half-century. The king did indeed take care to keep them informed; he levied no taxes without their consent; but their share in decision-making now depended upon his grace. Much of their law-making power passed into his hands; and when he needed the Diet's cooperation he increasingly turned, not to the Estates as a whole, but to their Secret Committee. The Secret Committee had first been set up in 1627, with the special object of dealing with delicate questions of foreign policy. At first all four Estates had been represented on it, but the participation of representatives of the Peasants became less frequent with the passage of time. In the 1680s so wide a variety of matters was referred to it that it became virtually a miniature Diet, and indeed the only element in the Diet with any spark of life left in it. It was therefore almost natural that when after 1718 a parliamentary régime was once more established the Secret Committee should from the very beginning have assumed to itself the functions of leadership at the expense of the rights of the *plena*, and of the Council also. But for the rest, the Estates in Charles XI's time acquiesced in the Absolutism almost without resistance: Charles XI, they thought, was the kind of ruler that the times required; Absolutism seemed for the moment the answer to Sweden's problems. They manifested their confidence in the king – and more specifically in his peaceable foreign policy – by authorising in advance the levying of additional taxes and the raising of necessary loans in the event of war: so in 1683, 1686, 1689; and in 1693, as a reward for Charles's success in contriving to live of his own in peacetime, they renewed this authorisation – but without limitation of time. This open-ended commitment proved disastrous; for it left Charles XII free to tax his subjects to the limit – or beyond it – during a war of twenty years. During the whole of his reign Charles XII never called the Estates together. And when in 1713 the Council, in despair, summoned them in order to give some sort of validity to their efforts to make peace, Charles from his Turkish exile peremptorily ordered them to disperse.

Thus the Estates, which had accepted the Absolutism with satisfaction, as giving them security for better governance, found themselves thrust aside and powerless, impotent spectators of the country's ruin. The position of the Council under Charles XII was no better: diminished in numbers, unable to influence the king, wishing but fearing to disobey his orders, they offered no very promising alternative government, if a chance bullet should put an end to Charles's career. The new efficient bureaucracy which Charles XI had built up, and over which he had presided as the arch-bureaucrat, had likewise been supplanted in the closing years of his son's reign by officials unknown to the constitution, responsible to the king alone, who overrode the law and violated private rights in obedience to his insistence that means must be found, at whatever cost, to carry on his campaigns. For the bureaucrats of the *Collegia*, and for their colleagues in the local government of the provinces, the situation had become intolerable; and they too looked forward to the moment when the country should cease to be governed by emergency measures and constrained to live in a siege-economy, and when the old official hierarchies, the old regularity and order (and the payment of their salaries) might be restored.

For all these elements – Council, Estates, bureaucrats, and victims of the Absolutism – the death of Charles XII offered a unique opportunity. It consisted in the simple fact that Charles left no heir. There were two possible claimants. One was the young Charles Frederick of Holstein, son of Charles XII's elder sister Hedvig Sophia; the other was Charles XII's younger sister Ulrika Eleonora, who in 1715 had married Frederick of Hesse-Cassel. By entering into this marriage she had doubly compromised her claim: first, because Frederick was a Calvinist; and secondly because the Diet of Norrköping in 1604 (and Charles XI's Testament also) had laid it down that in the event of failure of heirs male the throne should pass to the eldest daughter 'who was unprovided for' – and after 1715 Ulrika Eleonora was no longer in that situation. In 1713–14, before her marriage, she had been invited (without Charles's approval) to sit in the Council, and there had even been a suggestion that she should be made Regent. In December 1718 she still believed, with an obstinacy which was characteristic of her, that she was entitled to claim the throne by hereditary right. But she was mistaken. When Charles XII fell at Frederikshald the Crown once again became elective: the situation reverted to what it had been before 1544. And there was virtually no element in Swedish society that was not determined to extract the maximum advantage from this fortunate accident. Whoever succeeded Charles XII – for there were already Hessian and Holstein partisans – whatever the outcome of any struggles for power, one thing was certain: the new monarch would be a limited monarch.

The constitutional revolution was carried through very swiftly. Frederick of Hesse, apprehensive of the rival claims of the young Duke of Holstein, advised Ulrika Eleonora at once to renounce Absolutism and summon a Diet. That advice she had little option but to follow; for the officers of the army gave notice that they would swear no oath of allegiance to her unless she had been elected by the Estates. In January 1719 she formally renounced her supposed hereditary right; and the Diet, having declared *all* hereditary right to be extinguished, unanimously elected her queen. A month later she gave her Accession Charter and put her signature to the Constitution of 1719.

The Constitution of 1719 stood for no more than a year; and by 1720 it was found necessary to replace it. Ulrika Eleonora had signed it without troubling to read it; she never seems to have understood its terms and implications, which on occasion she violated; she was dilatory and stubborn in the conduct of business; and she strove to place her husband on the throne beside her, after the manner of William and Mary. For this proposal she found no support whatever. But it became clear that a situation in which Frederick, as consort, was becoming the irresponsible power behind the throne, could not be tolerated: much better if the queen would agree to step down in her husband's favour. To this she at last assented; and Frederick of Hesse, having conveniently discovered that he was at heart a Lutheran, gave what amounted to a preliminary Accession Charter, and was in March 1720 invited to take the Crown – an invitation which he lost no time in accepting.[4]

Though the men who were responsible for the revolution were united in their determination to end the Absolutism, in much else they were at odds with one another. The Council – and notably its leader, Arvid Horn – together with the high nobility and the representatives of the old families who had dominated affairs before 1660, hoped to restore the tradition of aristocratic constitutionalism as it had existed in the previous century, and dreamed of a return to the state of affairs established in the Form of Government of 1634: some of them hoped also for the restitution – at least in part – of the lands they had lost by Charles XI's *reduktion*. But the lesser nobility, who cared little about reversing the *reduktion* (of which, indeed, they had been the most eager supporters in the 1680s) and who had retained their hostility to the old Council-aristocracy which they had helped Charles XI to overthrow, had other views: it is significant that they called the Council-party 'Tories'. Massive ennoblement by Charles XI, and again by Ulrika Eleonora in her brief reign, had produced an Estate of Nobility in which great numbers had no landed estates of their own, but were dependent for their livelihood on the service of the Crown – for most of them in the army, but also in civilian office. The officers of the militia were settled on small farms which had been 'allotted' to them

---

[4] This was almost a return to 1544, for it gave the succession to Frederick's heirs male (or to Ulrika Eleonora if he died before her). The precedent was followed in 1743, on the election of Adolf Frederick as heir-apparent. But this in no way meant that the monarchy, now once again declared hereditary, was not strictly limited: the Constitution of 1720 bound it so tightly that the reversion to hereditary monarchy no longer mattered.

for their maintenance out of the noble lands which Charles XI had resumed
to the Crown, and the last thing they wanted was any interference with
the 'allotment-system' (*indelningsverk*) and the recovery of these lands by
their former owners. The nobility was becoming democratised; and one
sign of this was the abolition, in 1720, of the division of the Estate of
Nobility into three classes.[5] And for this numerous nobility, living in
modest circumstances, necessitated to carve out for themselves a niche
somewhere in the king's service, the matter and manner of appointments
and promotions was of vital importance. Hence the careful provisions in
the Constitution of 1720 which defined the rights of king, Council and
Collegia in the nomination to jobs. Nor was it surprising that the Nobility
in 1719 should seek to protect their position, or to improve it, by
extracting from the queen a grant of privileges more extensive than any
they had enjoyed before. But the three lower Estates were not prepared to
see the revolution accompanied by the reinforcement of what they
considered to be social injustice overdue for correction; and throughout
the years 1719–20 the debate on the constitution was complicated by a
strife of Estates which on occasion was very bitter. The privileges of 1719
were in fact never applied, and they were destined to be considerably
curtailed in 1723.

But the most important part in carrying through the revolution was
played by the bureaucracy, now renascent after its eclipse in the last years
of Charles XII. As in 1680 the bureaucrats had helped to make Charles XI
an absolute monarch, so now they were mainly instrumental in
transferring his sovereignty to the Estates. A main motive for their
attitude in 1680 had been a determination to put the monarchy on such a
financial footing that it would be enabled to pay their salaries punctually
and in full; and in 1719 they were equally determined to use the
opportunity to ensure that they be paid in good money, and not in a
devalued token currency. And in 1719–20 the bureaucrats dominated the
Diet, because they dominated the Secret Committee. Already at the Diet
of 1713–14 the Secret Committee had shown its readiness to encroach
upon what had hitherto been considered to be the concern of the Council;
and in 1719 it was perhaps the only element in the state which combined a
clear idea of what to do with the strength to do it. The Estates no doubt
remembered the constitutional advances they had made in the years
before 1680; but it was the Secret Committee which most resolutely
revived the parliamentary tradition. The Constitutions of 1719 and 1720
were drafted by committees on which they were strongly represented;
and it is significant that the Constitution of 1720 had not yet obtained the
approval of the *plena* at the time of Frederick's coronation, and was not

[5] The division into three classes had been established by the *Ordinance for the House of Nobility*
(1626). Class I comprised Counts and Barons; Class II, descendants of former members of the
Council; Class III the untitled nobility.

even submitted to the Council until after it had been signed by the king.

The revolution of 1719–20 thus resulted in the defeat of the old tradition of Council-constitutionalism, the ending of the Nobility's claim to be the historic guardian of liberties – and hence, by clear implication, of its claim to those privileges which had hitherto been considered to be its due in return for its discharge of that function. Power passed to the Estates, as the legitimate heirs of a rival tradition. The revolution was thus pregnant with social consequences: the democratisation of the Estate of Nobility, the revival of the claims of the three lower Estates to a greater measure of political equality. Those claims, fiercely asserted in the early 1720s, would revive with increased intensity in the decade before the revolution of 1772, and they would be a decisive factor in the double crisis which the *coup d'état* of Gustav III temporarily resolved.

It was not only in regard to Swedish domestic affairs that the death of Charles XII produced a revolution. It marked the transformation of a system of international politics that had remained, substantially unchanged though occasionally threatened, since the Peace of Westphalia in 1648. It was a system dominated by a handful of major powers, of which Sweden had been reckoned as one. At Westphalia Sweden had stood forth as the equal of France and the Emperor, one of the three *partes principales paciscentes*, and with them co-guarantor of the great settlement. Since 1631, with short intervals, she had been France's ally, and France had been Sweden's most faithful friend. Twice – in 1660, and again in 1679 – French diplomacy had been exerted to extricate Sweden from predicaments into which she had been led by unfortunate war. After 1660 there were indeed statesmen who began to feel that the status acquired at Westphalia was becoming too much for the country's limited resources to maintain. Charles XI himself was one of them: after 1680 he devoted his attention to conserving and improving those resources, and took care to refrain from any attempt to emulate the warlike achievements of his predecessors. But the exploits of Charles XII in the first decade of the next century had more than restored any recent loss of reputation, and at the climax of his career in the years around 1707 he blazed like some portentous comet in the European sky. But this brilliance had been dimmed by Pultava and Perevolotschna, and after his return from his Turkish exile in 1715 had been nearly extinguished. By this time, as a contemporary observed, 'a strange planet [ruled] in all the northern circles',[6] disturbing the old astronomy of Richelieu and Mazarin, Lionne and Torcy, shedding a baleful light and exercising an uncertain influence upon the European system, necessitating difficult adjustments to a wholly new situation. The strange planet was of course Russia. Hitherto Muscovy had been thought

---

[6] Lord Whitworth, quoted in Basil Williams, *Stanhope – A Study in Eighteenth-century War and Diplomacy* (Oxford 1932), p. 353.

of by most European statesmen as on the very periphery of their world, 'a distant glimmering star', an altogether minor element in their calculations. But now, as Chatham was later to remark, there was 'a great cloud of power in the North', a formidable expansive force. As yet they had formed no notion of how to harness that force; and therefore they must somehow strive to obstruct it. Peter the Great's armies had overrun Finland and the Baltic ports; his troops, to the consternation of all Europe, stood on German soil in Mecklenburg. Desperate adventurers, such as the Jacobites, or Alberoni in Spain, or Görtz in some of the twists and turns of his diplomacy, might be prepared to angle for Russian assistance; but the more cautious statesmen of the West were not prepared if they could help it to admit Russia as a participant in the intricate diplomatic game with which they were so familiar.

In 1719 it seemed to them obvious that the immediate victim of Russian expansion must be Sweden, and the question that confronted them was what they could do, what they were willing to do, what they could afford to do, to rescue Sweden somehow from the plight in which Charles had left her. But this was a problem which had many facets. Peter the Great was not the only predator at large. As the Swedish empire disintegrated, old enmities revived, and new ambitions developed from the opening of new opportunities for plunder. George I, as Elector of Hanover, saw his chance of acquiring Bremen and Verden. Frederick William of Prussia coveted Western Pomerania, which had been denied to Brandenburg in 1648. Frederick IV of Denmark aspired to undo the settlement of 1660, and to recover the southern provinces of Sweden which Denmark had then lost. It would not be easy to arrive at a general settlement of the North which conceded the minimum of satisfaction to these lesser vultures while denying its prey to the Russian eagle.

It was a piece of good fortune for Sweden that at this moment the two great powers of the West were in accord, bound together by the so-called Quadruple Alliance of 1718, and united in their determination to save what could be saved from the wreck that Charles XII had left behind him. But they differed as to what might safely be sacrificed, and what they must strive to retain or regain for their client. To Dubois it still seemed to be important that Sweden should retain a foothold in Germany, should still be a member of the *Reich*, for French statesmen were still influenced by their historic fear of the House of Habsburg, and therefore clung to that 'Eastern System' which was designed to maintain friends or clients – Sweden, Poland, the Turks – who would be available at need to threaten the Habsburgs with a war on two fronts, and so safeguard French influence in Germany. Stanhope, struggling in London or Herrenhausen with the ticklish task of balancing British against Hanoverian interests, looked at the question rather differently. He was prepared so far to satisfy George I as to support the idea of a Hanoverian acquisition of Bremen–Verden, but he would not willingly concede the lordship of the Baltic to the Tsar in order to save Pomerania. England could not view without alarm the prospect of a situation in which Russia would have a virtual monopoly of the supply of hemp and pitch, masts and spars, which were essential to the British navy. British policy, therefore, as against French, was to try for the restitution to Sweden of Finland, Estonia and Livonia (an uncommonly optimistic programme); and to secure the support of Prussia, as a useful barrier against Russian meddling in central Europe, by persuading the Swedes to sacrifice Stettin. And just as it would not suit British interests to have Russia in total control of the Baltic, so neither would it suit them to allow Denmark once more to straddle the Sound, and in an emergency perhaps to close it to British shipping, as had happened in 1652.

Both England and France were in 1719 represented in Stockholm by bold and able ministers who worked well together; and the pressure exerted by the devastations of Russian landing-parties on the Swedish east coast supplied them with a leverage which made their task less difficult than would otherwise have been the case. It proved possible to reconcile the British and French views of what ought to be done; and thanks above all to the exertions of Carteret, the British minister, the programmes of each were in fact realised – up to a point. In July 1719 Carteret persuaded the Swedes to agree to the cession of Bremen–Verden to Hanover; in August he renewed the Anglo-Swedish alliance of 1700, with a secret article pledging Sweden to hand over Stettin, Usedom and Wollin to Prussia – a pledge which was implemented by the Swedish–Prussian peace of January 1720. In return he promised subsidies which were essential if Swedish resistance was to be carried on at all; and he ordered up Admiral Norris from the Sound to cooperate with the Swedish fleet. It remained only to deal with Denmark and Russia. As to Denmark, England and France were at one in refusing to countenance the transference to Denmark of Wismar, or of the areas in Pomerania occupied by Frederick IV's troops; and England was inflexibly opposed to any Danish gains in Sweden itself. Carteret therefore undertook to mediate; and having extorted Sweden's abandonment of that exemption from the Sound Dues which had been her privilege since 1645, he carried it with a high hand in Copenhagen. In return for an indemnity Frederick IV renounced all his conquests except 'royal' Holstein, and France and England guaranteed his possession of Slesvig.

The problem of a settlement with Russia had still to be tackled, and the activities of Russian raiding-parties – who on one occasion reached the outskirts of Stockholm – made it a problem of the utmost urgency. It was in these circumstances that Frederick of Hesse, in conjunction with Carteret and Campredon, launched the idea of a great concert of powers which should by joint military and naval action force Russia to make concessions in the Baltic. It was to comprise England-Hanover, Prussia, Poland, and if all went well the Emperor, and was to be financed by heavy French subsidies. In the mind of Frederick I, it was conceived of as a Grand Alliance comparable to that which had brought Louis XIV to reason: Frederick, after all, had had a distinguished military career in the service of that cause. It may be doubted whether even under the most favourable auspices such a coalition, if it had been formed, would have long held together, or would have had much chance of success; but as it happened such prospects as it may have had were blighted by the domestic troubles of the two major powers that were behind it. For France, 1720 was the year of the collapse of Law's Mississippi scheme; for England, it was the year of the South Sea bubble. Few Englishmen felt any enthusiasm for fighting a war in the Baltic; few Frenchmen were disposed now to pay for one. The concert never got off the ground. And so the Swedes were left to themselves to make the best settlement they could with the Tsar. They had a strong feeling that the allies – and England in particular – had let them down. In return for the painful sacrifices which Carteret had cajoled them into making they felt that they had received virtually no assistance. They forgot that without the subsidies which France and England provided the government of the country would have been simply unable to carry on.

In 1721, therefore, Swedish and Russian negotiators met at Nystad to discuss terms. The Swedes were not only under overwhelming Russian naval and military pressure; they had also to face the possibility that the Tsar might support the claims of Charles Frederick of Holstein, and use the opportunity to install a Russian client on the Swedish throne. Their only real hope was that the Tsar was sufficiently anxious for peace to be more or less content with what he had got. And so it proved: by the terms of the peace of Nystad Sweden ceded to Russia Ingria, Estonia, Livonia; but she recovered (what she was certainly in no position to reconquer) all of Finland except Viborg and part of Karelia; she obtained the right to purchase 50,000 roubles' worth of grain from Russia each year, free of duty – a concession of real importance; she received two million *riksdalers* in cash, as compensation for her losses; and she obtained from the Tsar an undertaking that he would not interfere in Swedish domestic affairs, or disturb the order of succession, or permit the subversion of the Constitution of 1720.

The position in which Sweden now found herself was succinctly summed up by Carl Germund Cederhielm in a famous epigram:

> The glory of our age is dead and gone;
> We to our former nothingness are fated.
> King Charles is in his grave; King Frederick's consecrated;
> And Sweden's clock has moved from XII to I.[7]

The hands of the clock could certainly never be put back; but the clock, in spite of everything, was still going: it must be the task of the post-war generation to ensure that it continued to do so. They might luxuriate in the newly-won liberty which the Constitution of 1720 secured to them; but they could never forget that 'great cloud of power' which hung so menacingly over them. After 1721 it was an imperative task to contrive some system of foreign policy which might neutralise or deflect any thunderbolts which might in the future issue from it.

---

[7]   Vad i sin period den högsta punkten sett
    plär åter strax därpå sitt förra intet röna.
    Kung Karl vi nyss begrov, kung Fredrik vi nu kröna.
    Så har vårt svenska ur nu gått från tolv till ett.

MARSHALS OF THE DIET AND CHANCERY-PRESIDENTS

HATS AND CAPS

Marshals	Chancery-Presidents
1720 Arvid Horn	1720 Arvid Horn
1723 Sven Lagerberg	
1726–7 Arvid Horn	
1731 Arvid Horn	
1734 Charles Emil Lewenhaupt (H)	
1738–9 Carl Gustaf Tessin (H)	1739 Carl Gyllenborg (H)
1740–1 Charles Emil Lewenhaupt (H)	
1742–3 Matthias Alexander von Ungern-Sternberg (C)	1747 Carl Gustaf Tessin (H)
1746–7 Matthias Alexander von Ungern-Sternberg (C)	
1751–2 Henning Gyllenborg (H)	1752 Anders Johan v. Höpken (H)
1755–6 Axel von Fersen (H)	
1760–2 Axel von Fersen (H)	1761 Claes Ekeblad (H)
1765–6 Thure Gabriel Rudbeck (C)	1765 Carl Gustaf Löwenhielm (C)
1769–70 Axel von Fersen (H)	1768 Fredrik v. Friesendorff (C)
	1769 Claes Ekeblad (H)
1771–2 Axel Gabriel Leijonhufvud (H)	1772 Joachim von Düben (C)

Monarchs

Ulrika Eleonora	1719–20
Frederick I	1720–51
Adolf Frederick	1751–71
Gustav III	1771–92

I

The predicament of a minor power[1]

(i)

In 1721, after over twenty years of warfare, the peace of Nystad brought to Sweden surcease from misery and relief from a burden she could no longer bear. The imperial edifice which had been the work of the previous century had been dismantled; the Russian fleet dominated the Baltic; St Petersburg contradicted a century of Swedish policy. At home, Görtz's emergency measures had disrupted that established bureaucracy which had been the backbone of the state, and had substituted new authorities and new procedures for the old. New taxes, new devices, had conscripted the wealth of the country and subjected all classes to intolerable strains. The load of debt was so heavy that the state was really, if not formally, bankrupt. The king's armies were reduced to living at free quarters upon the countryside; the king's servants were either unpaid, or paid in the paper money and tokens with which Görtz had flooded the country in the last desperate months of the war. The drain of manpower had left the farmer with a shortage of hands. The casualties incurred in the war – or which arose from it as a result of plague and starvation – had been heavy; disproportionately so among members of the nobility, where by 1721 there were five women of marriageable age to three men.[2] Here and there it is possible to see fortunate groups who had done well out of the wars,[3] but still it is probably true to say that in 1721 Sweden was exhausted, prostrate, and without much hope of resurrection.

And when it was all over – when the last Russian galleys had returned

[1] Only two works cover Swedish foreign policy throughout this period. The more modern is Olof Jägerskiöld, *1721–1792*, which is volume II:2 of *Den svenska utrikespolitikens historia* (Stockholm 1956–9). The other is the classic work of Carl Gustaf Malmström, *Sveriges politiska historia från konung Karl XII:s död till statshvälfningen 1772*, I–VI (2nd edn Stockholm 1893–1901), which is very full on foreign policy. In their respective ways both are excellent.

[2] Sten Carlsson has calculated that some 15–20% of the total nobility served in the forces, and more than 1000 fell victims to the war: Sten Carlsson, ' "Många tappra drängar fått sitt banesår". Den svenska adelns personella förluster under stora nordiska kriget', in *Bland böcker och människor. Bok-och personhistoriska studier till Wilhelm Odelberg den 1 juli 1983* (Uddevalla 1983).

[3] See e.g., Kekke Stadin, *Småstäder, småborgare och stora samhällsförändringar. Borgarnas sociala struktur i Arboga, Enköping och Västervik* (Uppsala 1979), for some examples.

home to Kronstadt, and the Swedish prisoners of war at Tobolsk could begin to think of coming home too, when the veterans of Charles's armies transferred their energies to internal faction, *riksdag* debates, and the exploitation of the new constitution they had helped to give to the country, the picture remained sombre. Trade did indeed react feverishly to the end of hostilities, and Sweden was glad (for the moment) to welcome imported goods of which her people had long been deprived; Görtz's fiduciary currency was ruthlessly devalued; his administrative innovations were swept away; the old civil service bureaucracy resumed its place, and made sure for the future of its wages.[4] What nobody in 1721 could foresee was the astonishing resilience of the Swedish people, the vigorous demographic rebound from the losses of war, the recovery of old standards of living, which marked the two peaceful decades after Nystad. But none of this could alter the fact that the loss of the overseas provinces had reduced the standing revenue of the Crown by more than half; and it was a loss that could not easily be made good. However unpalatable it might be, the men of 1721 had to face the fact that their country had quite suddenly sunk from the status of a major power to being one of the weakest of European states.[5]

The psychological shock of this realisation was more serious, because more enduring, than the country's material exhaustion. Since 1648 Sweden had considered herself, and on the whole had been considered, as one of the great powers. In 1721 she found herself at the mercy of Russia – and even, perhaps, of Denmark – once the temporary and limited protection afforded by the interests of the western powers should be withdrawn. It was painful to make the mental adjustment required by this new situation: to many it was impossible. As the immediate post-war prostration lifted, as the immediate threat to security passed away, there remained a feeling of anger, of betrayal, of incredulity: the tradition of despising the Russians was of such long standing – and Narva, Klissow and Fraustadt had certainly not diminished it – that men could hardly bring themselves to believe that in fair fight one Swede could not beat five Russians any day. They could not accept the verdict of Nystad as final: given the opportunity, given a favourable international situation resolutely exploited, they fancied that the Baltic provinces could be recovered as easily as they had been lost. It must therefore be the natural aim of Swedish policy to prepare for – and, indeed, to contrive – what they were in the habit of referring to as 'conjunctures'.

[4] For this aspect of the transition see Werner Buchholz, *Staat und Ständegesellschaft in Schweden zur Zeit des Überganges vom Absolutismus zum Ständeparlamentarismus 1719–1720* Stockholm 1979).

[5] In 1769 Frederick the Great wrote that Sweden was 'the most disorganized and the weakest of all the European states': *Politisches Correspondenz Friedrichs des Grossen* (Berlin 1879–1939), XXVIII, 119.

But there were those who looked the truth in the face, and who, perceiving that there was no real prospect of a return to the great days of Gustav Adolf and Charles X, saw the best hope of retrieving Sweden's reputation, and even of attaining to a kind of greatness, in the development of their country's resources, material and human; in industrial progress, internal colonisation, and an expanding commerce; and, not least, through eminence in the arts, and above all in science. In this last regard the seeds had already been sown in the Age of Greatness; and here indeed the Age of Liberty would reap a rich harvest. More generally, the spirit of the age, with its widespread acceptance of 'utility' as a criterion, and its application of critical and 'scientific' approaches and techniques to matters which might have no direct relevance to science, produced an attitude which did something to temper the hankering for the old glories. Considerations of economic advantage, of social utility, offered an alternative to military ambitions, and the generally optimistic spirit of the century helped to make men disposed to look forward rather than to look back.

There were thus from the beginning two possible attitudes to Sweden's predicament: on the one hand, nostalgia for past splendours; on the other, the hope of greatness through the arts of peace. But they were far from being incompatible. It was typical of the age that they could, to a surprising extent, coexist in the same persons. The men who drove Arvid Horn from office in 1738, and who engineered the reckless attack on Russia in 1741, were also the vociferous promoters and champions of new industrial enterprises; the enthusiastic backers of the Swedish East India Company; the patrons of the arts; the lavish dispensers of premiums and rewards to deserving scholars and ingenious entrepreneurs. They had attacked Horn not only for compromising the chance of a war of revenge, but also for his alleged failure to give proper support to new manufactures. In the fifties prominent politicians such as Ulrik Scheffer and his brother could insist in the same breath – without any apparent sense of inconsistency – that the only road to security lay through expanding the country's wealth, but also that Sweden must seize any promising opportunity to recover her lost provinces by war.[6] Yet it may be conceded that it would have been too much to expect that a century of heroic memories, a foreign policy rooted in a long tradition, should be easily forgotten, or abandoned altogether: Arvid Horn himself, most prudent and realist of statesmen, looked forward to the recovery of the Baltic provinces – at some time in the future; though he differed from his impatient adversaries in thinking that that time had not yet arrived. And if

[6] Lars Trulsson, *Ulrik Scheffer som hattpolitiker. Studier i hattregimens politiska och diplomatiska historia* (Lund 1947), pp. 173–4, 177–8; Gunnar Carlquist, *Carl Fredrik Scheffer och Sveriges politiska förbindelser med Danmark åren 1752–65* (Lund 1920), p. 35.

the men of that age were always agonisingly tender of 'reputation', that was not wholly irrational either; for reputation (as Axel Oxenstierna and Cardinal Richelieu had both observed long ago) is a useful, and perhaps an indispensable, element in the conduct of a successful foreign policy.[7]

Nevertheless, Swedish statesmen after Nystad found themselves in a predicament which seemed to them to be new and strange. There had, indeed, been something like a precedent if they had cared to look for it: the Regents for Charles XI, from 1660 to 1672, had been confronted with a similar situation. But at that time the noonday sunlight of Charles X's spectacular victories was still bright enough for the reality of Sweden's weakness to be obscured; or, if perceived, to be seen as merely temporary and accidental. Whatever the true state of affairs after 1660, Magnus Gabriel de la Gardie and his colleagues had taken it for granted that Sweden was still a great power. No such comfortable obliquity was possible to Arvid Horn in the 1720s, when the smoke of Russian devastations, from Umeå to Norrköping, was still rank in men's nostrils. Horn and his successors had to frame their policies in terms which were unfamiliar to them, and within limitations which proved to be permanent. This was no easy task; and it is hardly surprising that at times it should have resulted in a tortuous diplomacy of apparently incompatible alliances.[8] Throughout the period they had to face two problems, and neither was ever really solved. One was the state of the finances; the other (which was a consequence of the former) was the state of the armed forces of the Crown.

(ii)

Swedish finances during the Age of Liberty were theoretically based on the budget of 1696, which provided for a fixed ordinary revenue. The loss of the Baltic provinces, however, had meant that it was now hopelessly inadequate to deal with the disastrous financial situation which Charles XII had left behind him: in 1718 expenditure was around twelve times the ordinary revenue.[9] At every meeting of the Estates thereafter it was necessary to ask for supplementary grants, and for one reason or another they were rarely adequate. Budgets were balanced, if they were balanced

---

[7] Compare A. J. von Höpken: 'A country which takes no care of its authority, its reputation, and its dignity can indeed have peace-treaties, but no security for trade or commerce': A. J. von Höpken, *Riksrådet Anders Johan von Höpkens skrifter* (Stockholm 1890), II, p. 105, and cf. II, pp. 37–8, 321.

[8] As C. G. Tessin wrote in May 1762: 'When one looks at all Sweden's different engagements to other European powers, one loses one's way in contradictions. Who is there who is capable of disentangling so many irreconcilable alliances?': [F. W. Ehrenheim], *Tessin och Tessiniana* (Stockholm 1819), p. 373.

[9] Expenditure for 1718, 34 700 000 silver *daler*; ordinary revenue 'less than half' the 6 886 000 laid down in 1696: Malmström, *Sveriges politiska historia*, I, 121.

at all, only with difficulty and often by borrowing from the Bank and by other undesirable devices. But in fact budget deficits were the rule, especially after 1741. In these precarious financial circumstances the best hope of avoiding either a deficit, or the unwelcome alternative of recourse to the Estates for increased taxes, seemed to lie in a subsidy from a foreign power. Sweden was not unique among the minor powers in this respect.[10] What perhaps marked her off from the others was the amount of support she seemed to require, and the very poor return that her supporters received upon their investment.

In the years immediately after 1721 the government would hardly have been able to meet the most urgent demands without the aid of French and English money. Thereafter subsidies in peacetime were thought of primarily as providing the means – which Sweden herself could not provide – for improving the armed forces: as preparations for war, in fact. After 1738 a succession of treaties with France gave Sweden subsidies – smaller in peacetime, larger in wartime – which continued until 1766; and French subsidies in peacetime came to be treated almost as a normal item of revenue, available for other purposes than those for which they had been bestowed. When they failed to turn up punctually the finances at once fell into serious disorder. As to subsidies in wartime, they were invariably inadequate. Swedish governments therefore proceeded upon the seventeenth-century assumption that war could be made to sustain war: *bellum se ipsum alet*. In 1758 Höpken said flatly that Sweden had never made war at her own expense, and had not the resources to do so;[11] and up to a point he was right. But *bellum se ipsum alet* was a maxim which the hasty improvisations and wretched generalship of 1741–3 put it out of their power to follow, and which in 1757–62 conflicted both with what was practicable and with common sense. It was precisely because the presupposition that war could sustain war proved to be a delusion that the amounts received in subsidy, however high they might screw their demands, however complaisant the subsidising power, fell short of what was needed to enable Sweden to give the military *quid pro quo* for which she had engaged.

The result of these expensive gambles – the Finnish war of 1741–3, the Pomeranian war of 1757–62 – was therefore a swollen national debt, and heavy deficits caused by the need to service it. It was the Finnish war that

---

[10] Frederick the Great once classified the states of Europe into three categories. In the first of these he placed England and France; in the second; all states more or less dependent upon one or other of the states in Class I; in the third he listed Sardinia, Denmark, Portugal, Poland and Sweden as all being incapable of carrying on a foreign policy without subsidies from another power; Gunnar Olsson, 'Fredrik den Store och Sveriges författning', *Scandia* xxviii (1961), p. 343.

[11] Höpken, *Riksrådet Anders Johan von Höpkens skrifter*, ii, p. 521. A century earlier Per Brahe had said exactly the same thing.

first tempted the government to those massive issues of paper money that fuelled the inflation of the late fifties and early sixties. Less than a third of the cost of the Pomeranian war was estimated to have come from subsidies, and not much more than a twentieth from contributions extorted from enemy territory. By 1762 the deficit was estimated at ten times what it had been in 1757; by the end of 1764 peacetime extravagance had piled up a debt almost as large as in 1720, with no means of paying the interest.[12] By that time the army was without weapons; no single regiment had common necessities; the fleet could be neither maintained, nor exercised, nor reinforced; the civil service was starving because its wages could not be paid; and the state was borrowing at 15%.[13]

Ulrik Scheffer once defined what Sweden really needed: an assured financial support from an ally, with no troublesome commitments in return.[14] This had been the ideal also of Magnus Gabriel de la Gardie in the 1660s, and it presupposed that the world owed Sweden a living.[15] At times it almost seemed as though the world acknowledged the obligation: as a member of the Alliance of Hanover, from 1727, Sweden's real commitments in return for the handsome subsidies paid by France and England were in fact negligible – as they also were for a few years in the early fifties when she was the pensioner of France. But unlike Denmark, which throve on subsidies paid to her to do nothing, Sweden could never long enjoy this enviable position. For in the diplomatic strategy of France, Sweden was cast for the 'active' power – in contradistinction to Denmark, which was to be the 'passive' power – and sooner or later she came under pressure to live up to that expectation. Not that much urging was required; for 'activity' implied the prosecution of plans of revenge upon Russia which men were sanguine enough to suppose would be at little or no cost to the country. It is true that after each of the wars in which Sweden was engaged there were fairly substantial increases in taxation; but the fact that they could be borne suggests that if governments had nerved themselves to levy them in peacetime they might have had some chance of escaping, or lessening, dependence upon foreign subsidies.[16]

[12] Malmström, *Sveriges politiska historia*, v, pp. 127, 145, 228, 251.
[13] Riksarkivet, Stockholm [RA], Sekreta propositionen. Inrikes. 1765: a highly-coloured account, designed to shock.
[14] Trulsson, *Ulrik Scheffer som hattpolitiker*, p. 174.
[15] The Danish statesman J. H. E. Bernstorff rationalised the relationship less invidiously: the payment of subsidies, he argued, was no more than equitable; they gave the subsidising power influence in the Baltic. And he feared that if once either of the Northern Courts accepted a treaty without subsidies, 'it will become a habit and a right': *Correspondance ministérielle du Comte J. H. E. Bernstorff* (Copenhagen 1882), II, 177–8.
[16] In 1766 the Caps, deprived of the hope of subsidies from either England or France, and finding drastic economies insufficient, increased taxation by a quarter of a million silver *daler*. Whereat Daniel Tilas sardonically commented: 'And that's all. We'll then be out of debt and entering the Golden Age. Hallelujah!': Daniel Tilas, *Anteckningar och brev från riksdagen 1765–1766*, ed. Olof Jägerskiöld (Stockholm 1974), p. 420.

Taxes, however – that is, new taxes – required the assent of the Estates, and governments shrank from summoning an extraordinary meeting of the Diet, and from the unpopularity of fresh taxation. Hence the Pomeranian war was fought without any new taxation at all; for the Diet was not summoned until it had been carried on for more than three years: the Council relied on the subsidies, on loans from the Bank and private persons, on a lottery, rather than face the prospect of presenting the Estates with the bill. The feeble performance of the Swedish forces in Pomerania was certainly not (as had been the case in the Finnish war) the result of bad generalship, nor (it seems) of the quality of the troops: it was a straight consequence of lack of money, which meant lack of the transport and equipment without which a successful offensive could not be undertaken. Successive commanders were either recalled for not attempting the impossible, or they resigned in despair; and the best of them – J. A. von Lantingshausen – twice saved the army by pledging his private fortune in order to supply essentials which a timid and unimaginative Council of State professed itself unable to furnish.[17] And as in wartime in 1760, so in peacetime in 1764, when once more the Council deferred calling an Extraordinary Diet until the financial situation had become plainly disastrous. Certainly they had no chance of breaking the chain of indebtedness and dependence by such methods as Charles XI had used after 1680. Charles XI had been able to liberate his country from the servitude of subsidies only thanks to the drastic expedient of the *reduktion*, and this was a once-for-all measure which could not be repeated (indeed, after 1720 the Crown was rather losing than gaining land); and his whole system had been based on good husbandry, careful accounting, and the renunciation of aggression – none of which made any appeal to the governments that controlled Swedish policy between 1738 and 1765. So subsidies became a determinant of foreign policy, and at times interfered with men's judgment about it. Perhaps it was not until 1766, when the hope of subsidies from either France or England was extinguished, that the conditions existed for a sober and rational appreciation of where Sweden's interest really lay.

The impact upon foreign policy of financial weakness was compounded by the military weakness which was its consequence, but which subsidies in peacetime had been designed to remove. That weakness was painfully revealed in the two wars in which Sweden engaged in this period, and even more humiliatingly in her inability to defend herself against a threatened Danish attack in 1743 without calling in a Russian army to rescue her. One might have supposed that any search for allies,

---

[17] There is a lengthy essay on von Lantingshausen, and especially on his part in the Pomeranian war, in Carl Gustaf Malmström, *Smärre skrifter rörande sjuttonhundratalets historia* (Stockholm 1889).

any solicitation of subsidies, was not made easier by the plain fact that Sweden had now become, militarily, a liability. That the search was as successful as it was is to be explained partly by the fact that she was regarded as a sort of international makeweight which must not in the existing delicate balance of forces be allowed to fall into the wrong scale; but almost as much by France's refusal for almost thirty years to face the truth about her ally's real military potential – or lack of it.

In Charles XI's time Sweden had been able (after 1680) to pursue her own line in international affairs, secure behind a well-trained native army carefully supplied with equipment, stores, and a precisely thought-out logistical system. Charles XI's national militia had been an army of soldiers maintained by being settled on the land; its degenerate successor in the eighteenth century was a collection of farmers with incidental military obligations which were seen as interfering with the business of wresting a living from the soil: in 1760 the army command was complaining bitterly that officers were being promoted on the basis of their success as farmers.[18] The regular training and periodic musters which had been the rule when the system was inaugurated in the 1680s diminished to the point at which it hardly became effective training at all.[19] One of A. J. von Höpken's arguments for embarking upon war was that 'It might well be a good thing to diminish attachment to their farms, to re-establish decayed discipline, to clear out from the army those who serve for peacetime and not for wartime . . . A long period of inaction is deleterious in Nature, and men are corrupted from the same cause.'[20] But it was not only inaction that subverted discipline: the 'Liberty' which Swedish politicians gloried in proved equally pernicious. A decade after Höpken, Anders Nordencrantz asked himself what discipline could be expected under a constitution,

where the subaltern can with impunity insult a field-marshal in the House of Nobility, and where on the other hand, a field-marshal often needs to cajole a subaltern to attach

[18] Malmström, Sveriges politiska historia, IV, p. 418 n. 2. And see Klingspor's comment (20 March 1762) in Sveriges ridderskaps och adels riksdagsprotokoll från och med år 1719 [SRARP], ed. Sten Landahl, XXIII (Stockholm 1955), p. 192.

[19] Malmström, Sveriges politiska historia, IV, p. 298. While Crown Prince, Adolf Frederick showed considerable insight into the defects of the army, and much energy in attempts to reform them; but those efforts necessarily ceased on his accession: the last thing the Diet wanted was a king with military experience and an admiration for Prussian methods: Birger Steckzén, 'Adolf Fredrik under kronprinstiden', Historisk tidskrift (1934), pp. 342–55. At the Diet of 1755–6 some reforms in this respect were determined on; but they can hardly have had much effect before the country was involved in war: Riksrådet och fältmarskalken m.m. Grefve Fredrik Axel von Fersens Historiska Skrifter, ed. R. M. Klinckowström, II (Stockholm 1866), p. 141.

[20] Höpken, Riksrådet Anders Johan von Höpkens skrifter II, p. 340. As he wrote, on another occasion: 'C'est un exercise continuel qui forme aujourd'hui d'excellents troupes, et comment y parvenir avec des gens qui doivent se nourrir du labourage?': ibid., I, p. 123.

himself to his party, and where in case of punishment for disobedience, revenge in a thousand forms can be practised at the Diet, and obtain backing in its exercise.[21]

The system as originally devised had had the great advantage that it provided a force of known size, immediately available, properly trained and easily mobilised. In the mid-eighteenth century none of this was true any longer. The native militia was not kept up to strength: during the Finnish war it appeared that there were 'vacancies' to the extent of 13.5% of its regular establishment.[22] With the passing of time, the rigidity and unalterability of the system became a disadvantage, for it took no account of changing circumstances or developments in the art of war: for instance, the ratio of cavalry to infantry in the militia was permanently fixed. Even supposing that no changes had been required, there was a disastrous decline from the standards which had obtained under Charles XI's unremitting personal supervision: the army he created would never have been called upon to march without shoes, stockings and trousers. There was now no supply-train, no properly organised commissariat. Nor was there much awareness of useful innovations: when during the Pomeranian war a commander complained that his men had no field-bakeries, he was informed that they were unknown in Swedish armies. The descendants of the Ancient Goths were expected to face climatic rigours and rotten rations with a Nordic hardiness which the armies of less fortunate lands could not be supposed to command. Even they, however, felt themselves disadvantaged when issued with bullets which were too large for their muskets.[23] The administrative machinery which might have rectified these deficiencies, or been capable of exerting pressure for reform, was either weak or lacking. The College of War, staffed mainly with bureaucrats, was not strong enough to stand against the amateur interferences of the Diet's committees, or to shift the inertia of the supply services. There was no member of the Council specifically responsible for military matters, though the constitution provided for a member with some acquaintance with naval affairs. Strategy, both in Finland and in Pomerania, was dictated by political considerations, and the directives of the Council or the Secret Committee might emanate from men with little or no military experience. Perhaps no commander could have made much of such conditions – though in the Pomeranian war Lantingshausen made a valiant attempt; but it unfortunately happened that commanders were

[21] Anders Nordencrantz, *Tankar om krig i gemen och Sveriges krig i synnerhet*, I–II (Stockholm 1767, 1772), I, pp. 76–77.
[22] Leif Dannert, *Svensk försvarspolitik 1743–1757 i dess utrikespolitiska sammanhang* (Uppsala 1943), p. 54.
[23] *Ibid.*, pp. 67–8; Höpken, *Riksrådet Anders Johan von Höpkens skrifter*, II, pp. 455, 537; Malmström, *Smärre skrifter*, pp. 282, 291, 293 etc.

too often either grossly incompetent – as Lewenhaupt, appointed by the Diet for political reasons, was in 1741–3 – or were incapable of controlling a highly politicised officer-class who put party considerations and private interest above patriotism and attention to duty, intrigued against their superiors, and did not hesitate to return to Stockholm for meetings of the Diet, in flat disobedience to orders. Few armies can have made a more disgraceful showing than the army of Finland in 1741–3; and though the record in Pomerania was better, the government's fear of a repetition of the Finnish fiasco had a disastrous effect upon morale.[24] In Nordencrantz's view (and he may well have been right) Sweden was simply incapable of fighting a modern war.[25]

This was far from being the opinion of those who launched the country into the Finnish and Pomeranian adventures. They had a sublime confidence in the traditions of Charles XII; they believed that the reputation of the Swedish soldier was enough to strike terror into their enemies. When in 1739 the Council of State sent 6000 men to Finland as a first move towards the war that they were planning, Carl Sparre considered that this might be enough to frighten the Russians into handing over Viborg, Ingria and St Petersburg; and his colleagues in the Council were much of his opinion.[26] Before war was declared in 1741 they formulated their peace-terms: in the event of victory (and who could doubt it?) the cession of all Sweden's former Baltic provinces, and all the country between Ladoga and the White Sea. And in the unlikely event of defeat their modest demand would be merely for Karelia and the Neva estuary, including St Petersburg and Kronstadt.[27] When they agreed to participate in the Seven Years War they stipulated as their reward the whole of Pomerania, as they had acquired it at Westphalia, and – Tobago.[28] In vain their French ally warned them to 'mesurer leur résolution plutôt au véritable état de leurs affaires qu'à leur zèle et à leur courage'.[29] It was left to A. J. von Höpken who – despite his shuffling attempt to evade it – had a fair share of moral responsibility for the Pomeranian war, to pronounce in his disillusionment the appropriate verdict, when he wrote that his countrymen apparently, 'believed that the land was ruled by King Gustav Adolf, the ministry and Chancery

[24] As appears from Höpken's nagging exhortations to his generals, culminating in the intolerably insulting letter which provoked G. D. Hamilton's resignation: Höpken, *Riksrådet Anders Johan von Höpkens skrifter*, II, pp. 522–4.

[25] Nordencrantz, *Tankar om Krig i Gemen och Sveriges Krig i synnerhet*, I, p. 76.

[26] Malmström *Sveriges politiska historia* II, pp. 368, 378.

[27] *Ibid.*, II, p. 429.

[28] *Ibid.*, IV, p. 288; on the curious ground that it had once belonged to the dukes of Courland and had been inherited by Adolf Frederick, though unfortunately the documentary evidence had been lost.

[29] Carlquist, *Carl Frederik Scheffer*, p. 166.

directed by Oxenstierna, and the armies commanded by Baner and Torstensson'.[30]

Until a considered policy was accepted in the 1750s, and work on Landskrona and the future Sveaborg was begun, neither the frontier with Denmark nor the frontier with Russia was provided with fortifications capable of seriously holding up an enemy; and both France and Prussia, when they became Sweden's allies, knew very well that Finland could not be defended, and were not prepared to waste their resources in defending it. Before the new fortifications in Finland made real progress Stockholm was in effect a frontier fortress, and her only defence against Russia was the navy. In the great days of the seventeenth century the navy had held the empire together and provided the shield of the metropolis. The disasters of the war of 1675–9, when Sweden lost almost all her capital ships and Pomerania was overrun because it could not be reinforced, offered a lesson which Charles XI had not been slow to learn. After 1680 the fleet had been given the highest priority, and at his death in 1697 it had numbered thirty-four ships of the line and seventeen frigates: the most powerful force Sweden had hitherto possessed, or was to possess again for many years to come. By the 1720s that force was virtually in ruins. In the last days of the war the Russian galleys harried the Swedish east coast at will; in 1726 and 1727 only the presence of an English squadron seemed to stand between Sweden and a repetition of that experience. Thereafter, attempts to make the fleet once more a force to be reckoned with ran up against two main obstacles. One was a chronic shortage of crews to man the ships; the other was lack of money for new building. Building programmes were indeed drawn up from time to time – in 1734, 1756 – but in 1743 the situation is said to have been as bad as twenty years before, thanks to incompetence and muddle in the College of Admiralty, and by 1756 there had been little improvement.[31] In 1765 the high seas fleet had only eleven ships fit for service; in 1769 the figure had sunk to eight; in 1770 it was decided to fit out a further nine unserviceable ships 'for the sake of appearances'. When the Age of Liberty came to an end on 19 August 1772 only three new vessels had been launched since 1756. The galley fleet was in rather better shape, thanks to a vigorous building programme in the years after 1749, and possibly as a result of its being transferred to the control of the army from 1756 to 1765.

Unlike the army, the navy was never tested in this period: in the war of 1741–3, when it might have proved a match for the still weaker navy of Russia, it was effectively put out of action by devastating epidemics

---

[30] Höpken, *Riksrådet Anders Johan von Höpkens skrifter*, II, p. 333.

[31] For the navy see *Svenska Flottans Historia. Orlogsflottan i ord och bild från dess grundläggning under Gustav Vasa fram till våra dager*, II ed. Otto Lybeck (Malmö 1942), and Dannert, *Svensk försvarspolitik*.

resulting from insanitary conditions and poor victualling which a more efficient administration would have taken care to remedy. In the war of 1757–62 it had no serious enemy to meet; but one may suspect that things would have gone ill with it if it had tried to bar the entrance to the Baltic of that British squadron for which Frederick the Great was clamouring. However that may be, it is clear that the Swedish navy in the years from 1720 to 1772 never came anywhere near to recovering the strength of 1697. The dominant naval power in the Baltic for all this period was not Sweden, nor Russia, but Denmark: in numbers of ships, maintenance, availability of trained crews, Denmark was – after Holland – the strongest of the minor powers. When in 1763 and 1764 Praslin tried to make an arrangement whereby Sweden would give naval aid to the extent of six ships of the line, if called upon to do so, in return for France's resuming payment of arrears of subsidy, the proposal reflected either France's urgent need for additional ships in the event of war with England, or Praslin's culpable ignorance of the true state of the Swedish fleet, or both: if aid on this scale had in fact been given, Sweden would have been left with no more than three ships for her own defence.[32] Lord Sandwich, who had at first been disturbed at the possibility of a Franco-Swedish naval agreement, soon decided that this was not a prospect that need alarm him.[33] Nevertheless, the Swedish navy, unlike the Swedish army, did not directly reduce the credibility of Sweden as an ally: since no one had seen it in action, no outsider really knew how little it was worth. Only a careful comparison with the resources at Denmark's disposal could demonstrate that the hope of naval aid from Sweden was not worth political or financial sacrifices by any power.[34]

Thus the subsidies which Sweden received – and she received them for some two-thirds of the years from 1721 to 1772 – availed neither to balance the budget, nor to equip her for efficient war, nor to bear the cost of waging it; and they almost unavoidably entailed, to a greater or less degree, a sacrifice of political independence. It was felt most painfully as the subsidies increased in size: at the time of the Pomeranian war Swedish statesmen could hardly move a step without the approval of the French ambassador.[35] This did not mean, however, that for most of the period Sweden lost all freedom of choice, or that her foreign policy was not in some senses her own. The conclusion of a subsidy-treaty, or an alliance, in itself involved a choice: it could represent an option between two

---

[32] As Baron Bunge remarked in January 1770: Daniel Tilas, *Anteckningar och brev från riksdagen 1769–1770*, ed. Olof Jägerskiöld (Stockholm 1976), p. 422.

[33] PRO, SP 91/74/118, Sandwich to Buckinghamshire, 20 November 1764.

[34] Such a comparison was made at the request of successive Secretaries of State several times between 1764 and 1772: Michael Roberts, *British Diplomacy and Swedish Politics, 1758–1773* (1981), pp. 124–5, 389.

[35] As Ulrik Scheffer confessed: Trulsson, *Ulrik Scheffer som hattpolitiker*, pp. 311, 418.

powers offering similar advantages; and it was always possible to opt for no subsidies at all, as Arvid Horn did for a few years after 1731. But once the choice was made, once the subsidy-treaty was concluded, then the options were limited, the freedom was restricted, foreign policy was bound with golden fetters: the French subsidy-treaty of 1738, for instance, debarred Sweden from concluding any other alliance without first notifying France; and though France undertook a reciprocal commitment, it was understood at the time that it would be unrealistic to expect her always to comply with it. It is true that the obligation was ignored by Sweden also in the years immediately after 1743, but the reality of the restriction appeared as late as 1766, when the point was seriously raised as a possible obstacle to the conclusion of a simple treaty of amity with England.[36]

(iii)

Was there, then, any feasible alternative to subsidies, given the position in which Sweden found herself in 1721? Was neutrality an available option? Was it impossible, with caution and patience, to repeat the achievement of Charles XI, and transform the Swedish lion into a hedgehog? Other minor powers in the eighteenth century made a success of neutrality: the Dutch, for one; Denmark, for another. Sweden's experience during the third Anglo-Dutch war – which was matched by that of the Danes and the Dutch in the Seven Years War – suggested that neutrality during a conflict between the major powers offered good prospects of annexing an increased share of international freights. What relevance, it might be asked, had the struggles of Bourbon and Habsburg, or the world conflict of England and France, to the interests of a power geographically remote, and already shattered by a generation of war? What, in general, were the preconditions for the successful preservation of neutrality, and how far were they applicable in Sweden's situation?

The preconditions for neutrality in the eighteenth century were much as they have always been, before and after. For neutrality to be possible it was necessary that the great belligerent powers should on the whole prefer the minor power's neutrality to its involvement: which meant, among other things, that its territory should not be of strategic importance to them, and that it should not lend that territory to the warlike designs of one party or the other. Necessary, too, that it should pursue a course which was perceived to be impartial: if not a policy of impartial refusal, then at least a policy of impartial concession to either side. So far, perhaps, Sweden satisfied the requirements. It was not in the interest of those whose Baltic trade was important to them to provoke one of the

[36] Roberts, *British Diplomacy and Swedish Politics*, pp. 199–200.

guardians of the Sound: a consideration which must weigh heavily with England and Russia, though admittedly to a less extent with France. In this respect Sweden's position was similar to that of Denmark. Again, for England – and for Russia also once the frontier with Finland had been pushed back in 1743 to a less uncomfortable proximity to St Petersburg – Swedish territory had no real strategic importance; and even for France its loss to the other side would mean no more than a weakening of that 'Eastern System' which by this time had become little more than a diplomatic habit inherited from the seventeenth century. It had been devised as a bridle upon the Habsburgs, and that was a function which Sweden had now no interest in discharging. And if the System were to be reshaped in order to provide a barrier against Russian penetration of central Europe, it was upon Poland and the Turks, rather than upon Sweden, that France must rely: Sweden's possible role was restricted to providing a diversion. But it was a diversion in which it was never intended that French troops or ships should be involved. The only occasion when there was any question of Swedish territory's being used by the forces of a belligerent was in 1759, when Choiseul conceived his design for a descent on Scotland based on Swedish west-coast ports; and that design was carefully aborted by Swedish procrastination. Nor was there any reason why a neutral Sweden should not apply the rules of neutrality as impartially as Denmark was to do under Bernstorff's judicious leadership.

There the parallel with Holland and Denmark stopped. The advantage to belligerent powers of Swedish neutrality was much less than in their case. The Dutch were the indispensable neutral carriers – so indispensable that England was prepared to bend the 'Rule of '56' in their favour; indispensable to France also, as the suppliers of masts, spars and ship's timber from the Baltic by routes which escaped the visitations of privateers or the British navy. As to Denmark, it was Denmark alone that kept alive England's trade with the Mediterranean during the Seven Years War.[37] The Swedish mercantile marine, though far from negligible, could render no comparable services; Swedish iron was of importance mainly to England, and could at a pinch be largely replaced by Russian; Swedish pitch and tar, also, were replaceable from other sources. But Amsterdam was the great continental banking and commercial centre, the regulator of rates of exchange, deeply intertwined by investment with her most formidable commercial rival, England.[38] Sweden, on the other hand,

[37] For this, and Danish neutrality in general, see H. S. K. Kent, *War and Trade in Northern Seas. Anglo-Scandinavian Economic Relations in the Mid-Eighteenth Century* (Cambridge 1973), *passim* and p. 128.

[38] For Dutch neutrality, see Alice C. Carter, *The Dutch Republic in Europe in the Seven Years War* (Coral Gables, Florida, 1972).

performed no obvious services to the international community which might entitle her to be rescued if destruction seemed likely to overtake her, once the western powers had resigned themselves to Russia's predominance in the Baltic: the most that could be hoped for were demonstrations, or threats of demonstrations, by the British navy, as in 1726–7. In the period 1721–72 Holland never seemed to be in danger of attack on land except for a moment in 1747; Denmark, except in 1761–2, was likewise safe on land from attack by any major power. But for nearly two centuries Sweden had had to face a possible war on two fronts; and though in this period the threat from Denmark became a reality only once (in 1743), the threat from Russia was obvious in 1723, 1726–7, 1743, and 1747–50. The Dutch and Danish armies were perhaps even weaker than the Swedish; but if the movement to strengthen the land forces was defeated in Holland, that was balanced by the success of the opposing policy of expanding the fleet. So too the efficient Danish navy made up for the inadequacy of her land forces, and ensured that the powers would prefer to keep on reasonably good terms with her. Holland and Denmark, unlike Sweden, had no significant territorial ambitions: they might have unresolved controversies of one sort or another, but no one could suppose them to be preparing for wars of aggression. Moreover, while Dutch and Danish statesmen were virtually unanimous in their commitment to neutrality, to many Swedes it seemed both delusive and disgraceful: it was unworthy of a nation with Sweden's great traditions to stand back from the great affairs of Europe, and by doing so lose not only friends but reputation.[39] The really essential precondition for neutrality was, as always, that the neutral power must be able to make itself respected; but the only means by which Sweden seemed to have much prospect of regaining that position, the only means of ensuring that her army and navy should indeed be respectable, were in fact irreconcilable with neutrality: the acceptance of foreign subsidies, the inclusion in a 'system'.[40] Finally, in 1721 neither Denmark nor the Dutch were in Sweden's lamentable situation: neither stood isolated. A power in the position in which Sweden then found herself dared not think of neutrality: an ally, almost any ally, seemed to be an imperative necessity.

But might not the ally be Denmark? If neutrality were ruled out, was not a Scandinavian alliance a reasonable alternative? The Sound controlled by allied powers, the Danish navy reinforced by the Swedish:

---

[39] Höpken, *Riksrådet Anders Johan von Höpkens skrifter*, II, p. 237.

[40] Compare the remark of Nils Brahe in March 1672: 'If we had means to equip another fifty ships, maintain a brave army on land, and garrison our fortresses, then I think our best policy would be to sit still'; and the answer of Magnus Gabriel de la Gardie: 'But since we are *not* in a condition to do these things out of our own pockets, it is reasonable to take that side with which we are *solennibus pactis* allied': Birger Fahlborg, 'Sveriges förbund med Frankrike 1672', *Historisk tidskrift* (1935), p. 310 *n*. 5.

this was a combination calculated to give pause even to the Maritime Powers – a combination strong enough, it might be hoped, to safeguard the North from molestation. It was an old idea, and it had a long future before it. On the Danish side Hannibal Sehested in the 1660s, on the Swedish Johan Gyllenstierna in 1679, had seen this as a way to peace and an escape from clientelage. In the 1690s the first Scandinavian Armed Neutrality had been a real check upon the maritime outrages of England and the Dutch. And now, when the great wars were over, and when the North above all needed peace, it was not surprising that men should from time to time have recurred to the Scandinavian ideal: twice – from 1734 to 1743, and again in the 1750s – it seemed for a little while that that idea might be realised. But in the 1720s, and for many years thereafter, there was one difficulty which cropped up again and again, and which constituted a formidable obstacle to any permanent arrangement on these lines: the problem of Holstein.

The settlements at the end of the Great Northern War had guaranteed Denmark's possession of Slesvig; and the history of the previous half century, when Denmark had been permanently menaced by a Holstein which was more or less a Swedish client, made this part of the settlement of vital importance to her. But the ruler of 'ducal' Holstein, Charles Frederick, the son of Charles XII's elder sister, was thought by many Swedes to have a better title to the Swedish throne than Charles XII's younger sister Ulrika Eleonora – and still more so than her husband, Frederick I. Until the late twenties there was a strong Holstein faction in Stockholm. And when in 1725 Charles Frederick married Peter the Great's daughter Anna, and Russia began to interest herself in the Holstein cause, a Holstein succession in Sweden looked possible, and a Russo-Holstein-Swedish coalition seemed to impend over Denmark.[41] However, the death of Peter in 1725, the withering away of Holstein influence in St Petersburg under his successors, and the corresponding decline of the Holstein faction in Sweden, removed the main obstacle to a Scandinavian alignment – for a time. With the accession of Christian VI to the Danish throne in 1730 such an alignment became an object of Danish policy; and in 1734 it became a reality with the conclusion of a Danish–Swedish alliance. But within a decade the Holstein problem cropped up again; and this time it brought the two countries to the brink of war.

[41] For the Slesvig–Holstein question in this century see Fritz Arnheim, 'Beiträge zur Geschichte der nordischen Frage in der zweiten Hälfte des 18. Jahrhunderts', *Deutsche Zeitschrift für Geschichtswissenchaft*, II–V, VII (1889–92); Otto Brandt, *Caspar von Saldern und die nordeuropäische Politik im Zeitalter Katharinas II* (Erlangen-Kiel 1932); idem, 'Das Problem, der "Ruhe des Nordens" im 18. Jahrhundert, *Historische Zeitschrift* 140 (1929); and the convenient orientation in the Introduction to *Recueil des Instructions données aux Ambassadeurs de France. Danemark.* (Paris 1895).

On the death of Ulrika Eleonora in 1741 the choice of a successor to Frederick I (who had no legitimate children) became – or was made to become – urgent. To Christian VI, godly but not without ambition, this seemed to offer an opportunity not only to reinforce the Scandinavian *entente* but to transform it into a Scandinavian Union by securing the election of his eldest son as successor to the Swedish throne: by a simple dynastic conjuring-trick the history of two centuries was to be wiped out, and the Union of Kalmar was to be restored. The chances looked not unpromising: the Swedish peasantry, who after the experience of the Finnish war were inclined to think that Danish Absolutism might be an improvement on the sovereignty of the Diet, were well-disposed; the city of Göteborg likewise. Elizabeth of Russia, however, had other views. Charles Frederick of Holstein was by this time dead; but his son was now adopted by the Empress as her successor, and in due time was to emerge as the luckless Peter III. The association of Russia with the Holstein cause was thus renewed; and it was strengthened when Elizabeth, as a condition for granting Sweden a lenient peace in 1743, forced the Diet to accept as Frederick I's successor an inconspicuous twig from the wide-spreading Holstein family tree. This was Adolf Frederick, the Protestant bishop of the secularised sees of Lübeck and Eutin; a *douce* man, formed for domesticity and a quiet life, and devoted to his turning-lathe – a man, in short, of whom Elizabeth might reasonably expect that he would be grateful for his elevation, and could be relied upon to give no trouble. Despite Adolf Frederick's inoffensive personal character, his election was for Christian VI a deeply disturbing development. It was bad enough to have a Holsteiner as heir-presumptive in Russia; it was almost worse to have another of the same family installed in Sweden. Denmark, he felt, was encircled. His reaction (in 1743) was to prepare an invasion of Sweden's southern and south-western provinces, in the hope of ejecting Adolf Frederick with popular support; and he abandoned his preparations only when the Swedes, in desperation, called in Russian troops to save them.

It might seem that the idea of a Scandinavian *bloc* had now no future. But in fact relations between the two countries slowly improved after the crisis of 1743. On the one hand Adolf Frederick was not prepared to be Elizabeth's poodle, and gradually emancipated himself from his over-bearing patroness; on the other, Bestuzhev had little interest in, or patience with, the views of the Holsteiners. A reconciliation was thus made less difficult; and by 1749–50, thanks to the good offices of France, the Holstein stumbling-block was once again cleared away: this time, it might seem, permanently. For Adolf Frederick was persuaded by his advisers to renounce his contingent claim to Holstein–Gottorp, and to agree that if ever the Holstein succession should fall in to him he would

accept Oldenburg and Delmenhorst in exchange; and by a typical piece of
dynastic diplomacy the reconciliation was sealed by the engagement of
Prince Gustav (afterwards Gustav III) to the Danish princess Sophia
Magdalena: this, it was supposed, would bind the two royal houses
together in amity. In fact, it poisoned relations between them for more
than a quarter of a century. In other respects also the agreements of
1749–50 did not produce all the beneficent effects expected of them. In the
new era of Scandinavian friendship most of the good-will was on the
Danish side. By J. H. E. Bernstorff, who directed Danish policy in the
fifties and sixties, a Scandinavian System was warmly desired, though not
always steadily supported; but in Stockholm friendship with Denmark
was by no means unanimously popular. The traditional hatred and
suspicion of Denmark was still very much alive; and it was reflected in
Höpken's pathological scepticism about Bernstorff's good faith. The
Naval Union of 1757, which was intended to act as another Scandinavian
Armed Neutrality, might seem to show that Scandinavianism could once
again be an effective force; but in fact it showed precisely the opposite. Its
history was a rather melancholy record of suspicion and failures of
cooperation; and when it seemed that there was some risk that it might
compromise Denmark's profitable neutrality, Bernstorff made it plain
that it was the Naval Union, and not Danish neutrality, that must be
sacrificed. And so, in petty wrangling about Norwegian lumbering, the
fortification of Landskrona, and Danish naval uncooperativeness, what
was perhaps the last chance in this period of realising the Scandinavian
alternative was allowed to slip away. Yet even when, as in 1750–7, a
Scandinavian System had seemed to be a reality, it had never been a really
independent association. As the *détente* of 1749–50 was nurtured by
France's care, so the resulting amity produced – and was designed to
produce – an alliance *within* the 'French System'. Neither Denmark nor
Sweden would have wished it otherwise; for neither was minded to
sacrifice French subsidies for the sake of the hazardous satisfactions of real
independence. Scandinavianism as a variant of neutrality was only
intermittently possible, and when achieved was very much a delusion.

(iv)

Since neither neutrality nor a Scandinavian *bloc* could do duty as a policy,
there remained only alliances; and the question presents itself why, at any
particular moment, Sweden should have chosen (or accepted) one ally
rather than another. Swedish and Danish statesmen well understood that
it was inexpedient for a weaker power to take the initiative in proposing
alliances to a stronger.[42] They realised too that a weak power would do

---

[42] As Bernstorff put it: 'Je suis très fidèle au principe que . . . lorsqu'il s'agit de liaisons et
d'alliances entre deux cours de forces inégales, ce n'est jamais à la moins puissante de faire des

well to cultivate good relations with some other state than that to which it was allied, in order to preserve an escape-route from possible servitude to a single imperious friend.[43] Each of them contrived at times to do this; hence the apparently irreconcilable engagements which give to Swedish foreign policy (and still more so, to Danish) the superficial appearance of lunatic inconsequence. Certainly the first alliance concluded by Sweden after 1721 appears at first sight improbable enough: the alliance, for twelve years, which Arvid Horn concluded with Russia in 1724. Arvid Horn, Chancery-President from 1720 to 1738, was a statesman of long experience. He had fought in Charles XII's wars, had been sent home by him to stiffen the Council, and had been the directing mind at the abortive Diet of 1713–14.[44] He had then taken the initiative in negotiations for peace, and had abandoned them only when it was no longer possible to ignore Charles's curt order that the Diet should cease meddling with foreign policy. On the question of the succession he had at first been of the Holstein faction; he was not well seen by Ulrika Eleonora, who virtually forced his resignation; and he represented, in constitutional and social matters, the high aristocracy's attempt to resume that control of the state which it had lost since 1680. In many respects he stood for the attitudes of an earlier generation (he was born in 1664); but his realistic appreciation of what was and what was not possible, his prudence, and his all-round ability, made him, in the first decade of Liberty, the necessary man. In 1724 he saw clearly that the Russian alliance, so contradictory of the hopes of those who wished to undo the verdict of Nystad, was in fact an unavoidable expedient. It represented a choice: a choice between Russia and Denmark. And the choice went in Russia's favour, partly because a choice of Denmark might have provoked Peter the Great into an attempt to put Charles Frederick of Holstein on the Swedish throne; partly because Sweden was in no state to repel threats from the Russian navy: safer to join Peter than to defy him.

The diplomatic upheavals of the mid twenties presented Horn with a chance to balance this unpalatable partnership; and in 1727, after much cautious manoeuvring, he felt himself strong enough at home to accept the pressing offers of England and France and add Sweden to the Alliance of Hanover. This too was a choice, for it meant the rejection of Austro-Spanish offers, and in particular of a proposal that the Emperor be invited to accede to the Russo-Swedish alliance of 1724. The new alignment brought handsome subsidies from Sweden's allies in the West,

offres ou des propositions': *Correspondance . . . du Comte J. H. E. Bernstorff*, II 379 (to Scheel, 6 February 1769). Ironically enough, he was at that precise moment violating his own principle by his approaches to Russia.

[43] So, for instance, the recommendation of the Lesser Secret Deputation in December 1746: Höpken, *Riksrådet Anders Johan von Höpkens skrifter*, II, p. 45.

[44] See Carl Lennart Lundquist, *Council, King and Estates in Sweden 1713–1714* (Stockholm 1975).

emancipation from an embarrassing dependence, and the protection of the British navy. But (and it was characteristic) it entailed no breach with Russia: the treaty of 1724 still stood, though the considerations which had dictated its acceptance had by this time disappeared.

The disintegration of the Anglo-French *entente* which followed upon the second Treaty of Vienna in 1731 put an end to this satisfactory state of affairs. It confronted Horn with the possibility of having to choose between the two allies of 1727, and it cut off the subsidies which had come from London and Paris in the previous four years. It was followed soon after by the War of the Polish Succession; and that war inaugurated an era in Swedish foreign policy which lasted in effect until 1762. For the first time since 1721 an opportunity seemed to present itself for striking a blow at Russia; for the first time French statesmen could think of harnessing Swedish aspirations and emotions to support French policy. Enthusiasm for Stanislaw Leszczyński was running high in Stockholm; for Leszczyński, after all, had been Charles XII's King of Poland, and Arvid Horn himself had played a major part in putting him on the Polish throne. The establishment in Poland of a patriot régime hostile to Moscow, the defeat of the Russian armies which had entered the Republic, appeared to almost all Swedes as the obvious initial step towards the recovery of the Baltic provinces. French diplomacy played upon these feelings to lay the foundation of a pro-French party in Stockholm. That party was to triumph in 1738, and it was to last through good times and bad until the Age of Liberty came to an end. But for the moment France's attempt to induce Sweden to pull Polish chestnuts out of the fire for her was unsuccessful: the French intervention in Poland was tardy and tentative, its results were ignominious, and Arvid Horn, justifiably suspicious of French good faith, was too much of a realist to allow himself to be enlisted in Fleury's ill-executed enterprise, or to believe that the débâcle at Danzig offered Sweden any rational hope of recovering her lost dominions.

Nevertheless, the episode left behind it diplomatic consequences which were to be determinant of much that was to follow. For in 1734 England and France, almost simultaneously, offered Sweden subsidy-treaties. Of the two, the French offer was considered to be the better; and in 1735 a treaty of alliance on these lines was duly signed, and sent to Paris for ratification. But about the same time a Russian proposal to renew the alliance of 1724 was accepted also, with the assent even of Horn's political opponents. Nobody in Stockholm, apparently, considered it to be repugnant to the treaty recently concluded with France – or at least, nobody said so at the time. Fleury and Chauvelin, however, had other views. The war in Poland was almost over, and France was already in secret negotiation with Russia (as Horn well knew); but for a French client and pensioner to ally with France's successful antagonist in Warsaw was

not to be tolerated. The French retort took the form of a refusal to ratify
the treaty which had been sent to Paris. And by taking this line Fleury
prepared the way for Horn's fall three years later, and for the passing of
power to France's pensioned partisans.[45]

For by 1738 the political situation in Sweden had undergone an
ominous change. When the Diet met in that year Horn's political enemies
– the men who formed the nucleus of what was coming to be known as
the party of the Hats – made frenetic efforts to drive him from office: an
enterprise backed by heavy financial support from the French ambassador. And the most damaging of the charges they brought against Horn
was that by his renewal of the treaty with Russia in 1735 he had lost the
French subsidy-treaty, had in effect ranged himself with the national
enemy, and had obstructed the laudable designs of all good patriots. The
Hats came to the Diet, determined not only to get rid of Horn, but also to
prepare the country for an attack on Russia: Caroline officers living in
straitened circumstances on half-pay, young hotheads who felt impatient
and contemptuous of Horn's cautious policies, pamphleteers fee'd by
French gold – all rode on the crest of the first great wave of enthusiasm for
the memory of Charles XII.[46] The Russians were now deeply involved in
a Turkish war, and were reported to be suffering enormous losses; and the
Hats set much dubious diplomacy in motion in the hope of an offensive
alliance with the Porte, directed against their common enemy.[47] The
prancing chauvinism of the hour was memorably expressed by Carl
Gustaf Tessin, when to the thunderous applause of the Estate of Nobility
he declared his conviction that they 'would always, when the occasion
arises, be more disposed to an honourable participation in the general
motions of the world, than to an ignominious quiescence and a craven
repose': brave words, which four years later his friends would be sorry
for. For the moment, all this euphoria produced no perceptible effect; for
it assorted ill with French policy, and without France's approval even the
Hats must think twice about risking the venture. Fleury's immediate
concern was somehow to rescue the Turks from their predicament; he
had no sympathy whatever with the idea of a Swedish–Turkish offensive
alliance; and he might hope that the peace of Belgrade would suffice to
prevent any rash escapades in the North.

The ardour of the Hats was not to be damped so easily. In vain did
Fleury warn them that they had better sit still. For two years they dabbled

[45] For this episode see Hilding Danielson, *Sverige och Frankrike 1736–1739* (Lund 1956), pp.
32–41; Malmström, II, pp. 162–95, 202–12, 230–9.
[46] For discussion of the types of men from whom enthusiasts for the war were drawn, see
Ingemar Carlsson, *Olof Dalin och den politiska propagandan inför 'lilla ofreden'* (Lund 1966), pp.
211–3; idem, *Parti – partiväsen – partipolitiker. Kring uppkomsten av våra första politiska partier*
(Stockholm 1981), pp. 166–81; Göran Nilzén, *Studier i 1730 talets partiväsen*, pp. 201–8.
[47] Danielson, *Sverige och Frankrike*, pp. 239–40.

ineffectively with the preliminaries to their Russian war. The French had little faith in their ability to make a success of it, and no desire to see their expensive ally involved in a fiasco. But then, in 1740, the 'conjuncture' for which the Hats had been impatiently waiting unexpectedly presented itself; for in that year the pattern of international relations underwent a sudden and portentous change. The deaths of the Emperor Charles VI and of the Empress Anna, the accession of Frederick the Great, the virtual certainty of a war to uphold or overturn the Pragmatic Sanction – these things gave to Sweden's half-baked designs a new importance. For France a Swedish attack on Russia was now desirable, to prevent the despatch of Russian troops to the assistance of Maria Theresa; it appeared now to have better prospects of success, in view of the confusion, actual and potential, of Russian domestic affairs; and it became absolutely necessary when Frederick the Great threatened to cancel his French alliance if Sweden did not move soon.[48] Peter the Great's daughter Elizabeth was calculating that a Swedish advance upon St Petersburg would give her an opportunity to seize the throne; and she gave verbal promises of cessions of territory in exchange for Swedish support of her plans. And so, in 1741, the long-projected, eagerly-awaited war with Russia began, this time with France's blessing. The days of ignominious quiescence were over; ahead lay ignominious capitulation. Two years hence a Swedish army of 11 000 men would lay down their arms without attempting resistance.

There had been reasons, of a sort, for this disastrous adventure: the belief that Russia was in a weakened state; the chance of exploiting a palace revolution; the incitements of France. But the war was made against the opinions of the military experts,[49] in the frivolous expectation that since one campaign would decide it no provision, financial or otherwise, need be made for its continuance beyond that time; and it was made upon the basis of political calculations which were mere gossamer fantasies. To suppose that the Turks, at a moment when Villeneuve's diplomacy was being exerted to obtain peace for them, might pledge themselves to go on fighting the Russians until Sweden had recovered her lost provinces;[50] or that the support of Denmark and Prussia might be bought by promises of Livonia and Courland;[51] to imagine that any Russian government, even after defeat, would be prepared to buy peace by retroceding St Petersburg and Kronstadt – these were notions so romantic that only men intoxicated by memories of former glory could have believed in them for a moment. The events of 1738–41 might

---

[48] Malmström, *Sveriges politiska historia*, I, p. 419.
[49] Dannert, *Svensk försvarspolitik*, p. 17.
[50] Danielson, *Sverige och Frankrike*, p. 378.
[51] The Danes indicated that they would be more interested in Bohuslän, and the offer was in fact never made.

suggest that while such men were in power Sweden could hardly have a rational foreign policy at all.

The history of the later forties, however, offers a corrective to any such hasty judgment. In the immediate post-war years Sweden had of course to pay for her follies: ten thousand Russian troops in Södermanland and Östergötland, to discourage any Danish attempt to replace Adolf Frederick by the Danish crown prince; a Russian alliance in 1745 which bound Sweden to maintain the Holstein pretensions, and in effect registered a return to the state of affairs in 1724. France, preoccupied with the War of the Austrian Succession, had neither the ability nor the inclination to rescue the victim of her solicitations; and d'Argenson, to the scandal of the Swedish minister in Paris, appeared to regard his ally with indifference.[52] For the moment French diplomacy was more active in Denmark. Thus it happened that in 1744 the men who had made the Finnish war, no less than those who had opposed it, were looking to England rather than to France to extricate them from their vassalage to Russia.[53] They looked in vain; for England was content for the present to act as Russia's auxiliary in Sweden. Nevertheless, the idea was to be of importance in the future. In the later thirties British diplomacy had been active in support of Arvid Horn, and in the forties Horn's political heirs, who were beginning to be known as the Caps, continued to pin their hopes on England if only because the Hats soon reverted to their normal stance and once more looked to France: already it was possible to discern a polarisation of politics into French and English supporters. But this emerging pattern was distorted in the late forties by the failure of England to provide the Caps with the alternative to France for which they were looking, and by the long break in Anglo-Swedish diplomatic relations which began in 1748, and was to last until 1764.[54] The Caps were driven into the arms of Russia for lack of anything better; and they became for a time a party which seemed willing, in their struggle against the Hats, to use Russian aid and accept Russian leadership in ways which came near to treason. In these circumstances the Hats were able, from 1746 onwards, to retrieve their past errors by standing forth as the champions of Sweden's independence, and could claim with some plausibility that they were not only a French but a *national* party.

They would scarcely have been able to effect this transformation if Russia had not played into their hands. Adolf Frederick, whom Elizabeth had imposed on the unenthusiastic Swedes as successor to Frederick I,

---

[52] Göran Behre, *Underrättelseväsen och diplomati. De diplomatiska förbindelserna mellan Sverige och Storbritannien 1743–1745* (Göteborg 1965), pp. 200–1.

[53] *Ibid.* pp. 67–9, Birger Sallnäs, *Samuel Åkerhielm d.y.: en statsmannabiografi* (Lund 1947), p. 144.

[54] For the circumstances that led to the breach, and its long continuance, see Roberts, *British Diplomacy and Swedish Politics*, pp. 4–5, 8–12, 15–17.

proved much less pliable than she felt that she had a right to expect. Successive Russian ministers in Stockholm – Korff in 1746–7, Panin in 1749–50 – gave pungent expression to her displeasure. Korff demanded the dismissal of the new Chancery-President, Tessin, who was now Adolf Frederick's political ally; Panin delivered successive Declarations couched in terms of ever-increasing menace: on more than one occasion threats were followed by Russian military demonstrations on the Finnish border, and war seemed very near: Bestuzhev – though not, perhaps, his sovereign – seems to have intended it. The Hats' reply, in 1746, was the so-called 'National Declaration', which called upon men of good-will to unite against the intolerable interference of a foreign state in Swedish domestic affairs. And they followed this, in 1747, by an alliance with Prussia, and the renewal for a further ten years of the alliance with France.[55]

The opportunity thus to escape from their condition of subjection or isolation was provided by the movements of European diplomacy during the War of the Austrian Succession; for as Russia moved closer to the participation in that war which became a fact in 1747, she became, for Prussia and for France, an enemy; and hence the anti-Russian cause in Stockholm became once more a cause to which France must give active support. One corollary of this new situation was the reconciliation of Sweden and Denmark; for it was also to France's interest to save Denmark from being forced by Russian pressure into collaborating in an attack on Sweden. The reconciliation was achieved, as we have seen,[56] by the agreements of 1749–50, which seemed to remove the Holstein issue as a source of controversy between the Scandinavian powers. In these circumstances Russian attempts to bully Sweden collapsed before the firmness of the Hat government, the warnings of France, and the restraining counsels of Russia's allies: nobody wanted another European war so soon after the peace of Aix-la-Chapelle. Thus by 1751 France could register complete success in the North: the Hats triumphant, Bestuzhev forced to back down, the reconciliation of the Scandinavian powers effected. The Hats could claim with some justice that their policy had been the right one, that a courageous assertion of their country's independence had brought its reward, and that Sweden's battered reputation had been repaired. All of which, in a measure, was true. But it was true also that Sweden's ability to resist still inspired no confidence in her allies;[57] that her army, despite the energetic and intelligent efforts of Adolf Frederick to give it some training and discipline, was still wofully

[55] For the diplomacy of this period see J. R. Danielsson, *Die Nordische Frage in den Jahren 1746–51* (Helsingfors 1888).
[56] Above, p. 31.
[57] Dannert, *Svensk försvarspolitik*, pp. 251, 264.

unfit for any serious fighting; that the programme of naval building had made virtually no progress; that work on the defences of Finland had barely begun. And, not least, that for any speedy remedying of such deficiencies Sweden was heavily dependent upon French subsidies. The French ally had rescued her from immediate danger; but there was no use blinking the fact that the alliance locked her into the 'French System' more inescapably than she had ever been locked into any system before. If for the moment it seemed to give security, it went far to deprive the country of its freedom of manoeuvre.

(v)

The long crisis with Russia at the end of the forties introduced a new element into Sweden's relations with foreign powers, an element which would continue to affect them until it was removed by Gustav III's *coup d'état* of 19 August 1772. This was nothing less than the Swedish constitution itself. By article 7 of the peace of Nystad Russia had promised that there should be no interference in Sweden's domestic arrangements, 'nor in the Form of Government . . . established and unanimously sworn to by the Estates, . . . but that [the Tsar] . . . will endeavour to hinder and to forestall everything that may be contrary to it'. This, it was assumed, was designed as a pledge of non-intervention;[58] but already in the twenties there had been attempts by Russia to interpret it as a right to intervene whenever the Russian government might choose to allege that the constitution was in danger.[59] It had been one of the few successes of the Swedish negotiators of the peace of Åbɔ in 1743 that on this occasion the clause was omitted. In 1744, however, Adolf Frederick married Frederick the Great's sister, Lovisa Ulrika: it was the first step towards that alliance with Prussia which was to follow in 1747. It had also domestic implications. For the marriage had been very largely the work of Carl Gustaf Tessin; and on Lovisa Ulrika's arrival in Sweden she lost no time in identifying herself with the Hats and drawing her amenable husband into the same political camp. She hoped that this political alliance might be used to liberate the monarchy from some of the stringent limitations which the constitution imposed on the prerogative: Frederick I's health was breaking, and Adolf Frederick's accession might come at no distant time. Tessin and the Hats, for their part, were anxious to bind the

---

[58] It has been contended that the real object of the clause was to provide a safeguard against any possible pact between Frederick I and Peter the Great to extend the prerogative; and also against any attempt by Peter to force Charles Frederick of Holstein upon Sweden as successor-designate: Göran Wensheim, *Studier kring freden i Nystad* (Lund 1973), pp. 214–15.

[59] And also by at least one member of the Holstein faction in Sweden, D. N. von Höpken, in 1726: see Malmström's indignant comment in Malmström, *Sveriges politiska historia*, I, pp. 477–8.

successor to their party, and Tessin personally was fascinated by Lovisa Ulrika's intelligence and charm. They were therefore ready (for the moment) to contemplate some modest constitutional concessions. Thus for domestic reasons Elizabeth's protégé became an open supporter of the anti-Russian party in Stockholm. Elizabeth, understandably chagrined by this development, retorted by resurrecting article 7 of the peace of Nystad. Her concern for the integrity of the constitution seems in fact to have been genuine; and in the years that followed the maintenance of the constitution was more than simply a useful peg upon which to hang menacing declarations, or a possible pretext for armed intervention. Panin seems really to have believed that the Hats and the young Court were hatching a revolution, and that the death of Frederick I would be the moment for making the attempt. As far as the young Court was concerned Panin was perfectly right; but by 1750 Tessin and the Hats (or such of them as had been in the secret) had abandoned any ideas of that sort. Panin's threats of war were defied; the intention of revolution was disavowed; and the accession of Adolf Frederick in 1751 took place not only without Russian interference but almost with Elizabeth's blessing: Bestuzhev had been made to feel that Europe disapproved of his bullying tactics. Nevertheless, in the course of the next twenty years the integrity of the constitution, or its possible amendment, would remain a question which influenced Sweden's relations, not only with Russia, but also with Denmark and with France.

From the point of view of any who might be interested in a more effective conduct of foreign policy the constitution might well have been all the better for a little amendment – though not necessarily in the ways which Lovisa Ulrika and those who sympathised with her had in mind. For the conduct of foreign policy was undoubtedly prejudiced by the authority which the Form of Government gave to the Estates. The Diet, regarding itself as virtually a sovereign body, assumed to itself the right (and, indeed, the duty) of supervising and correcting the work of the executive in all its branches,[60] including foreign policy and diplomacy. The permanent body in charge of these matters was the College of Chancery, headed by the Chancery-President, who sat in the Council of State and was more or less equivalent to a Foreign Secretary. Only rarely, however, was he in a position to pursue the course he thought best without regard to other considerations; for he was responsible to the Diet, and accountable to it for his actions. When the Diet was sitting he was simply its functionary, carrying out the policies prescribed to him by the Secret Committee, under whose supervision foreign affairs fell; and on occasion the Committee did not hesitate to do his work for him: in 1738 they took it upon themselves to negotiate directly with foreign ministers in

[60] For a fuller treatment of this element in the constitutional situation see chapter II, below.

Stockholm, to appoint diplomats, and to send orders to Sweden's representatives abroad.[61] In the intervals between Diets the Chancery-President was bound to conform himself to the Secret Instruction which they left behind as a directive; and from its injunctions he departed at his peril. In the meantime, of course, the international situation might have altered radically: if so, he had to guess how best to meet it within the instructions that had been bequeathed to him, and what course of action would be likely to commend itself to the next Diet – which might be of a different party complexion from its predecessor. It could happen that the Secret Committee had such complete confidence in the Chancery-President and the Council that it was prepared to take the risk of leaving matters to their discretion, without any specific instructions: this happened, for instance, at the end of the Diet of 1747.[62] But such occasions were rare. And in two critical instances, in 1734 and 1756, the Secret Committee left behind it instructions which were either self-contradictory or capable of differing interpretations.

In other respects also the Chancery-President was in an unenviable situation. Members of the Chancery College who were nobles had seats in the House of Nobility; some of them might well be elected as members of the Secret Committee. Diplomats, too, often contrived to come home to attend a Diet, bringing views of their own, and not hesitating to express them. All of these were officially the Chancery-President's subordinates, but all of them might on occasion use the opportunity to oppose or controvert their chief, or to impose a policy upon him which was not necessarily his own. This did not conduce to good order and departmental discipline.[63] Although foreign affairs were strictly secret, and only the Secret Committee could take cognisance of them, in a committee of a hundred members leaks inevitably occurred, and details of foreign policy could be communicated from party motives (and, often enough, for bribes) to the ministers of foreign powers. When absolute secrecy had at all costs to be preserved, as while they were planning the attack on Russia in 1741, the Committee might delegate the decision to a *sekretissimum* of up to a dozen members, who would embody their directives in a sealed memorandum, to be opened only when the expected emergency arose: that of 1739 was so secret that its very existence was known only to two members of the Council. The effect of these procedures was to produce a Council which was lacking in initiative and

[61] Malmström, *Sveriges politiska historia*, II, pp. 344–5.
[62] *Ibid.*, III, p. 422.
[63] In 1765, for instance, when the Lesser Secret Deputation (which was a sub-committee of the Secret Committee) was preparing charges against the Hat Council for their conduct of foreign policy, the membership included two leading civil servants in the Chancery – who thus used their expertise against their official chief: Lennart Linnarsson, *Riksrådens Licentiering* (Uppsala 1943), p. 187.

wanting in nerve in a crisis: they did not dare, for instance, to deprive the incompetent Lewenhaupt of his command in Finland, since he had been appointed by the Diet itself. But if Sweden were to pursue a Hat-style foreign policy of exploiting 'conjunctures', she needed a strong government prepared to risk responsibility on its own account. Yet at two critical moments the Hat Council – under Carl Gyllenborg in 1741, and again under A. J. von Höpken in 1757 – was rather weak than strong. The only really strong Councils before 1765 were those dominated by Arvid Horn in the twenties and early thirties, and by Carl Gustaf Tessin for half a dozen years after 1746; and as it happened both of these were committed to peace and recovery. It was Höpken himself who in June 1757 confessed that the Swedish constitution 'n'est fait que pour la paix et le repos, puisque . . . ses mouvements sont arrêtés par des formalités continuelles et qui amènent pour l'exécution des lenteurs que les grandes affaires ne comportent point':[64] a state of affairs, he ruefully reflected, which made absolutist Denmark a more eligible ally.[65] And in 1766 Choiseul was to write that Sweden possessed 'une administration métaphysique, et qui ne seroit soutenable et possible qu'autant que tous les Suèdois seroient assez sages d'esprit et de moeurs que pourroit être Platon':[66] successive Secret Committees can hardly be said to have satisfied that requirement, either in the one respect or the other. It is no doubt true that the devastating description of the ignorance of the Estates in matters of foreign policy which the historian LagerBring penned after the end of the Age of Liberty is to be considered less as a faithful representation of the truth than as an example of the acid wit of a disillusioned provincial professor;[67] but it was not entirely without foundation, and it would not be unfair to say that one weakness in Swedish foreign policy in the Age of Liberty was that the constitution ensured that a matter which above all ought to be handled by well-informed experts was delivered over to the control of imperfectly-enlightened and irresponsible amateurs.

(vi)

The 'French System' held firm throughout the fifties. At home, the Hats were in command, and a disastrous attempt at a royalist *coup* in 1756 only

[64] Höpken, *Riksrådet Anders Johan von Höpkens skrifter*, I, p. 123.
[65] *Ibid.*, II, p. 602.
[66] *Recueil des Instructions données aux Ambassadeurs de France. Suède.* (Paris 1885), p. 407.
[67] Sven LagerBring, *Sammandrag af Swea-Rikes Historia* (Stockholm 1779), V. iii. 52: '. . . alliances, peace, war and defence were sometimes determined by people who needed the almanack to know whether it was Catherine II that ruled in Russia, or Louis XV in France, and on occasion it was a sign of unexpected *expertise* if a man was aware that France and England were located west of the Kattegat. . .'

confirmed their ascendancy.[68] The Caps were in the political wilderness; Russian ministers abandoned any attempt to meddle in Swedish domestic politics; for the whole decade England was without a diplomatic representative in Stockholm. When the Diplomatic Revolution transformed European alignments in 1755–6, Swedish policy conformed to that of the country's paymaster.

The approach of another continental war, however, presented the Council of State with an uncomfortable problem. The Diet of 1756 had left behind it an instruction – drawn by Ulrik Scheffer, a diplomat home on leave – which on the one hand enjoined a policy of caution, peace, and concentration on economic development, but on the other placed upon the Council the responsibility of using any 'conjuncture' to ensure that Sweden's 'reputation, advancement, and (if it be possible) *expansion*' be not neglected.[69] As to the correct interpretation of this instruction the Council was divided; the Chancery-President (A. J. von Höpken) did his best to avoid personal responsibility; but in the end Sweden entered the Seven Years War (after taking care to secure the promise of much increased French subsidies) essentially because Höpken and his colleagues were afraid that the next Diet might charge them with criminal negligence if they did not.[70] It was clearly illegal, as they knew full well, to embark upon an offensive war without the consent of the Estates: even in 1741 that assent had been asked and obtained, though then it had been virtually a formality. But in 1757 a timid government nerved itself to ignore the law; and the formality was dispensed with.

They cloaked their action in a cloud of worn-out sophistries and pompous rhetoric. Since Pomerania was a member of the *Reich*, was it not clearly Sweden's duty to respond to the Emperor's appeal for a Declaration condemning Prussian aggression upon Saxony? But if the Declaration were to have any force, did it not follow that weight must be given to it by the transference of troops to Pomerania? Such a measure, of course, in no way implied active military intervention. But as the historic champions of the Protestant Cause, as one of the guarantors of the treaties of Westphalia – 'the only surviving memorial of Sweden's former glory and reputation in Europe, which cost the life of a great king and the blood of many Swedish men in its attainment'[71] – their honour obliged them to maintain that Cause and do their duty as guarantors; though the argument became a little confused when at the same time it was contended that by

[68] See below, chapter v.

[69] Trulsson, *Ulrik Scheffer som hattpolitiker*, p. 177: my italics.

[70] And also, perhaps, in the hope of strengthening their party (and annoying Lovisa Ulrika) by a successful military enterprise against Lovisa Ulrika's brother. Malmström did not hesitate to call the Pomeranian war 'a party-question in the highest degree': Malmström, *Sveriges politiska historia*, IV, p. 304.

[71] Höpken, *Riksrådet Anders Johan von Höpkens skrifter*, II, p. 318.

joining Catholic Austria and France against Protestant Prussia, Sweden had prevented the struggle from assuming the aspect of a religious war.[72] 'What could be more honourable', wrote Höpken, in a burst of factitious enthusiasm, 'than to be called to the aid and rescue of the Empire, and see that day break again which once dawned upon the beginnings of the rise of Sweden, and of its potent participation in the affairs of Europe!'[73] – a sentiment which Gustav Adolf, we may suspect, would have found only partially intelligible. Yet, after all, they denied that they were really making war at all: all that they were doing was arranging for a peaceful demonstration to give credibility to a diplomatic action directed against a disturber of the peace.[74] Hence when they proceeded to invade Prussian territory, they were careful to do it without a declaration of war. As they had done before, in 1675: a memory which may account for Höpken's panic fear of a Fehrbellin to follow.

Once again they had embarked upon a war which they knew that they were unready to fight and unable to pay for, though their ally France had warned them against undertaking what they were unfitted to carry out. But this time, at least, the 'conjunctures' bore more relation to reality than in 1741. Frederick the Great was fighting Austria, France and Russia simultaneously: on any reasonable calculation only a short war would be needed to bring him to his knees; and provided it was short the Council believed that Sweden could stand the strain. In the event, it took nearly five years to get the Swedish army into anything like decent trim, by which time they could no longer afford to use it. The war exposed them to no obvious risk: the old enemy Russia would this time be fighting on the same side. They had legitimate grievances against Prussia, arising from Frederick the Great's diversion of trade from the Swedish Pomeranian ports to Stettin;[75] and they were not without an uneasy feeling that a monarch who had snatched Silesia might one day hit upon the idea that Pomerania was to be had for the taking. And Pomerania meant much to them. It was a symbol: the last remnant of Sweden's empire, the basis of their claim still to have a voice in the affairs of Germany and Europe; a province mutilated in 1679 and 1720, but still conceivably capable of restoration to its former integrity after a fortunate war. But this feeling, though even Arvid Horn had shared it, was after all

---

[72] Höpken, *Riksrådet Anders Johan von Höpkens skrifter*, II, p. 546–7 (to Ulrik Scheffer, February 1759).

[73] *Ibid.*, II, p. 303 (to the Council of State, 6 December 1756).

[74] These were faithful echoes of seventeenth-century arguments: see the Council debates of December 1654 (especially Erik Oxenstierna's remarks), or Magnus Gabriel de la Gardie's self-justification, 1678; both printed in translation in *Sweden as a Great Power. Government. Society. Foreign Policy*, ed. Michael Roberts (1968), pp. 163–9, 175–9.

[75] Nils Holmberg, 'Oderhandeln, Preussen och svenska Pommern vid mitten av 1700-talet. Ett historiskt perspektiv', *Scandia* (1941), pp. 120–49.

a sentimental illusion. Pomerania provided a lucrative governorship for second-rate or troublesome politicians; but it was not, as Finland was, a vital interest: in 1765 Frederick the Great was wondering whether the Swedish government might not be willing to sell it as a way out of their financial embarrassments.[76]

Whatever defence can be attempted for the intervention in the Seven Years War, it was an unlucky venture. Frederick declined to be overwhelmed; with the French, collaboration was ruled out by their defeats; with the Russians, by their victories; and the ill-found Swedish army was left to struggle on by itself. When Peter III made peace with Prussia it became impossible to go on; and by the aid of Lovisa Ulrika's good offices with her brother peace was made at Hamburg in 1762.

The peace of Hamburg marks the beginning of a new phase in Sweden's international relations. First, a weakening of the French connexion, though not its dissolution. Both sides had reason to be dissatisfied with the other: Sweden had never been able to provide the number of troops stipulated for in the subsidy agreement; France's strained finances made it impossible for her to avoid falling into arrears with her subsidy payments. Choiseul's plan for involving Sweden in a descent on Scotland had revealed the risks which the French alliance might entail. Choiseul and Praslin were already beginning to think that in the existing state of the Swedish forces it was a waste of money to go on paying subsidies in Stockholm.[77] Höpken's inveterate suspicion of Denmark, and the squabbles with Bernstorff over Danish failure to cooperate heartily in the Armed Neutrality, had combined to destroy what had been Tessin's most solid political achievement – the reconciliation of 1749–50. And finally, the peace of Hamburg, though this was not apparent at the time, put an end for the remainder of the Age of Liberty to the policy of 'conjunctures'. There would be no more gambles: they must now come to terms with reality. And since this was so, perhaps the Pomeranian war had not been fought wholly in vain.

(vii)

The war and the peace left the Hats divided; their inflationary policies and their maladministration had aggravated an already severe post-war economic crisis; the general election at the end of 1764 swept them from power; and there followed a period of Cap rule which lasted until the

---

[76] *Politisches Correspondenz Friedrichs des Grossen* (Berlin 1879–1939) XXIV, 194 (to Cocceji, 14 May 1765).

[77] In 1762 Ulrik Scheffer, the Swedish ambassador to France, wrote: 'The most humiliating thing is that they consider us as annihilated and practically reduced to complete anarchy; from which they conclude that we are neither dangerous nor deserving of support': C. T. Odhner, *Minne af Riksrådet m.m. Grefve Ulrik Scheffer* (Stockholm, n.d.), pp. 31–32.

spring of 1769. In their last days the Hats had sought to escape retribution by a tactical alliance with the Court; and in return for Lovisa Ulrika's support they had once again given imprecise promises of constitutional concessions to the Crown – promises which some of them were, but more were not, prepared (at some time in the future) to make good.[78] For the moment, this seemed to accord well enough with their relations with France; for Choiseul and Praslin were beginning to think along the same lines: if ever Sweden were to be a useful ally, the constitution must be revised to curb the authority of the Diet, and to give more power to the Council and to the king.[79] But Choiseul, at least, soon made up his mind that such a reform of the constitution would be no more than a half-measure. No mere tinkering with the balance of the constitution would do France's business: what was required was a radical reform. On 25 April 1766, in a famous despatch, he laid it down that what France should aim at was nothing less than a revolution; a revolution which should emancipate the monarchy from parliamentary control, and leave the king free to follow the foreign policy of his choice – or at least, such foreign policy as Choiseul might urge upon him.[80] It was a decision which directly affected Swedish foreign policy. For the Hats, now under the leadership of Axel von Fersen, had no intention of allowing France to use them to engineer a revolution of this sort; while Choiseul for his part was adamant in his refusal to resume payment of subsidies until the revolution had been carried out. And so when the Hats returned to power in 1769 that did not mean – could not mean – a return to the close identification of Sweden with French policies which had existed in the fifties.

The victory of the Caps in the election of 1764 coincided with, and was assisted by, the reappearance of an English minister in Stockholm, and was followed by the resumption of that close collaboration with his Russian colleague which had marked the politics of the mid-forties. It also marked the final polarisation of parties into supporters of England or of France. The Danish minister to Sweden, J. O. Schack-Rathlou, described this alignment as traditional, hereditary and universal;[81] and this was so far true that for the Caps the situation of 1765 represented a long-sought reversion to normality: at long last they could be, what they had always felt themselves to be, an English party. The Russians for their part asked

[78] Riksarkivet, Stockholm [RA], Stavsundsarkivet, Smärre enskilda arkiv, [S. Piper], 'Pro Memoria, 1771'; Olof Jägerskiöld, Hovet och författningsfrågan 1760–1766 (Uppsala 1943), pp. 64–72, 102–115, 125–6, 151–7; Michael F. Metcalf, Russia, England and Swedish Party Politics 1762–1766, (Stockholm and Totowa, N.J., 1977), pp. 28–9, 103, 119. See below, chapter v.
[79] RA. Malmström avskrifter, Breteuil to Praslin, 12 February 1764.
[80] Recueil . . . Suède, pp. 407–13.
[81] Rigsarkivet, Copenhagen [DRA] TKUA, Sverige B 152, Schack to Bernstorff, 19 March 1765. Schack no doubt exaggerated: he was trying to head off Bernstorff from any idea of attempting to form a Danish party.

for nothing better, being well aware – despite Panin's hopeful instruction to his minister in Stockholm to try to make Russia beloved[82] – that a Russian party could never be popular there, and being also inclined to hope that if England could be persuaded to take the lead, she might be manoeuvred into paying the piper. Like the French, the Russians had been brooding on the experience of 1757–62; and like them they had reached certain conclusions about the Swedish constitution. What impressed them most forcibly was that the Council had been able, in defiance of the law, to enter the war without consulting the Diet. What had been done once against Prussia (they argued) might be done another time against Russia, by a Council which was the tool of France. Panin and Catherine, therefore, looked for a reform of the constitution, but in a very different sense from that desired by Choiseul. They wanted a curb upon the powers of the executive, and a strengthening of the authority and control of the Estates. Their aim, unlike that of France, was essentially defensive; and in the long run it suited well enough with the views of the Caps, who were probably even more committed champions of the sovereignty of the Diet than were their enemies the Hats. It accorded also with the views of Denmark. For if the constitution were transformed into something like an Absolutism, as Choiseul appeared to intend, Bernstorff had no doubt that Adolf Frederick could be relied upon to denounce the agreements of 1749–50, and so reopen the whole Holstein controversy. That Sweden should remain 'French' was to Bernstorff much less important than that she should remain 'free'.[83] By the end of 1764 Denmark's French alliance had been allowed to lapse; Bernstorff's faith both in the Hats and the French had been badly shaken; and when Catherine II indicated her readiness to promote a scheme of territorial exchanges which would leave Slesvig and Holstein in Danish hands, the Holstein factor and the constitutional factor combined to persuade Denmark to change sides. In the spring of 1765 a Russo-Danish alliance was concluded: it was the end of France's Northern System. In the autumn of 1766 Denmark and Russia joined hands with the Caps in forcing through modifications of the constitution conformable to the views of all three of them.[84] Thus for the Caps – in contrast to the Hats – the constitutional issue reinforced the foreign policy that they preferred.

For England the constitution was of no particular importance, save as being the concern of her friends. The object of British Secretaries of State

---

[82] *Sbornik Imperatorskago russkago istoricheskago obshchestva*, 57, pp. 126ff; Erich Amburger, *Russland und Schweden 1762–1772. Katharina II, die schwedische Verfassung und die Ruhe des Nordens* (Berlin 1934), pp. 113–4.

[83] *Correspondance ministérielle du Comte J. H. E. Bernstorff*, II, 107, 114–5; *Correpondance entre le comte Johan Hartvig Ernst Bernstorff et le duc de Choiseul, 1758–1766* (Copenhagen 1871), p. 14.

[84] The *Ordinance for the Better Execution of the Laws*: Roberts, *British Diplomacy and Swedish Politics*, pp. 222–7. See below, chapter IV.

was as it had long been: the preservation of peace in the North; and they believed that this could best be done by destroying French influence in Stockholm. After 1764 they came increasingly to hope that by making an alliance with Sweden they might provide a bridge to that alliance with Russia which was now their grand objective. As for the Caps, though their Chancery-President, Löwenhielm, professed to be attracted by Panin's plan for a great Northern League, and though they had no doubt that if the league came into being they must join it,[85] what they really wanted was an English alliance – with subsidies. An innocuous treaty of amity they did obtain in 1766; but no British Secretary of State, of whatever political complexion, was now prepared to agree to subsidies in peacetime. Thus by the end of 1766 it had become very unlikely that subsidies would be forthcoming from England on any terms, and certain that they would be forthcoming from France only in return for a constitutional revolution for which the Hats had no stomach. And this position remained unaltered until Louis XV put up the money for the *coup d'état* of 19 August 1772.

Each party was now forced to reconsider the reasons for the foreign policy that it advocated. It was no longer sufficient for the Hats to declare, as they had done in 1752, that a French alliance was Sweden's 'natural system, necessarily implicit' in the circumstances of the time.[86] Their Council of State, putting up a last-ditch defence of its policies at the beginning of 1765, had so far modified its former attitude as to claim only that their object had been to 'strengthen the late peace and carefully to cultivate friendship with Sweden's neighbours, and with all foreign powers'.[87] But something better than this anodyne utterance was clearly necessary; and before the year was out it was provided by the Hats' leader in the House of Nobility, Axel von Fersen. Fersen reaffirmed the Hats' traditional commitment to France; but he justified it on the ground that France was now an essentially pacific power, linked to Sweden by common interests in Germany and at the Porte, able to do good offices to Sweden's trade with the Bourbon monarchies, and with the Levant. England, on the other hand, was essentially a bellicose power, concerned to organise attacks on France in order to keep her occupied on the Continent and divert her from improving her navy; above all, a power aiming at a monopoly of commerce at the expense of other nations:

---

[85] PRO SP 95/106/72–5, Goodricke to Sandwich, 1 February 1765; RA. Svar på sekreta propositionen (13 October 1766), for the Lesser Secret Deputation's views. For Panin's Northern League, see Roberts, *British Diplomacy and Swedish Politics*, pp. 85–6, 119–21, and the still useful Niklas Tengberg, *Om kejsarinnan Catharina II:s åsyftade stora nordiska alliance* (Lund 1863).

[86] Malmström, *Sveriges politiska historia*, IV, p. 76.

[87] *Sveriges Ridderskaps och Adels Riksdagsprotokoll från och med år 1719*, [*SRARP*] ed. Sten Landahl, XXIV. App., p. 3.

friendship with England, therefore, involved the sacrifice of Sweden's economic interests and the ruin of her trade. England and France were 'the true rivals who divide the influence of Europe between them', and it was futile for Sweden to try to be friends with both.[88]

Fersen thus enunciated a quite new criterion for determining his party's choice of allies: they must be peaceably inclined. It was a very necessary condition, now that Sweden had no longer subsidies at her disposal, and had at last realised the implications of her military inadequacy; and in the next few years the Hats erected it into a central principle of their foreign policy. In 1768, for instance, a judicious and moderate member of the party, Anders Schönberg, published anonymously an essay entitled 'On Alliances between States',[89] in which he argued that offensive alliances are extremely dangerous; that to think in terms of any fixed and unchangeable system is folly; and that the object of Swedish statesmen should be 'to keep foreign policy to a minimum'. Though he was impartially severe upon the prejudices of the rabid partisans of England and of France, he reiterated Fersen's view of England's commercial jealousy and greed, and instanced the case of Portugal as a warning of the 'trade-slavery', which could follow upon attachment to an English system. Two years later, at the close of the Hat Diet of 1769–70, the Hats' Lesser Secret Deputation drew up what was to be almost their last official pronouncement on foreign policy.[90] Once again it insisted on the dangers of economic subjection to England, which since Cromwell's time had aimed at an *Imperium Maris*; but essentially it advocated the kind of foreign policy which Tessin in more confident times had stigmatised as 'an ignominious quiescence and a craven repose'. The only road to security lay through developing the country's wealth; to that end peace was imperatively necessary; the objective (despite Fersen) should be good relations with all states; no new alliances – not even a defensive alliance – must be contracted before the next meeting of the Diet. The Family Compact was no danger to peace, and therefore required no balancing combination; and anything like Panin's Northern League was 'if not chimerical, yet for Sweden unnecessary and injudicious'. If Sweden were attacked, France could be relied upon to give assistance, even though no alliance existed; but if Choiseul were prepared to renew the alliance, they were now ready to drop the plea for French subsidies – which meant, in effect, that they

[88] Fersen's arguments are transcribed in Goodricke's despatch of 28 Jan 1766: PRO SP 95/109/48–57, and are dated 20 December 1765. The notes printed by Trulsson (pp. 508–9) are a direct copy of this, dated 22 February 1766, and not Scheffer's own work.

[89] [Anders Schönberg], 'Om förbund, mellan stater' *Gjörwells Statsjournal*, II (Stockholm 1768). For Schönberg's authorship see *Anders Schönbergs bref till Bergsrådet Adlerwald*, ed. Sam Kellin (Stockholm 1920), p. 66.

[90] RA. Svar på sekreta propositionen, 5 februari 1770 (Riksens ständers brev 1765–1770: Utrikes ärenden).

were ready to forgo the hope of any rapid and effective rearmament.[91] The world had altered since the days of Tessin's expansive rhetorical flourishes: the Hats had learned their lesson.

This appears from their attitude to Poland, and to the Turks, in 1768 and 1769. In 1734 they had been all agog to intervene on behalf of Stanislaw Leszczyński. In 1751 the Hat politician C. F. Scheffer – who had the misfortune to be initiated into 'le secret du Roi' – was revolving plans to prevent Poland from becoming a Russian puppet: all that was required, he thought, was a joint Swedish–Prussian army of 25–30 000 men, and the succession of the Prince of Conti: a choice example, this, of French influence and Hat frivolity.[92] But when in 1768 Repnin was riding roughshod over Polish liberty and deporting Polish bishops to Siberia, no Hat invective assailed the passivity of the Cap government: the only person to be seriously perturbed seems to have been the future Gustav III. So too with the Turks. The outbreak of the Russo-Turkish war at the end of 1768, which provoked festive fancy-dress celebrations on the part of Lovisa Ulrika, and persuaded Choiseul that this was the appointed moment to carry through a revolution in Stockholm, was received by Fersen and the Hats with a marked absence of that enthusiasm which had prevailed in similar circumstances thirty years before. They recalled with relief that their alliance with the Porte bound them to give assistance only if the Turks were attacked (and in this war – fortunately – they were the attackers); they took care to give England and Russia ample reassurances that they did not intend to meddle; and no surge of chauvinist feeling complicated their policy of prudence.[93]

The Caps, for their part, had less need to re-think their foreign policy. At the beginning of the Diet of 1765 the abrasive Bishop Serenius in a brimstone sermon had denounced the warlike enterprises of the Hats, 'begun with Saul's folly and Moabitish boasting';[94] but he and his colleagues had been singing that song since 1743. After the Caps came to power in 1765 their characteristic foreign policy was laid down in the Lesser Secret Deputation's instruction of October 1766;[95] and it was reiterated – with some significant additions and variations – in Anders Nordencrantz's *Thoughts on War in General, and on Sweden's Wars in particular* (1767), Esbjörn Christian Reuterholm's *Information for the Swedish People* (1769), Claes Frietzcky's memorandum of 1771, and the anonymous *Thoughts on Alliances and which is most advantageous for Sweden*,

[91] RA. Kungl. Maj:ts Nådiga Proposition öfver Utrikes ärenden till Riksdagen 1771.
[92] Carlquist, *Carl Fredrik Scheffer*, pp. 35–6.
[93] RA. Kabinettet för utrikes brevvexling. Presidentskontoret. Koncept, Ekeblad to Creutz, 4 July 1769; DRA TKUA Sverige B 163, Juel to Bernstorff, 29 April 1769.
[94] L. A. Cederbom, *Jacob Serenius i opposition mot Hattpartiet 1738–1766* (Skara 1904), p. 117.
[95] RA. Riksens ständers brev 1765–1766 uti utrikes ärenden, no. 210½.

which appeared in the same year.[96] The policies they advocated coincided in many respects with those which the Hats had now been forced to swallow: to a considerable extent there was now a consensus of opinion between the two parties. Sweden's main concern must be the preservation of peace. Security could best be achieved by concentrating on economic development, the fostering of trade and industry, and the effective utilisation of the large tracts of land which still lay unproductive. All war meant impoverishment; subsidies never covered the cost; the notion that war can sustain war was a delusion inherited from a previous age. But they went further than the Hats would have been prepared to go; for some of them insisted that all attempts to recover Sweden's lost provinces were a disastrous mistake, and even if successful would mean only 'a revival of old causes of new bloodshed'.[97] Nordencrantz condemned all overseas possessions in principle; Frietzcky suggested that perhaps Pomerania might be sold in order to provide the finance for a necessary currency reform at home.[98] Already in 1766 Serenius had denounced French subsidies as committing Sweden to six times as much expenditure as the amounts she received from them; the Lesser Secret Deputation in 1766 had been prepared, in the last resort, to accept an English alliance without subsidies; Reuterholm, Frietzcky and Nordencrantz were at one in rejecting all subsidies as inadmissible. There may well have been an element of sour grapes in this attitude: both Serenius and the Lesser Secret Deputation would have been glad enough of an English subsidy if they could have got one; and no doubt there were many Caps who privately resented the fact (or what they believed to be the fact) that England stole Sweden's trade and was then mean enough to refuse a subsidy by way of compensation: the ironic comment of Daniel Tilas on the Anglo-Swedish treaty of amity of 1766, and the loss of the French subsidies which was its consequence, may well represent a reaction which was not peculiar to himself.[99]

Translated into a programme for foreign policy these views tended to two related conclusions: the first was that England, rather than France,

---

[96] Anders Nordencrantz, *Tankar om Krig i gemen och Sveriges Krig i synnerhet*, i; [Esbjörn Christian Reuterholm], *Uplysning för Swenska folket om Anledningen, Orsaken och Afsigterne med Urtima Riksdagen 1769*; Claes Frietzcky, 'Reflexioner till Riksdagen 1771', in UUB 378; *Tankar om Alliancer, Och hwilka kunna wara för Swerige de förmånligaste* [1771].

[97] Nordencrantz, *Tankar om Krig i gemen och Sveriges Krig i synnerhet*, i, p. 43.

[98] *Ibid.*, i, pp. 44, 47, 49; Frietzcky (unpaginated).

[99] 'And so we are now, praise the powers, free of the French alliance, we have become a great and glorious people, we are now independent, we can now take our economic measures and be prosperous again. I and some others sat as scared as rabbits lest the gentlemen in question [the French] should come up and plank all 12 millions [of arrears of subsidy] on the table before we had managed to complete this admirable proceeding, for what is such a bagatelle compared with independence . . . Hallelujah ! Goddam the fransh Dogg [*sic*]': Tilas, *Anteckningar . . . från riksdagen 1765–1766*, pp. 460–1.

must be Sweden's ally (and, they hoped, protector); the second was that
every effort must be made to keep on good terms with Sweden's most
dangerous neighbour, Russia. The standard argument for an English
alignment was that England was not (in Europe) a bellicose or aggressive
power liable to involve an ally in hostilities, provided that care was taken
to refuse any obligation to participate in wars arising from colonial
controversies. Moreover, England could offer (as against France, whose
navy rarely ventured into the Baltic) effective naval protection if need
arose – supposing, of course, that British statesmen were prepared to take
the matter as seriously as they ought: wishful thinking led the Cap leaders
to suppose that England's interest in, and enthusiasm for, the Swedish
connexion matched their own. That this was an error had been perceived
more than thirty years before by one who was a Cap before the Cap party
was born: J. W. Arckenholtz. In his MS pamphlet of 1732 Arckenholtz
analysed the nature of the relationship with England more perceptively
than any of his successors.[100] He argued that only if Sweden's very
existence was threatened would the government in London contemplate
intervention: certainly they would not lift a finger to help her to regain her
lost provinces, foreseeing that success in that enterprise might be
followed by something similar directed against Bremen–Verden.[101] The
real reason why Sweden must seek England as an ally was not because
British statesmen had any predisposition in Sweden's favour, but for the
sake of trade. Sweden's most important export was iron; and for this, as
all later Cap writers did not fail to point out, England was Sweden's best
customer. The balance of trade was heavily in Sweden's favour: a
consideration important to those – and they were a majority, in both
parties – who thought in mercantilist terms.[102] But Arckenholtz reminded
his readers that Swedish iron exports were threatened by Russian
competition; that England's commercial ties with Russia were far too
important to be sacrificed for Sweden's sake; and that in contrast with a
Sweden embattled behind protectionist tariffs Russia was a relatively
open market for British manufactures. And the moral he drew from all
this was that an English alliance was necessary in order to prevent Russia
from extending and entrenching her position in the English market.

   Few later Cap writers were able take so dispassionate a view of
England's interests and obligations; but all agreed with his argument
about trade. For Britain was not only the major importer of Swedish

[100] J. W. Arckenholtz, *Om Sweriges nu warande intresse i anseende till andra riken och stater i Europa* (1732). I have used the MS copy in RA. Sjöholms samlingen.
[101] *Cf.* Sir Richard Lodge, 'The first Anglo-Russian Treaty, 1739–1742', *English Historical Review*, xliii (1928), p. 354, who made the same observation.
[102] Not quite so heavily as appeared: smuggling was an important offset, and there were other countervailing factors: see Kent, *War and Trade in Northern Seas*, pp. 89, 101–11.

iron,[103] she was also the provider of the *Verlag*[104] without which Swedish ironmasters could hardly have carried on: in 1739 the British minister in Stockholm wrote exuberantly that 'England's trade is, alone, of more value [to Sweden] than the Friendship, not only of France, but of the Universe together';[105] and this was a consideration which touched Hats even more than Caps, since a majority of the big ironmasters were of the Hat party: hence the indignant complaint of Sir John Goodricke, thirty years later, that the Hat ironmasters financed their anti-British election campaigns out of the profits of their trade to England.[106] Swedish exports of iron remained steady throughout the period; but increasing British demand could be satisfied only by larger imports from Russia, which in 1765 exceeded imports from Sweden for the first time; and though the fine Öregrund iron had no Russian competitor, and the Royal Navy would use no other, it represented only a small percentage of British purchases.[107] It was thus always possible, in theory, for a British government to blackmail Sweden by threatening to clap heavy duties on Swedish iron, and to buy as much as possible from Russia; and such a step was actually considered in 1769.[108] Nor was this the only instance in which it might seem that England had a Swedish enterprise at her mercy. The Swedish East India Company really conducted its operations on sufferance: at any moment its trade could have been disrupted and its factory taken over by its English rival. It had been the fear of reprisals that had induced Arvid Horn (and the Hats after him) not to press the Porto Novo affair (1734) to a crisis.[109]

Yet as far as the iron trade was concerned, at any rate, Cap apprehensions as to what might happen if Sweden and England ceased to be friends were to some extent unrealistic. The British position was not as strong as they supposed, nor was the Swedish iron industry in practice at England's mercy. Ministers in London realised very well that punitive

[103] Staffan Högberg, *Utrikeshandel och sjöfart på 1700-talet. Stapelvaror i svensk export och import 1738–1808* (Stockholm 1969), pp. 66–8, 71–5.

[104] By the *Verlag*-system the Swedish wholesale exporter owned the Swedish producer's iron before it came to the market, since he had advanced the capital for its production; and the wholesaler himself was no more than a commission-agent for the British importer, and operated with his money.

[105] Quoted in Nilzén, *Studier i 1730-talets partiväsen*, p. 83.

[106] PRO SP 95/113/165–8, 114/109–10, Goodricke to Rochford, 27 December 1768, 10 January 1769.

[107] Kent (p. 68) puts it at 15%, or 3–4000 tons; but in 1769 the Navy Board stated it at only 700 tons in peacetime: PRO SP 95/134, Navy Board to Admiralty, 23 June 1769.

[108] Roberts, *British Diplomacy and Swedish Politics*, p. 277.

[109] For the Porto Novo affair see Conrad Gill, 'The Affair of Porto Novo: an Incident in Anglo-Swedish Relations', *EHR*, lxxii (1958); Nilzén, *Studier i 1730-talets partiväsen* pp. 112–15; Göran Behre, 'Ostindiska Kompaniet och hattarna. En storpolitisk episod 1742', *Historisk tidskrift* (1966). For other examples of fear of English reprisals, Högberg, *Utrikeshandel och sjöfart på 1700-talet*, pp. 102–5, 138–40.

measures against Swedish iron would hurt British interests which were too considerable to be lightheartedly jeopardised: too much British capital was invested in mines and forges by way of *Verlag* for tough action to be resorted to except in an extreme case. Again, another of the staple Cap arguments for the English alliance was that Sweden had a large, and consistently large, favourable trade balance with England. On the official figures this was certainly true; and it was a matter of concern to successive British governments. They complained of Sweden's protective tariffs; they hoped for a commercial treaty which would lower or abolish them. Yet among English exporters there seems to have been no great popular demand for any action: despite the duties, English legitimate trade to Sweden seems to have been doing quite well, and smuggling – in both directions – even better.[110] The suggestion, sometimes made on the British side, that if Sweden would only agree to a commercial treaty involving the lowering of duties she would gain more than any subsidy could give her[111] was (as the Hats insisted) fallacious: the result would be the swamping of struggling Swedish industries by cheap manufactures. Experience amply proved that there was a ready market for English textiles and leather goods, which were notoriously smuggled into the country; for they were of better quality – and cheaper – than the corresponding Swedish articles. On this point the Hats certainly had the better of the argument, even though it may be conceded that the industries they were so concerned to protect were hothouse plants cultivated at extravagant cost, and often very inefficiently run;[112] and the Caps' replies were, on the whole, shuffling and disingenuous in their attempts to deny this consequence.[113] Moreover, the Hats were entitled to point out that though England might indeed be the biggest buyer of Swedish iron, she was by no means the only one: not far short of half of iron exports went to Latin ports in exchange for salt and wine. Portugal was an especially important market for the poorer sorts;[114] for in the 1760s rather more than 80% of salt imports came from there, and salt was of particular importance at a period when the Swedish west-coast herring

[110] Kent, *War and Trade in Northern Seas*, pp. 89, 101–111. Smuggling of tea was an important item: in 1763 Goodricke reported that the British Isles had imported 800 000 lbs of smuggled Swedish East India tea every year for the last five years, at 2s. 6d. a lb.: PRO SP 75/115/80; and *cf.* *ibid.* 108/191.

[111] E.g. PRO SP 95/113: Conway to Goodricke, 8 January 1768.

[112] For the Hats' industrial policy see chapter III, below.

[113] E.g. RA Svar på sekreta propositionen (13 Oct. 1766): 'As regards . . . trade and industry . . . there may indeed be some rivalry . . . between the two countries; but as all such matters are independent of the friendship and alliance which may be established in political matters, they offer no other difficulty with England than such as may arise with all other countries (to a greater or less extent) as they seek gain by trade and a market for their goods'. And *cf.* an equally disingenuous passage in [Esbjörn Reuterholm], *Uplysningar*, p. 67.

[114] Karl-Gustaf Hildebrand, 'Foreign Markets for Swedish Iron in the 18th Century', *Scandinavian Economic History Review*, VI (1958), pp. 38–41.

fishery was booming.[115] Where the Hats went wrong was in supposing that the destruction of Swedish trade and native industry was the main objective of British policy. No doubt a commercial treaty was *one* objective which all Secretaries of State kept intermittently in mind. But from the British point of view the Swedish trade was too small to be of major importance; and in the period after 1765 it was political rather than commercial advantages that led British statesmen to interest themselves in Swedish affairs. A Swedish treaty was regarded in London as the most convenient stepping-stone to that alliance with Russia which now seemed to be the main *desideratum*, and which was certainly much more important in British eyes than the obtaining of easier access to the Swedish market. It was just because this was so that the Caps could risk evading all proposals for a commercial treaty. So, when in 1771–2 it became clear that not even the Caps were prepared to agree to a trade treaty which entailed a lowering of their tariff walls, England's tardy recognition of that fact in no way affected her Swedish policy. In this respect the weaker power could impose its terms on the stronger. But the Caps could put themselves in this satisfactory position only at the cost of admitting that Hat fears for the future of Swedish industry had not been without foundation.

If then the arguments for the Caps' policy of alignment with England, in so far as they were based on economic grounds, were less solid than might appear at first sight, how was it in regard to the other limb of their programme? Was their policy of friendship with Russia the right one? Were its risks and its advantages justly calculated? It is clear that in so far as Sweden was seriously threatened by any power, that threat came from Russia. Russian armies had occupied the whole of Finland twice during this century: another time they might not be so ready to quit it. In 1769 there was talk in St Petersburg of erecting Finland into an independent principality under Russian protection, on the analogy of Courland.[116] Nor was it so certain that Sweden herself might not be reduced to that status: in 1763 Bernstorff suspected that Catherine's object was to make Sweden a vassal kingdom, with Adolf Frederick as a Russian viceroy.[117] From time to time the example of Poland occurred to Swedish observers – even to those who favoured friendship with Russia – as a disquieting possibility.[118] The Hats' fear and hatred of Russia, born of two centuries of history, embittered by their own humiliation in 1743, and reinforced by Russian bullying in the forties, was understandable. But the foreign policy which they derived from it was ill-considered. It presupposed that

---

[115] Högberg; *Utrikeshandel och sjöfart på 1700-talet*, pp. 217, 226.
[116] RA. Tengberg avskrifter. Scheel to Bernstorff, 16/27 April 1769.
[117] *Correspondance ministérielle . . . de Bernstorff*, II, 109–10.
[118] Sallnäs, *Samuel Åkerhielm d.y.*, pp. 273–4.

Finland could be defended against a determined Russian attack; and that was probably not true. The fortification of Sveaborg was begun too late; its construction took too much time, and there was never enough money to hasten it;[119] and Sveaborg alone could not guarantee Finland's security. The shortcomings of the Swedish army remained, very little abated; the navy grew if anything weaker; by the end of the chapter Russia – whose fleet Catherine had once contemptuously dismissed as a collection of herring-busses – was numerically superior at sea. But any reinforcement of the exiguous army in Finland was likely to be seen as a provocation rather than as a deterrent: it is significant that in 1769 the Hats judged it wiser to abstain from any such troop movement. Their ally France was in practice incapable of defending Sweden – much less Finland; and as long as the Hats denied to Choiseul the constitutional revolution on which he insisted, there would not even be subsidies. After 1741 France never again incited a Swedish attack on Russia; and in 1773, when d'Aiguillon's only concern was Sweden's protection, he saw the best – perhaps the only – means of achieving it in a concert with England; and on that occasion his hope was frustrated by the refusal of England to tolerate any French naval squadron in the Baltic.[120]

The Caps faced the situation more realistically, and drew different conclusions from it. They liked the Russians no better than the Hats did; and if they took Russian money for their party funds, that was because they must have resources to match what the Hats drew from France, and because British Secretaries of State were not normally disposed to be open-handed. But apart from such financial considerations they honestly believed that the right policy – the only safe policy – was to maintain good-neighbourly relations, avoid provocations, and rely on their English friends to temper any Russian disposition to aggression. As long as Russia felt that she had nothing to fear from Sweden, she had no particular reason to molest her.[121] After 1750 this was probably a sound argument. But it was pushing the argument too far to assert, as Nordencrantz did, that 'if at any time since 1720 we had sat still, no one would have attacked us', – or, if they had done so, that Sweden in some

---

[119] Fersen, *Historiska skrifter*, II. 39.

[120] Michael Roberts, 'Great Britain and the Swedish Revolution, 1772–73', in *Essays in Swedish History* (1967).

[121] At least one prominent Hat inclined (at times) to this opinion. In 1762 Tessin, now an elder statesman in retirement, recalled that when he was in the Council he more than once minuted that Sweden might be safer with a Russian alliance. But he added 'O! what pressure from the West upon Sweden's trade and manufactures. O! what danger from the East to Sweden's political interests. The future enchainment or liberation of Europe depends . . . upon Revolutions in America. America's discovery first threw Europe into confusion, and the strength of the colonies may well soon be such as to be able to set all to rights once again': *Tessin och Tessiniana*, p. 371.

unspecified fashion would have been rescued:[122] an assumption reminiscent of the Hats' argument in 1770 that France could be relied upon for assistance, even without an alliance. If Nordencrantz supposed that England could be trusted to imperil her good relations with Russia for Sweden's sake he was likely to be disappointed: Arckenholtz had known better. England might at a pinch use diplomatic good offices, or even exert some pressure, as at the end of the forties or again in 1773; but no more than that. By the time the Caps were in a position to determine Sweden's foreign policy the situation had altered greatly from that which had existed a generation before. Catherine and Panin, like the Caps themselves, wanted a period of peace and recuperation. Both were concerned about Russia's economic difficulties; and Panin in particular was not anxious for any enlargement of the Russian dominions, which he considered to be already too extensive.[123] The very fact that he hoped that England would assume the lead (and bear the expense) in Stockholm is as good an indication as any that he was not thinking in terms of making Sweden a Russian puppet-state. His projected Northern System was conceived as a defensive organisation designed to safeguard Russia from 'the formidable League of the South'; though in reality France, too, was anxious (for the moment) for peace in Europe, and the Family Compact was directed essentially to colonial and naval issues. Yet it was understandable that Russian intervention in Warsaw might appear to have ominous implications for Sweden: it could not be known that the Polish imbroglio – and the Turkish war which arose out of it – were developments neither envisaged nor desired in St Petersburg, and that they amounted in fact to a defeat for Panin's policies. And the sabre-rattling of 1769 underlined the defensive nature of Russian attitudes to Sweden. The new treaties of alliance with Denmark and Prussia which Russia concluded in the autumn of that year, and which undoubtedly contemplated armed intervention in Sweden, and even in certain circumstances partition, were provoked by the *fears* of Bernstorff and Panin: fears that the Hats might after all accept Choiseul's terms, might agree to a revolutionary alteration of the constitution, and might confront them with an unlimited monarch who would denounce the Holstein agreements of 1749–50, make a diversionary attack on Russia at France's behest, and give active support to the Turks at a moment when Catherine was heavily committed in Poland and fighting a full-scale war in Moldavia. To Panin it must have seemed that 1738 had come again. No

---

[122] Nordencrantz, *Tankar om Krig i gemen och Sveriges Krig i synnerhet*, I, p. 68.
[123] David L. Ransel, *The Politics of Catherinian Russia. The Panin Party* (Yale 1975), pp. 53, 136, 143; David M. Griffiths, 'The Rise and Fall of the Northern System: Court Politics and Foreign Policy in the First Half of Catherine II's Reign' *Canadian Slavic Studies*, VI (1970); and Amburger, *Russland und Schweden*, pp. 113–14, 125, 187, 267–8.

doubt he ought to have been reassured by the failure of the Hat leadership
to give adequate support to a plan of constitutional reform which from
the Russian point of view was relatively innocuous;[124] but the episode
served to emphasise the point that the support of the Caps, who appeared
to be more solidly committed to resisting reform than the Hats were, was
an interest which Russia must take care to uphold, however backward
England might be in sending guineas to Sir John Goodricke.

On the whole, then, the Caps gauged the situation correctly. Yet when
the Age of Liberty ended, the Hats were still by sentiment and tradition a
French party, as the Caps were an English party; but both in future would
be wary of committing themselves to exclusive alliances. Common sense
had prevailed over nostalgia; ends (it was now agreed) must be
proportioned to means. The Hats might feel, and be entitled to feel, that
there was something humiliating and degrading in their rivals' dependence upon Russian money for their party funds, and their acceptance of
the Russian minister almost as a party-leader; though they might have
found it embarrassing to attempt to explain the difference between
Osterman's relationship with the Caps, on the one hand, and their own
dependence on Casteja in the thirties, d'Havrincour in the fifties, and even
Breteuil after 1764. Moreover, the Caps had shown in 1766, and would
show again in 1771–2, that Russian bribes and Russian leadership could
not restrain them from taking their own way, even if that way was not
Russia's. And they could retort that as a matter of practical politics their
tenure of power was the best security that Sweden had for immunity from
Russian molestation. But such polemic, such party traditions, no longer
stirred more than the surface of policy, and could no longer obscure the
great change which had overtaken Swedish statesmen in the years since
the mid-century: a change which was to prove irreversible, a change
which did much to prepare the way for the Sweden of the nineteenth and
twentieth centuries. After fifty years of unhappy experience, Sweden by
1771 had at last made the painful adjustment to her new status as a minor
power. But though Hats and Caps might now be in tacit agreement about
neutrality, the country still lacked – as it had lacked ever since 1721 – the
resources, military and financial, to make that option really available,
and to ensure that neutrality would be respected. It would require the
reforms of Gustav III to give some credibility to Sweden's foreign policy;
it would be another half-century after him before Swedish sovereigns
finally abjured foreign adventures; and it would be much longer before
the Swedish people squarely faced the fact that the neutrality which they
so jealously watched over must rest upon their willingness to bear the
burden of defending it.

[124] See below, chapters II and V.

II

Swedish Liberty: in principle and in practice

(i)

It was not only the historians who devised the term 'The Age of Liberty' to describe the period in Swedish history which lies between 1719 and 1772. Swedish contemporaries used it also, for they felt it to be appropriate to their circumstances.[1] The great majority of the political nation exulted in the liberty which the Constitution of 1720 was considered to have given to them; they treasured that constitution as a precious national monument; they believed it to be of unique excellence. In 1759 the Swedish Church altered a form of prayer so that it ended 'To the Honour of Thy Holy Name, and the safeguarding of each and all of us in our blessed Liberty'.[2] In 1766 a Swedish politician remarked that the constitution could not have been improved upon, 'though it had been writ by angels'.[3] He was not alone in his opinion: Voltaire pronounced Sweden to be 'the freest country in the world'; Mably called the Swedish constitution 'that masterpiece of modern legislation'; for Rousseau it was 'an example of perfection'.[4]

In Sweden in 1719, no less than in England in 1689, politicians were forced to have recourse to constitutional fictions in order to secure a settlement:[5] in England a supposititious abdication; in Sweden, the fiction

[1] For an example of the use of the expression 'frihetstidehwarfwet', see *Bondeståndets riksdagsprotokoll*, 12 (Stockholm 1978), p. 415.

[2] Hilding Pleijel, *Hustavlans värld* (Stockholm 1970), p. 47.

[3] Erik Fahlbeck, 'Studier öfver frihetstidens politiska ideer', *Statsvetenskaplig tidskrift* (1916), p. 104.

[4] Fredrik Lagerroth, *Frihetstidens författning* (Stockholm 1915), p. 734; Erik Fahlbeck 'Studier öfver frihetstidens politiska ideer' (1915), p. 328, citing *De l'étude de l'histoire* pp. 257ff.; *ibid.* (1916), p. 125.

[5] The nature of the changes of 1719–20 is a matter of controversy. To Erland Hjärne and Lennart Thanner they constituted a revolution; while Lagerroth, in his determination to see the Constitution of 1720 as essentially a native growth, contended that Sweden experienced no revolution until 1809: Lennart Thanner, *Revolutionen i Sverige efter Karl XII:s död* (Uppsala 1953); Fredrik Lagerroth, 'Revolution eller rättskontinuitet?', *Scandia* (1936); *idem*, 'Det rättsliga utgångsläget för de stora författningsförändringarna i Sveriges historia', *Scandia* (1970), and especially 'Svensk konstitutionalism i komparativ belysning', *Historisk tidskrift* (1966), pp. 129–59.

that the Diet of 1719 was a continuation of that of 1713–14, and thus required no royal summons in order to meet. In each case the upshot was the accession of a ruler who held the throne by parliamentary title. But in both countries an attempt was made to disguise the violence of the change by the pretence that what had happened was really the restoration of a historic constitutional situation: the Diet of 1719 announced that its purpose was 'to restore the government of the country to its old state and nature, which from former times has proved so happy'.[6] The Swedish revolution was thus in one aspect an appeal to history, and to positive law, rather than to any doctrine of natural rights.[7] In imposing electoral monarchy the Swedes felt themselves to be reverting to a long historic tradition, first interrupted in 1544, but never wholly forgotten thereafter. But in another aspect the Swedish revolution invoked the idea of fundamental law.[8] Whereas the English revolution marks the beginning of the end of fundamental law as an element in practical politics, the Swedish ushered in a period of half a century during which the concept came to be of central importance. All this is not to deny, of course, that both revolutions were concerned with specific issues, abuses of power, demands for better governance: Daniel Silvius, one of the more influential political writers of 1719, deals much with typically English issues such as standing armies, control of taxation, regular meetings of the Diet, ministerial responsibility; and indeed the Constitution of 1720 included provisions – usually reiterations of accepted principles – designed to cover these matters.[9] It is also possible, of course, to see the Swedish revolution as simply the work of a selfish upper class of bureaucrats, landowners, merchants and mine-owners, propelled by the greed of the bureaucracy for its pay: thus not essentially an issue of constitutional principle at all.[10] That such considerations played a part in the years between 1719 and 1723 has long been obvious. That they dictated the nature of the constitutional settlement is unproven and improbable.

[6] Hugo Valentin, *Frihetstidens riddarhus. Några bidrag till dess karakteristik* (Stockholm 1915), p. 9.

[7] Fredrik Lagerroth, 'Positivrätt eller naturrät? Ett statsrättsligt dilemma från svenska 1700-talet', *Scandia* (1967).

[8] Daniel Silvius, e.g., was concerned that the constitution should be based on the law of Nature, and on reason: Erik Fahlbeck, 'Studier öfver frihetstidens politiska ideer' (1916), p. 328; cf. J. W. Gough, *Fundamental Law in English Constitutional History* (2nd edn, Oxford 1961), pp. 161ff.

[9] For Ludvig Stavenow this was the essence of the revolution: the pamphleteering on political theory no more than an incidental: Ludvig Stavenow, *Det adertonde århundradets parlamentarism i Sverige* (Uppsala 1923), p. 7. Ulrika Eleonora's Accession Charter did in fact include points such as the promise of no taxation without consent, freedom of election, free speech in parliament: Axel Brusewitz, ed., *Frihetstidens Grundlagar och konstitutionella stadgar* (Stockholm 1916), pp. 51–2.

[10] The theory is aggressively expounded in Werner Buchholz, *Staat und Ständegesellschaft in Schweden zur Zeit des Überganges vom Absolutismus zum Ständeparlementarismus 1718–1720* (Stockholm 1979).

Though the makers of the Swedish revolution may have thought in terms of a 'restoration', in fact they ended up with something which was in many respects new. Their immediate object may indeed have been only to wipe out Charles XI and Charles XII; but in attempting this they succeeded in wiping out Gustav Adolf and Axel Oxenstierna too. It is not easy to see the Constitution of 1720 simply as an historic growth, or an empirical adaptation to changing situations. No doubt it gathered up into itself precedents and demands stretching back for more than a century. No doubt it preserved the historic trinity of King–Council–Estates (with the Estates now in the place occupied by the monarch in 1682); and it certainly owed something to the Absolutism of Charles XI. Before 1719 the constitution had meant (in general) the Rule of Law, and (in particular) a handful of important acts of state: Magnus Eriksson's Land Law, the Succession Pacts of 1544 and 1604, the Charter of 1611, the Form of Government of 1634, the *Additament* of 1660. But in 1719 Sweden for the first time acquired a full, precise, written constitution, which was something more than a mere administrative statute, something more than an ampler version of the Form of Government of 1634. It inaugurated a new epoch in the constitution's history. The worn-out formularies which connected the new constitution with the old were not links strong enough to stand the weight of organic development in the style of Burke; and the next two generations would find them more a source of embarrassment and controversy than an asset.[11] Certainly Sweden owed something to English political experience, and also to English political thought. The men of 1719–20 were influenced by Locke, but also by Algernon Sidney; and it is even possible that they may have had the Instrument of Government in mind.[12] Yet despite such influences the differences were profound. The English constitution remained piecemeal and flexible, a matter largely of conventions and precedents;

[11] E.g. that decision of the Diet of 1602 which laid it down that the Council 'shall give counsel, but shall *not* govern': see the case of Creutz in 1739, who was voted out of the Council by the Estates for not having resisted an objectionable appointment by Frederick I, and vainly adduced this principle in extenuation: Lennart Linnarsson, *Riksrådens licentiering. En studie i frihetstidens parlamentarism* (Uppsala 1943), p. 83; and cf. the interpretation in Isak Faggott, *Swea Rikes Styrelse efter Grund-lagarne* (Stockholm 1768), pp. 128–30. Similar difficulties were experienced with the old constitutional watchword from the Form of Government of 1634, 'The King's majesty, the Council's authority, and the proper liberties of the Estates': on this see Ludvig Stavenow, 'De politiska doktrinernas uppkomst och första utveckling under frihetstiden', in *Festskrift tillägnade Carl Gustaf Malmström* (Stockholm 1897), pp. 17–18.
[12] Silvius seems to have been influenced by Sidney's *Discourses concerning Government* (1698). For a discussion of these influences, see Erland Hjärne, *Från Vasatiden till frihetstiden* (Stockholm/Uppsala 1929) pp. 129–30, 163–4; Frederik Lagerroth, *Frihetstidens författning*, pp. 285, 301, 466. The influence of the Instrument of Government has been doubted (Lennart Thanner, *Revolutionen i Sverige efter Karl XII:s död*, p. 47), and no doubt the suggestion rests only on the much later authority of Anders Schönberg. But if they were looking for a model of a written constitution, where else were they to find one?

the Swedish was now logical and rigid. The rigidity was by no means absolute; the growth of constitutional conventions was possible, and it proved necessary. But though the Diet was free to *interpret* the constitution, and even to *improve* it, it could not *alter* it; for the constitution, like the constitution of the United States later, was a fundamental law.[13] Constitutional controversy therefore came to centre on the interpretation of a group of fundamental documents – the Constitution of 1720, the Accession Charter of Fredrick I, the *riksdagsordning* of 1723. An essential skill of the politician came to be *exegesis*. The constitution became 'static'.

The English and Swedish revolutions differed not only in spirit, but in their practical consequences. In England, the result was a constitutional monarchy and the sovereignty of king-in-parliament; in Sweden the way was opened to the sovereignty of the Estates. The Absolutism of the Diet stepped into the shoes of the royal Absolutism which had been overthrown. The first three Georges all enjoyed large undisputed rights within the constitution: the right to appoint and dismiss ministers; the right to dissolve parliament; the right to create, or not to create, peers. They were a part of the legislative, and their consent to bills could not be taken for granted. Though they never used the veto, that was because they had no need to do so, since no minister if he were wise would try to pass legislation without securing the prior acquiescence of his sovereign. The Crown in England had patronage; it had influence. It was a working wheel in the machine. Kings were not merely entitled to defend the constitution against assault, but felt a positive duty to do so. It followed that they must be allowed to have a view as to what the constitution really meant; and that they were free to have conscientious scruples about the implication of their coronation oaths.

Very different was the situation of Frederick I or Adolf Frederick. In Sweden, as in England, the doctrine of the irresponsibility of the Crown, with its corollary of ministerial responsibility, was now generally accepted; and the consequences of that doctrine were drawn in Sweden immediately, with a stringency of logic which was still alien to English politics. In Sweden, the irresponsibility of the king necessarily entailed his political impotence. He could not veto legislation, since he had promised in his Accession Charter 'always to agree with the Estates'.[14] He could not dismiss a minister; he could appoint to the Council of State only from a list of three presented to him by the Estates; he could not dissolve parliament and appeal to the country, as George III did in 1784;[15] his

---

[13] The preamble to the Constitution of 1719 would have permitted alteration; but the word 'alter' was deliberately dropped from the Constitution of 1720.

[14] Brusewitz, *Frihetstidens Grundlagar*, pp. 60, 74.

[15] He did not obtain this power until 1866.

influence on policy was limited to having a double vote and a casting vote in the Council, and the right to record his dissent: when in 1756 Adolf Frederick refused to sign nominations which his Council had approved, they made a name-stamp to take the place of his signature. The king's power of creating peers was usually subject to the Diet's approval (though in the crisis-year 1756 he risked creating a batch of fifty in an attempt to strengthen his political position);[16] and his opportunities for acquiring influence were limited.[17] The Estates made him an allowance for his private disbursements: not for Sweden the antique confusions of royal finance in England. His oath bound him to comply with the constitution, not only as it now was, but as it might chance to be if the Diet should 'improve' it. His right to have a conscience was denied.[18] The Accession Charter which was imposed on Gustav III in 1772 took from him even his ultimate resort, for it bound him not to abdicate: the monarch might be a nullity or a mere decoration, but since by the fundamental law of the constitution Sweden could never be a republic, it followed that abdication was illegal. In 1756, after the discovery of a royalist plot, Adolf Frederick was forced to assent to an *Act of State* which recited his misdeeds in terms which might have come from the Grand Remonstrance, and declared that the Estates could dissolve the tie which bound king and subjects together, if he should break his oath.[19] All officials had, no doubt, to take an oath of loyalty to the king; but they had also to swear not to support by any means the introduction of Absolutism – which meant any measures which in the opinion of the Estates might be considered, even remotely, to have that tendency: an obligation which extended even to such unlikely persons as members of the Society of Surgeons.[20] When in December 1768 Adolf Frederick plucked up courage and struck work,[21] the Council invoked the principle of the Double Majesty, and claimed the *majestas realis*.[22] It is true that the king had some rights which were not unimportant. He was entitled to appoint to subordinate civil and military office from a list of candidates presented to him, and to senior posts in a session of the Council of State – though subject to their veto if they

[16] Per-Erik Brolin, 'Ståndsutjämning som historiskt problem', *Historisk tidskrift* (1951), p. 88; and though in fact that approval was usually given, and given too freely, especially around 1760.
[17] For the extent to which the ambiguities in the constitution gave the king some freedom of manoeuvre, see Birger Sallnäs, 'En kraftmätning mellan konung och råd 1723', *Historisk tidskrift* (1950), pp. 113–27.
[18] Carl Gustaf Malmström, *Sveriges politiska historia från konung Karl XII:s död till statshvälfningen 1772*, v pp. 149–50. C. F. Scheffer laid it down that a king has no moral responsibility before God if he acts according to his Council's counsel: F. Lagerroth, 'En frihetstidens lärobok i gällande svensk statsrätt', *Statsvetenskaplig tidskrift* (1937), p. 209.
[19] Printed in Fersen, *Historiska skrifter* (Stockholm 1867–72), ii, Appendix.
[20] Wolfram Kock, *Olof af Acrel* (Stockholm 1967), p. 98.
[21] See below p. 173.
[22] E. Fahlbeck, 'Studier öfver frihetstidens politiska ideer', (1916), pp. 39–40.

considered that he was overstepping the law. His right of presentation in cases when an advowson was in the hands of the Crown (and since Charles XI's time such cases were numerous) was a reality which even a political bishop could not brush aside.[23] His two votes in Council might be decisive on critical occasions, especially in regard to foreign policy – as they were, for instance, in 1727, in 1741 and in 1764. And in Frederick I's time it was certainly worth a politician's while to cultivate the royal mistress. But it remained true that the only legal way to increase his power and influence was to show that the Constitution of 1720 had intended it, and had been perverted by mistaken interpretations; an argument which proved unfruitful in practice, and insecurely based in theory.[24] All in all, Charles Sheridan was exaggerating only a little when he wrote that in Sweden the monarch 'had the title of King, with hardly the privileges of a subject'; and Sven LagerBring not much more when he observed that the prerogative was virtually restricted to the right to eat and sleep.[25]

The English revolution had been made of the ground of a broken contract, or so it seemed to Locke; and that contract (if we may believe Blackstone) had been subsequently formalised in the coronation oath.[26] In Sweden it was quite otherwise. There, contractualist theory soon came to be branded as a heresy. The settlement of 1719–20 was held to have produced no contract, implicit or explicit, between king and nation: a doctrine which was finally declared orthodox when in 1755 the Diet endorsed the Lesser Secret Deputation's *Memorial on false and erroneous ideas*, originally drafted by Bishop Browallius in 1752.[27] Erik Sparre, the father of Swedish constitutionalism, had in the 1590s based hereditary monarchy upon contract; the founders of the Age of Liberty now threw the one overboard with the other. For a contract implies reciprocal obligations; and the Estates for their part recognised no obligations whatever. Frederick I and Adolf Frederick were simply elected to the throne on a take-it-or-leave-it basis, which left the Estates free to alter the arrangements without their having any right to object. Their views on the constitution, their ideas about their duty, were simply irrelevant; and such powers as they enjoyed under the constitution were not rights: they were a revocable *concessio*. It was a doctrine long resisted by an obstinate minority; and the theory of a contract would survive to become one of the

[23] Björn Ryman, *Eric Benzelius d.y. En frihetstida politiker* (Motala 1978), p. 131.
[24] Ludvig Stavenow, 'De politiska doktrinernas uppkomst', pp. 37–43.
[25] Charles Sheridan, *A History of the Late Revolution in Sweden* (1778), p. 29; Sven LagerBring, *Sammandrag af Swea-Rikes Historia* (2nd edn, Stockholm 1780), v. iii. 52.
[26] 'As to the terms of the original contract between king and people, these I apprehend to be now couched in the coronation oath': Sir William Blackstone, *Commentaries on the Laws of England*, (9th edn, 1783), I, 234.
[27] Printed in Malmström, *Sveriges politiska historia*, IV, pp. 453ff.

intellectual forces behind the movement for constitutional monarchy which triumphed in the revolution of 1772.[28]

The question of how the constitution was to be interpreted, and by whom, came to be of importance also in eighteenth-century England. It lay at the root of the American revolt, which was in one aspect a challenge to the doctrine of the sovereignty of parliament, and an appeal to an authority higher than parliament: to the Law of Nature, or the Law of God, or even to the right of every man to decide for himself which law he would obey, and which not. But in Sweden the constitution was presumed to embody both the Law of Nature and the Law of God: in 1758 Nils Palmstierna wrote: 'if only one follows strictly *jus naturae*, one thereby describes *jus publicum svecanum*';[29] and the interpretation of the constitution must necessarily rest with those that made it – that is, with the Estates themselves:[30] not for a moment would they have been willing to place it in some extraneous body, still less leave it to the vagaries of the royal conscience. The constitution was indeed a sort of Holy Writ (in 1769 Burgomaster Sundblad compared it with the Lord's Prayer),[31] and only the trained theologians of the Diet could be relied upon to interpret it in an orthodox sense. To *mis*interpret it was, almost literally, heresy; and those who did so were pursued with inquisitorial rigour. Carl Gustaf Tessin could write that 'any man who follows his own opinion, after it has been rejected by a majority of the Estates, betrays his duty, and acts from vanity': a contumacious heretic, in fact.[32] Thus an intimate knowledge of the fundamental documents of the constitution, and dialectical subtlety and readiness in making quick deductions from them, were important prerequisites for an aspiring statesman. It was no wonder that Johan von Engeström always carried a copy of the constitution in his pocket.[33]

Between Crown and Estates there was now no such mediating power as the Council had been in the middle of the previous century, or as the eighteenth-century House of Lords liked to fancy itself to be. The Estate of Nobility certainly did not cast itself for that part; still less see itself, as the Lords did, as the hereditary bulwarks of the Crown.[34] The Council's

[28] But even in the citadels of Hat orthodoxy language on this subject could be somewhat loose on occasion: as late as 1751 Carl Gustaf Tessin could write that 'King and Estates are the two *contracting* parties of which our constitution is composed': for this, see Ludvig Stavenow, 'De politiska doktrinernas uppkomst' pp. 8–9, 37–43. And see Grönhagen's *Memorial* in *Sveriges ridderskaps och adels riksdagsprotokoll* [SRARP], xix, Appendix, pp. 119ff.
[29] Martin Weibull, *Lunds Universitets historia*, I (Lund 1918), p. 271.
[30] Even in 1765 Bishop Jacob Serenius, a bitter critic of many aspects of the constitution, could say 'No man can interpret the law but he who made it': L. A. Cederbom, *Jacob Serenius i opposition mot Hattpartiet 1738–1766*, p. 132.
[31] Erik Fahlbeck, 'Studier öfver frihetstidens politiska ideer' (1916), p. 35.
[32] *Carl Gustaf Tessins dagbok 1748–1752* (Stockholm 1915), p. 12.
[33] Johan von Engeström, *Historiska Anteckningar och Bref från åren 1771–1805*, ed. E. V. Montan (Stockholm 1877), p. xiv.
[34] Blackstone, *Commentaries on the Laws of England*, I, p. 158.

attempt to assert such a mediating power had been decisively crushed by Charles XI, as an infringement of his sovereignty; and it was equally objectionable to the absolutism of the Diet. The age of ephors was over for good. No doubt the settlement of 1719–20 had been based on the idea that the king should be controlled by the Council; but it had also supposed that the Council should be controlled by the Estates. For as long as Arvid Horn retained power it was still probable that the Council might have some real part to play in the working of the constitution. But from the beginning the Estates had been jealous of it; and after Horn's fall it was reduced, as a rule, to a position in which it was powerless to provide any check upon the sovereign Diet, and often lacked even the will to attempt it.[35]

The alteration in the constitutional situation which occurred in 1720, and the way in which that situation was exploited in practice, produced in the middle years of the century a body of political theory designed to justify and interpret it. Whereas in eighteenth-century England the constitution is for nearly half a century more or less taken for granted, in Sweden it becomes the subject of interminable narcissistic debate.[36] The starting-point for much of this political theory is Locke: so, for instance, in that *Memorial concerning false and erroneous ideas* drawn up by Bishop Browallius in 1752; so too with Isak Faggott, who in 1768 published an account of the Swedish constitution which in places is clearly a direct translation of Locke.[37] Both derive from Locke the principle of the supremacy of the legislative in the body politic. But it was possible to begin with Locke and reach very un-Lockean conclusions. A pamphlet written in 1747 laid it down that the People, on entering society, had divested itself of rights in favour of the sovereign Estates, and could not subsequently resume them; and if the Estates abused their trust, there was no remedy.[38] A decade or so earlier than Faggot, Carl Fredrik Scheffer, in a manual intended for the instruction of the future Gustav III, had asserted that the Estates were not simply representatives, not merely a body to which the people had entrusted power: they were themselves the people;

---

[35] That Serenius in 1765 should have suggested that the Council was an intermediary *Estate* between king and Diet was a heresy which could hardly have been risked ten years before: Linnarsson, *Riksrådens licentiering*, p. 320.

[36] It was no accident that during the Age of Liberty undergraduates at Uppsala were required to pass an examination in constitutional law, nor that Gustav III should have abolished this requirement, as unnecessary: Nils Ahnlund, *Jonas Hallenberg* (Stockholm 1957), pp. 29–30.

[37] E.g. when he writes that men entered society 'in order to enjoy peace, security and protection, for Honour LIFE and PROPERTY': Isak Faggott, *Swea Rikes Styrelse efter Grundlagarne*, p. 39. And *cf.* the passages on pp. 4–6, where he explains that the power of the legislative does not extend to life, since a man cannot give to government something he does not possess, and no man possesses the right to take his own life – a dictum which the Estates on occasion found it convenient to ignore.

[38] Erik Fahlbeck, 'Studier öfver frihetstidens politiska ideer' (1915), pp. 337–8.

and as such were invested with an *imperium*.[39] But when one Swedish
theorist asserted that the sovereignty which thus inhered in the Diet was
immutable because any attempt to revoke it would plunge men into the
terrors of the state of nature, that was an argument which Locke would
not have relished, and which is in fact an odd attempt to reinforce Locke
with Hobbes.[40] It was indeed generally conceded that the Estates were
bounded by the law (though at least one Swedish writer maintained that
they were *legibus soluta*),[41] and in particular by the fundamental laws; but
this might not mean much in view of their power to 'amend' or 'improve'
the constitution, and their monopoly of the testing-right. And since they
were absolute and sovereign,[42] it followed that they were not responsible
to their constituents.[43] It followed also that they enjoyed the dispensing-
power: a man whose application for leave to marry his deceased wife's
step-daughter had been refused by the courts applied to the Estates to
dispense him from compliance with the law, and his request was
granted.[44] Thus one fundamental presupposition of the constitution –
namely that power and responsibility are correlatives – was contradicted
in practice. Locke had argued that a legislative which broke the law *eo ipso*
ceased to exist; the men of the Age of Liberty turned Locke on his head by
arguing that since the Diet did exist, all that it did must necessarily be
legal.

Even the warmest champions of Swedish liberty grew pensive on
reaching this conclusion. There was much inconclusive debate as to
whether any remedy would be available if the Estates should violate the
constitution. Faggott was content to reiterate that the Diet was under the
law, and took it for granted that it would not threaten life and property;[45]
the editor of *En Ärlig Swensk* (1755) – who doubled the parts of Censor
and Hat pamphleteer – entangled himself in an elaborate distinction
between a man's right to resist Estates which violated the fundamental
law, and his duty of passive obedience in all other cases; though he offered
no guidance as to how the one situation was to be distinguished from the
other, or by whom.[46] Certainly the Estates did break the law from time to

---

[39] Fredrik Lagerroth, 'En frihetstidens lärobok i gällande svensk statsrätt', *Statsvetenskaplig tidskrift* (1937), pp. 198–200.

[40] Erik Fahlbeck, 'Studier öfver frihetstidens politiska ideer' (1915), pp. 335–6; (1916), p. 32; Lagerroth, *Frihetstidens författning*, p. 380.

[41] Lagerroth, 'Positivrätt eller naturrätt?', p. 291.

[42] The Estates prudishly avoided calling themselves sovereign: the expression they preferred was 'maktägande och lagbundna' – i.e. 'vested with authority within the limits of the law'. But on the whole they paid more attention to their authority than to the limits on it.

[43] Lagerroth, *Frihetstidens författning*, pp. 367, 374.

[44] Frederik Lagerroth, J. E. Nilsson, Ragnar Olsson, *Frihetstidens maktägande ständer* (Stockholm 1934) [*Sveriges riksdag*], I vi 243.

[45] Faggott, *Swea Rikes Styrelse efter Grundlagarne*, pp. 6–9, 139, 147.

[46] Stavenow, 'De politiska doktrinernas uppkomst', pp. 27–8.

time; and there was none to call them to account. Not until the Ordinance of 1766,[47] which gave the electorate a chance to reject a party which proposed to 'improve' the constitution, was there any real acknowledgement that the Diet was not at liberty to do exactly as it pleased.

It may be argued that Blackstone endowed parliament with as absolute a power as that which Scheffer attributed to the Diet. Certainly the Septennial Act was an extreme assertion of the view that no limit could be set to the exercise of parliamentary sovereignty. But after all, George I could have vetoed the Septennial Act, if he had thought it expedient to do so. A king of England's right to dissolve parliament, to 'recur to the sense of his people', was a vital reserve power against a tyrannous or lawless legislative. The want of any such power in Sweden was not the least of the causes which led to the crisis of December 1768 and the débâcle of August 1772. Moreover, though the Septennial Act might make clear the *fact* of the absolute sovereignty of King, Lords and Commons, it left the question of *right*, and still more the question of expediency, still debatable. Half a century later Burke would be reminding his hearers that, 'It is not what a lawyer tells me I *may* do, but what humanity, reason and justice tell me that I ought to do'; and that was a consideration which was – usually – kept in mind. So much so, that Professor Dickinson has argued that the opponents of the doctrine of unlimited parliamentary sovereignty in the end succeeded in convincing its champions that it was to be regarded as a legal fiction.[48]

In the years between 1739 and 1772 the overwhelming concentration of power in the hands of the Estates was only once seriously challenged, and that was by the Diet's own constituents. Between 1743 and 1747 debate raged on the question whether or not members of the three lower (elected) Estates were responsible to their constituents, accountable to them for their actions, and bound by such instructions as might be given to them. It was a question which cropped up from time to time in England also, most notably in 1769–70, and its appearance in Sweden to some extent reflects English influence; for Christopher Springer, who first raised it, seems to have believed that the imperative mandate was the rule in England, and was perhaps influenced by a misinterpretation of Locke's view of the accountability to the nation of a legislature which abuses its trust.[49] In Sweden, as in England, the doctrine of the delegate and the

[47] The *Ordinance for the Better Execution of the Laws*: for this see below, pp. 168–9.
[48] H. T. Dickinson, 'The Eighteenth-Century Debate on the Sovereignty of Parliament', *Transactions of the Royal Historical Society*, 5th Series 26 (1976), pp. 209–10.
[49] Torgny Höjer, 'Christopher Springer och principalatsstriden vid 1742–43 års riksdag', *Studier och handlingar rörande Stockholms historia*, I (Uppsala 1938). The question was whether 'Estates' meant elected representatives, or the whole electorate, as cl. 47 of the constitution might seem to imply. Samuel Åkerhielm, a prominent supporter of the delegate-theory, is known to have possessed a copy of Locke: Birger Sallnäs, *Samuel Åkerhielm*, p. 183.

mandate was firmly rejected; but it was rejected on grounds other than those upon which Burke rejected it. Burke might contend that he represented not Bristol only, but England; Scheffer insisted that members of the Diet did not represent anybody, for they *were* the Swedish people. And more fundamentally, it was rejected also on the characteristic Swedish argument that to question the decisions of the Diet was unconstitutional.[50]

Thus after 1747 the absolute authority of the Estates appeared to be beyond challenge; and in 1752 their pretensions were pushed to the limit of logic when Bishop Browallius enunciated the famous maxim that 'the idea that the Estates can err, is contrary to the fundamental law of the land'.[51] Fundamental law and parliamentary sovereignty, which in England came to be irreconcilable adversaries, were in Sweden joined in nefarious alliance.

(ii)

Of the four Estates which made up the Diet the Nobility was for long the true centre of Swedish political life, and was at times able to exercise strong (and occasionally quite violent) pressure upon the others.[52] It was much the largest of the Estates: on occasion more than a thousand members would be crammed into the *Riddarhus* for debates which were often labyrinthine, and on occasion tumultuous. Each noble family was represented by its *caput* or his proxy: younger sons of the peerage were thus excluded from politics since they were debarred from sitting in any other Estate. The suggestion that a seat in the House should depend upon the possession of landed property had been decisively rejected in 1720, with the result that a sizeable portion of the membership was made up of representatives of families in more or less modest circumstances. From time to time (for the last time in 1734) proposals were made for the replacement of this unwieldy body by a smaller assembly of representative peers; but the Nobility recoiled at the spectacle of English elections, and feared the corruption and influence which might follow such a change.[53] The history of the Scottish representative peerage suggests that they had a point.

The other three Estates were elective.[54] The Clergy returned members

---

[50] *Sveriges riksdag*, I, v, 152   [51] Malmström, *Sveriges politiska historia*, IV, 454.

[52] For an example from 1739 see Gustaf Bonde, *Historiska uplysningar om Tillståndet i Swerige under Konung Frederic den Förstes Regering* (Stockholm 1779), p. 51; for others, Ingemar Carlsson, *Parti–partiväsen – partipolitiker 1731–43. Kring uppkomsten av våra första politiska partier* (Stockholm 1981), pp. 87, 109.

[53] Hugo Valentin, *Frihetstidens riddarhus. Några bidrag till dess karakteristik.* (Stockholm 1915), pp. 106–32.

[54] Bishops sat *ex officio*, and for some of the smaller towns burgomasters virtually did so.

by diocese; and every beneficed clergyman within the diocese had a vote. Theirs was the smallest of the Estates, and numbered no more than fifty-one members.[55] For the Burghers, each of the ninety-seven towns was entitled to return at least one member; but the size of the Estate might vary considerably, since towns were free to combine to send a representative; and on occasion three of them might agree to choose a common member in rotation, somewhat in the manner of the Scottish burghs.[56] The franchise lay with all who had been admitted as burghers, were resident, paid scot and bore lot, and paid taxes; which in the majority of cases – especially of the smaller towns – meant that it was possessed by a majority of the adult male inhabitants: in Stockholm, however, the percentage was no more than 21%, and in Falun as little as 2%.[57] Votes were weighted according to the financial contribution of the elector; and elections in some of the larger towns were at two degrees.[58] As for the Peasants, election – once again, indirect – was by hundred (härad); and as with the Burghers, constituencies might club together to return a member. The basic principle was that every peasant who owned land within the constituency, and was not in any respect open to the objection that he was 'dependent' on a member of another Estate, or that his status was compromised by some sort of association with another Estate, was entitled to vote, his vote being weighted according to his stake in the country. The Estate of Peasants might number up to 180 members,[59] and was thus the largest of the non-noble Estates, as befitted the number of voters included in it. All members of the non-noble Estates received an allowance from their constituents for the period of their attendance at a Diet; and one reason for the combination of constituencies was a desire to spread this burden. By the end of the period election by secret ballot was appearing (notably among the Clergy); and both Burghers and Peasants admitted suitably qualified women to the franchise.[60]

Though, as we shall see, the political nation in Sweden was by no means all-inclusive, and though it shut out social categories whose

[55] The dioceses of Uppsala and Stockholm returned eight members each; Kalmar, Karlstad, Borgå and Visby only two: Sveriges riksdag, I.v. 227.

[56] Stockholm returned ten members. The Estate varied in size from 86 (in 1738–9) to 121 (in 1721–2), as a result of these combinations: usually it was around 101: Sveriges riksdag, I. v. 238–42.

[57] Gunnar Carlsson, Enköping under frihetstiden (Uppsala 1977), pp. 14–15.

[58] Notably in Stockholm and Göteborg.

[59] 139 in 1765–6; 162 in 1769–70; 182 in 1771–2. Forms of voting varied, and on occasion members were even chosen by lot: Ragnar Olsson, Riksdagsmannavalen under den senare delen av frihetstiden (Lund 1948), p. 12. The Peasants firmly resisted attempts to impose literacy as a qualification for election: Sveriges riksdag, I. v. 303.

[60] In Köping in the fifties one of the most formidable political bosses was a woman: Ulla Johansson, 'Hattar och mössor i borgarståndet', Historisk tidskrift (1973), p. 504.

omission was unfortunate, still it is sufficiently obvious that this was a representation very much superior to that which existed in contemporary England. The Established Church had a voice in the councils of the nation, and – towards the end of the period especially – used it not only to ventilate the grievances of necessitous curates, but also to support important reforms: in contrast to England, the Church in parliament meant much more than the bishops. In regard to the towns, the difference was no less striking. We look in vain for anything resembling a rotten or pocket borough. The franchise never rested in the corporation, or in the freemen: it was a kind of blend of scot-and-lot and burgage franchise. But the notorious abuses of English burgage boroughs did not occur in Sweden for the simple reason that burgages there were not attached to the possession of specific houses or properties. As to the English counties, it is probably safe to say that only if the forty-shilling freeholders had been reinforced by the copyholders would they have possessed as representative an electorate as the Swedish *härad*. It is evident also that the distribution of seats was free from the indefensible anomalies which formed so grotesque a feature of the electoral map of England: Sweden had no Dunwich, no Old Sarum. No *härad* was under-represented, as Yorkshire was; Stockholm's ten seats compared well with London's four. All in all, there was no representative system in Europe which was so firmly based on a broad sample of the population. And this high degree of social diversity, even though for the present it was confined within the straitjacket of the concept of 'Estates', might well seem to offer a better prospect of constitutional progress than the overwhelming homogeneity of the eighteenth-century House of Commons.

There was however one element of diversity which Sweden might have been better without, and which had no parallel in England. This was the representation of the armed forces. For more than a century there had existed a kind of quasi-Estate under the name of 'The Army Command' (*krigsbefälet*), which met when the Diet met, attempted to take care of the army's interests, and considered matters which the Estates remitted to it. It was a body elected by the territorial militia (*indelta armén*), each regiment of which returned two members; and perhaps the most useful service it performed was to act as a forum for the views and complaints of the non-noble officers, all of whom were debarred from sitting in the Diet. In 1719 it made an effort to secure recognition as a fifth Estate. The effort was unsuccessful; and in practice its influence does not seem to have been very great.[61] The army's interests were however more than adequately taken care of by other means. For the armed services (and

[61] For *krigsbefälet* see the disappointingly scanty account in *Sveriges riksdag*, I. v. 223–224. It should be noted that the interests, economic and professional, of the territorial militia by no means coincided with the interests of the 'recruited' regiments.

especially the army) offered a career, and something like a livelihood, to
the nobleman of modest fortune. The effect of this was that the House of
Nobility was full of men who were either on the active list, or had at one
time been in the army. The military thus constituted – at least potentially
– an extremely powerful parliamentary interest. How far they acted *as* an
interest, how far political behaviour was determined by the particular
views of the officer corps, is another matter. It is perhaps possible to see
them as acting for corporate advantage in 1739, and again in 1772;[62] but
otherwise the officers do not seem to have acted together as a group with
consistent and definable policies: what they were mostly concerned about
was the question of promotion and 'prejudice'. The officers, of course,
were not the only parliamentary interest: one can discern identifiable
groups of landowners, industrialists, financiers, exporters, the staple-
towns, debtors,[63] and so forth. But just as the military interest was confined to the Estate of Nobility, so the others tended to be predominantly
the concern of one Estate, or at most of two; and though Sweden, like
England, had an East India Company, the electoral system offered no
scope for carpet-bagging nabobs.

It is accordingly still not very rewarding to put the sort of questions
about the Diet which English historians are concerned to ask about
parliament. Information about contested elections is scanty, apart from
one study for the Burghers in the early sixties;[64] and even if such
information were available, the nature of the electoral system would
hardly permit the emergence of a Swedish Namier. The rigorous
requirement of residence in the constituency marked a decisive, and
possibly beneficial, difference from English conditions. Voting in the
constituencies was not influenced by landlords or patrons.[65] The Crown's
electoral influence was nil. There were complaints, especially from the
peasantry, about pressure by local government officials; but corruption in
the constituencies never seems to have been a problem, though candidates
might try to underbid their rivals by offering to take less than the normal
subsistence allowance for members, or none at all. The passionate

[62] See Gunnar Artéus, *Krigsmakt och samhälle i frihetstidens Sverige* (Stockholm 1982), who
argues strongly for the 'praetorian role' of the army officers: for their part in the events of 1739,
pp. 338–43; for their share in the revolution of 1772, pp. 352–60.

[63] For debtors as a pressure-group, see Gunnar Kjellin, *Rikshistoriografen Anders Schönberg.
Studier i riksdagarnas och de politiska tänkesättens historia* (Lund 1952), pp. 162–3. For the question as
to how far parties aggregated interests, see below, pp. 127–8.

[64] Per-Erik Brolin, *Hattar och mössor i borgarståndet 1760–1766* (Uppsala 1953). For the problems
presented by the scantiness of material, see Carlsson, *Parti – partiväsen – partipolitiker 1731–43*.

[65] Except in the Estate of Clergy, where bishops exercised influence: see the case of Bishop
Benzelstierna in the election of 1764, and that of Bishop Forssenius in the election of 1769: S. P.
Bexell, *Riksdags-historiska anteckningar eller Bidrag till svenska kyrkans och riksdagarnes historia . . .
1755–1778,* (Christianstad 1839), pp. 164, 188–91. And cf. Tessin's ironical comments on Serenius
in Sigrid Leijonhufvud, *Carl Gustaf Tessin och hans Åkerökrets* (Stockholm 1933), II 203–4.

involvement at all levels in party and national isues, which had
characterised English politics in the reign of Queen Anne, in Sweden was
manifest only in the capital, and in a handful of the larger towns: in
Örebro or Härnösand, Söderköping or Växjö, the waters remained
remarkably untroubled by the storms which agitated the politicians and
the Court.[66] Before 1766 there was nothing to compare with the use of the
press for political propaganda as it had developed in the age of Defoe,
Swift and Steele. There was certainly a considerable literature of
manuscript political pamphlets, whose extent has been charted, and its
authorship investigated, by the invaluable labours of Ingemar Carlsson;[67]
but its circulation was necessarily limited and select. Nevertheless, the
Swedish electoral system was so superior to the English that it could on
occasion rise above these disadvantages and pronounce a real electoral
verdict. We can see the operation of a floating vote, which could on
occasion be cast against the policies of the men in power: so in 1764, and
again in 1769.

The Diet possessed one characteristic which would have aroused
disquiet in England, and which did in fact affect its functioning. It was a
parliament of placemen, to an extent which would have seemed
disastrous to 'Country' opinion in England in the second quarter of the
century, and to economical reformers thereafter. Inheriting the Absolutism of Charles XI, the Diet inherited too the bureaucratic cast of mind
which had been one of the Absolutism's most conspicuous characteristics. Office, moreover, – all office – in law, and usually in practice also,
was liable to forfeiture only upon judicial conviction, or for physical
incapacity.[68] This had one very important consequence: in Sweden there
was nothing like a spoils system. But the need for judicial conviction as a
prerequisite for depriving a civil servant of his post permitted abuses to
flourish, despite the Diet's attempts to eliminate them. In the Estate of
Nobility, especially, placemen were very numerously represented: men
who held commissions in the army, or less frequently jobs in the civil
service, and were often dependent upon their pay for what they
pathetically termed 'their meagre bread'. In 1720 Ehrencrona wrote that
there were 'very few (Peasants excepted) who are not in H.M.'s service,
or intend to be so';[69] and his remark was echoed forty years later by Claes

[66] Cf. Geoffrey Holmes, British Politics in the Age of Anne (London 1967), and W. A. Speck, Tory and Whig. The Struggle in the Constituencies 1701–1715 (London 1970).
[67] Ingemar Carlsson, Frihetstidens handskrivna politiska litteratur. En bibliografi, (Göteborg 1967).
[68] Brusewitz, Frihetstidens Grundlagar, p. 63 (Frederick I's Accession Charter, cl. 11): the principle had first been laid down in Gustav Adolf's Accession Charter of 1611.
[69] Lennart Thanner, 'Frågan om ämbetstillsättningarna i belysning av Ehrencronas anteck-ningar 1720', Historisk tidskrift (1956), p. 406. In Sweden, as in England, military commissions were purchasable; and the system spread to civil offices too. Office thus became a form of property to be safeguarded (like other property) in terms of the constitution.

Frietzcky.[70] They sought office from motives which were social as well as economic: a pamphlet of 1770 alleged that some of them sold their estates in order to buy commissions, or even honorary titles (*karaktärer*); though office, whether civil or military, was not very lucrative, for this was a period of inflation and salaries were tied to the normal budget of 1696. Whereas in England men contended for jobs which had pay but no work, in Sweden they were prepared to struggle for jobs – or even for the reversion to jobs – which had work but no immediate prospect of pay; and if no established post happened to be vacant they sought an unpaid post additional to the establishment: on an average such persons had to wait seven years before they could hope for emolument.[71] But office brought prestige: Isak Faggott, analysing the Swedish national character, remarked that 'the nation's innate deference extends to all officials in the kingdom'.[72] It was a somewhat sanguine assessment, and as far as the Estate of Peasants was concerned it was almost the exact reverse of the truth; but perhaps it offered some consolation to *pauvres honteux* such as Johan Gabriel Oxenstierna, as he wearily fair-copied interminable minutes, and wondered how he could afford a new pair of shoes.

The same official character as marked the Estate of Nobility attached to two of the other Estates: the Clergy were, and considered themselves to be, office-holders whose duty it was to serve the state in all ways proper to their office; the Burghers tended to be represented in the Diet, particularly during the earlier part of the period, by their burgomasters.

Recent research has tended to play down the traditional insistence on the predominance of the bureaucratic element in the Diet. It is pointed out, for instance, that the aristocracy, despite its passion for office, was basically a landowning class;[73] that office-holding in itself is no indication of a man's centre of interest or source of income: one could hold the office of historiographer-royal, but be essentially a *rentier* or a landed gentleman.[74] Officials do not often seem to have acted together as a political group. The percentage of nobles in the higher civil service was declining: in 1750 it was about 66%; a decade later it had dropped to about 50% out of a total of higher civil servants that never exceeded 300.[75] Most entrants into the higher civil service were non-noble, though many of them acquired a patent of nobility in the course of their career; and it has been suggested that for those born into the peerage the civil service had no

[70] Lagerroth, *Frihetstidens författning*, p. 550.
[71] P. J. Edler, *Om börd och befordran under frihetstiden* (Stockholm 1915), p. 149.
[72] Ingvar Elmroth, *Nyrekryteringen till de högre ämbetena 1720–1809* (Lund 1962), p. 151.
[73] Elmroth, *Nyrekryteringen till de högre ämbetena 1720–1809*, p. 1. Though often on a very small scale: e.g. army officers who were dependent in peacetime on farms allocated to them.
[74] Gunnar Kjellin, *Rikshistoriografen Anders Schönberg*, p. 21.
[75] Elmroth, *Nyrekryteringen till de högre ämbetena 1720–1809*, pp. 66–8, 13.

great attractions.[76] Nevertheless, when these reservations have been made, there still remained a substantial civil service membership of the first Estate. But it was much inferior in numbers to the hundreds of the nobility who were actually serving in the armed forces, or had at one time done so.[77] Göran Nilzén reckoned that in 1740 there were 478 army officers in the Estate, as against 429 civilians;[78] Gunnar Artéus calculated that the percentage of army officers, which had averaged around 60% between 1726 and 1747, was 67.7% in 1755–6, and rose steadily thereafter to 72.8% in 1771–2.[79] They were certainly a potentially powerful corporate interest; but they hardly correspond very closely to the ordinary idea of a bureaucracy. So too with the Clergy: their concern at the Diet was to safeguard orthodoxy and good order in the Church, and to mount guard over their privileges and in particular their tithes. They might be Crown appointees, they might perform useful services without reward, as J.P.s did in England, but that scarcely qualifies them as bureaucrats.

It was not individual Estates, or categories of member within an Estate, that gave the Diet a bureaucratic character; it was the fact that their constant intervention in, and supervision of, the ordinary work of the executive induced a bureaucratic attitude of mind which was independent of whether members held a Crown appointment or not. Even if it be conceded that the Estate of Nobility was an assembly of placemen to a far greater degree than was the House of Commons, from a constitutional point of view it obviously mattered very much less. The very fact that they held office with security of tenure rendered them immune to the pressures which in England could be applied by the Crown, or by its minister. The Swedish office-holder was not dependent: he could vote as he chose without risk. It was not the liability to dismissal that made the petty noble vulnerable to influence and bribery: it was his poverty. And this explains their passionate, unremitting concern with jobs and promotions, and the countless hours of parliamentary time devoted to wrangles on such issues. The matter was also, of course, of constitutional importance: a king with a real influence on military appointments might provide himself with an army at his devotion; a Council with an unsupervised right of appointment might use it to bolster an 'aristocracy'. Sweden, like England, had an ingrained fear of a standing army; and every movement of troops – even the parading of a detachment for purely ceremonial purposes – had, in terms of clause 21 of the *riksdagsordning* of

[76] Ibid., p. 262; and cf. pp. 133, 151.
[77] Per-Erik Brolin estimated that the service nobility in 1760 numbered 44% of the total male nobility of the kingdom: 'Ståndsutjämning som historiskt problem', *Historisk tidskrift* (1951), p. 88.
[78] Göran Nilzén, Studier i 1730-talets partiväsen (Stockholm 1971), pp. 203–5.
[79] Gunnar Artéus, *Krigsmakt och samhälle i frihetstidens Sverige*, p. 52.

1723, to be notified in advance to the Estates, and receive their sanction. The control of appointments affected the incomes or prospects of so many members of the Diet that they felt it expedient to keep a sharp eye on its exercise; and they did in fact increasingly interfere directly in appointments and promotions. The *Memorandum on the Services* (1756) was designed to curb such abuses[80] by laying down the absolute rule that promotion should be based on length of service;[81] but this only made it easier for those who felt that they had been unfairly passed over to argue their case. And it was to the Estates that they turned for redress: the Diet of 1765–6 considered no less than 1400 such applications, and only the most credulous can suppose that all these cases were decided on their merits.[82]

The four Estates exercised powers such as no English parliament had wielded since the Interregnum. The Constitution of 1720 provided for triennial meetings of the Diet, and expected each to last for three months; but in fact they might last as long as twenty-one months in almost continuous session, without adjournment or prorogation save for a brief Christmas holiday. And when the Estates were in session, they ruled the country: ruled it in minute detail. They did it through standing and *ad hoc* committees; and they did it with the less hesitation since many of them were in fact officials with some administrative experience. The most important of these bodies was the Secret Committee of one hundred members: fifty from the Nobility, twenty-five each from the Clergy and Burghers; the Peasants were only very rarely admitted. All important business, everything which could plausibly be represented to be of a secret nature, was dealt with here; and in particular foreign affairs and finance.[83] When the Diet was sitting the Secret Committee became the effective government of the country. From the late thirties to the mid-sixties it showed a tendency to assume greater powers to itself; thereafter the *plena* to some extent reasserted their control. Side by side with it were a dozen or so of standing committees dealing with almost every aspect of national affairs:[84] the amount of committee-work was so

[80] And, of course, to strengthen the barriers against any possible influence by the Crown: see Gustaf Johan Ehrensvärd, *Dagboksanteckningar förda vid Gustaf III:s hof*, ed. E. V. Montan (Stockholm 1877), I, p. 197, for a frank admission of this aspect of the matter.
[81] Printed in Brusewitz, *Frihetstidens Grundlagar*, pp. 191–206.
[82] Ingvar Elmroth, *Nyrekryteringen till de högre ämbetena 1720–1809*, p. 48 note 48; P. J. Edler, *Om börd och befordran under frihetstiden*, p. 83.
[83] The Secret Committee had as sub-committees: the Lesser Secret Deputation (which dealt with foreign affairs); the Defence Deputation; the Estimates Deputation; the Commerce Deputation; and the Currency Deputation.
[84] Among them may be noted the Grand Secret Deputation, whose main function came to be to act as interpreter of the constitution in cases of doubt. Deputations and committees tended to generate subcommittees: thus the Fisheries Deputation, first set up in 1765, had by 1769 sprouted four standing sub-committees: Sigbrit Plaenge Jacobson, *1766 års allmänna fiskestadga. Dess uppkomst och innebörd med hänsyn till Bottenhavsfiskets rättsfrågor* (Uppsala 1978), p. 89.

great that the Estate of Clergy, with only fifty-one members, had difficulty in finding sufficient representatives to man them all. In virtue of clause 13 of the *riksdagsordning* of 1723 the Estates through these committees and deputations kept the administration under constant surveillance for as long as the Diet lasted. It has been said that if they had met every year, no other central government would have been necessary.

The end of the session, however, did not mean that for the next three years their control of government would cease. For the Estates had developed a special administrative apparatus of their own, distinct from the governing boards (*Collegia*) of the central government, and this apparatus continued to function between meetings of the Diet. The Estates alone controlled the Bank, the National Debt Office, and the Manufactures Office; and in conjunction with the Estimates Office their Estimates Commission kept an eye on the finances between one budget and the next.[85] At the close of every Diet, moreover, the Secret Committee, and its sub-committee the Lesser Secret Deputation, left behind a sort of political testament, containing binding instructions to the Council of State upon the policies to be pursued between this Diet and the next. And when the Diet met again, the Estates set about investigating everything that had been done by the executive since they last met. The Secret Committee scrutinised the Council's conduct of foreign policy; the Judicial Deputation scrutinised its decisions as Supreme Court of Appeal; the Secret Deputation combed all its other proceedings, on the look-out for the most trivial error. Those proceedings were read aloud *in extenso* – a process which might take weeks. Full minutes of the Council's meetings were insisted upon, every utterance of every member upon matters of policy was duly recorded, and all this mass of material was now subjected to the jealous inspection of the Diet's committees: any member of the Council might find himself called upon to explain and justify anything he had said or done during the previous three years.[86] By these inquisitorial proceedings the principle of ministerial responsibility to parliament was rigorously enforced. And the process was applied not only to the Council, but to the whole administration of the country. In 1734 the Estates set up a Minutes Committee, charged with the formidable task of reading all the reports and all the minutes of every government department. In 1738 their competence was enlarged to include all judicial decisions; in 1760 to the records of the College of Medicine; in 1765 to the provincial administration. If Sweden had possessed Justices of the Peace, the records of petty- and quarter-sessions would have been subjected to

---

[85] In 1766 these Committees (except that for the Bank, and the Estimates Commission) were abolished: Brusewitz, p. 446.

[86] Not surprisingly, members of the Council at times took care to speak with an eye to the record: Göran Behre, *Underrättelseväsen och diplomati*, p. 70.

the examination and censure of a jealous parliament: which might not, on occasion, have been a bad thing.

Thus the Diet, though primarily a legislative body, spent much of its time acting as a sort of superior executive; surveying, admonishing, correcting, the normal organs of government, and particularly the Council, which it seems habitually to have regarded with suspicion. To de Lolme, who thought that it was the duty of the legislative to check the executive, it seemed paradoxical – indeed, impossible – that the Swedish Diet should discharge that duty; for the Diet was itself the executive, and could hardly be expected to exercise self-control.[87] It is true, no doubt, that parliament in England acted as a kind of executive too: all that mass of legislation for repairing bridges, abating nuisances, enclosing commons, granting divorces, and so forth, was really an attempt to govern, to administer, in quite petty detail. It is also true that the control of the executive by parliamentary action was a familiar feature of English politics: enquiries into petitions, or into the conduct of individuals or departments, by special or select committees; power to compel the attendance of witnesses, and (after 1770) to examine them on oath; addresses for the removal of ministers; bills of pains and penalties. But a great part of the legislation which might give the impression that parliament was trying to administer the country was in fact only empowering legislation: parliament devolved responsibility upon magistrates or municipalities, equipped them with powers, and left it to their initiative to exercise them, or not; and it gave them such a wide discretion and undefined scope that often enough they became virtually subordinate law-making bodies – a state of affairs which would hardly have been tolerated in Sweden. In so far as parliament made any serious attempt at directly governing the country, it was casual and unsystematic. The Diet might govern Sweden; but broadly speaking England governed itself, with or without the powers provided by parliament. The Swedish method by no means excluded local initiatives, often of the greatest importance; and the Swedish parish meeting (*sockenstämma*) was a gathering democratic even by American standards:[88] the only Engish equivalent was to be found in the better type of 'open' vestry. The Swedes appear to have accepted supervision by the Diet as something suited to their needs, and a safeguard against an arbitrary or corrupt officialdom; but attempts by parliament to control the executive tended to be viewed with disquiet.[89] One decisive difference lay in the fact that parliament met

[87] J. L. de Lolme, *The Constitution of England* (4th edn 1784), p. 505.

[88] See K. H. Johansson, *Svensk sockensjälvstyrelse 1686–1862* (Lund 1937), pp. 194–201.

[89] The Commons' claim in 1693 to nominate the members of the new Board of Trade was unsuccessful; Fox's India Bill was attacked as an encroachment upon the executive power; Gladstone in 1855 denounced the appointment of a committee to investigate supplies for the

annually, and had thus no need to engage in marathon inquests into all the acts of the executive over the preceding three years.

If the Diet might seem to usurp the functions of government, it is undeniable that it could also effectively supplement them. A genuine concern to protect the subjects of the realm against administrative oppression led it to open its doors wide to any private citizen who imagined himself to have a grievance against an official; and attempts in 1766 and 1769 to make such appeals less easy were rejected. Apart from thus dispensing equity on a basis of common-sense, the Estates assumed to themselves the function of an Appeal Court, as a natural consequence of their scrutiny of the records of the three Supreme Courts,[90] and of the Judicial Division of the Council of State, which heard appeals from the Supreme Courts. This function was discharged by the Estates' Judicial Deputation; and from an early date there were justified misgivings about whether its members possessed the necessary legal expertise for the task. They did not hesitate to reverse or amend judicial decisions in civil cases;[91] and since judges, if otherwise qualified, were not debarred from sitting in the Diet, this could mean that they might find themselves overturning their colleagues' judgments – or their own.[92] Blackstone had been careful to limit parliament's jurisdiction: 'All mischiefs and grievances, operations and remedies, *that transcend the ordinary courses of law* (my italics) are within reach of this extraordinary tribunal'.[93] The *riksdagsordning* of 1723 did indeed include a similar restriction,[94] but the Diet in practice sometimes ignored the limitation. It would have agreed with Sir Matthew Hale, that 'it is most necessary, that the supreme decisive power of jurisdiction and the dernier ressort must be where the legislative power is'.[95] The Swedes justified it more pragmatically on the ground that litigants preferred to be dealt with by laymen rather than by lawyers or officials.[96] Professional lawyers, unless they happened to be ennobled, or were officials such as burgomasters, were not represented in the Diet; the

---

Crimea as being an executive act, derogatory to the authority which all ministries should possess. But these were exceptional cases: see Sir William Anson, *The Law and Custom of the Constitution* (5th edn, Oxford 1922), I 402, and generally *ibid.*, 381–409.

[90] Stockholm, Jönköping, Åbo.

[91] In 1766 the Minutes Committee reversed a decision of the Consistory of Åbo University (which they were perhaps entitled to do) and imposed a fine of 150 silver dalers upon each of its members – by what authority is a matter for speculation: *SRARP*, xxv, 441.

[92] Anders Nordencrantz, *Anmärkning wid åtskilliga utkomna Skrifter, angående Rättegångens förminskning och förkortande* (Stockholm 1756), p. 28.

[93] Blackstone, *Commentaries on the Laws of England*, I, 161.

[94] Brusewitz, *Frihetstidens Grundlagar*, p. 243.

[95] In *The Jurisdiction of the Lords' House of Parliament*, quoted in J. W. Gough, *Fundamental Law in English Constitutional History*, p. 173.

[96] Karl-Olof Rudelius, 'Författningsfrågan i de förenade deputationerna 1769', *Statsvetenskaplig tidskrift* (1935), pp. 353–4; Hugo Valentin, 'Det sociala momentet i historieskrivningen om 1772 års statsvälvning', *Scandia* (1941), p. 10.

profession of the law not being, as in England, a road to political eminence, and a favoured social escalator. On the other hand, we are assured that perhaps half the members of the Estate of Peasants were, or had been, either members of the standing jury of the hundred (*häradsnämnd*) or justices in the hundred-court (*häradsdömare*), and most of them carried a copy of the Law Code of 1734 in their pockets; so that some basic knowledge of the law could be assumed among them.[97] Nevertheless it seems likely that the Diet's Judicial Deputation, when it overruled the judgments of the Judicial Division of the Council, must often have done so by the light of nature, and sometimes by the darker gleam of party passion, rather than on a basis of legal expertise. Indeed, in the Council itself the law was by no means always adequately represented: in 1765 it was revealed that the Council's Judicial Division had been deciding cases without a single lawyer's being present.[98] The existence of abuses does not in itself invalidate a system; but it is difficult not to feel that the amateur and unpredictable interventions of the Estates did not offer a very secure guarantee of the dispensing of justice.

As to the Diet in its legislative capacity – which was, after all, its prime function – Lagerroth found its record 'depressing'.[99] An unexpected verdict. The business of government in the eighteenth century was not primarily to legislate but to govern; which meant in fact to take care of foreign policy, manage the finances and preserve law and order. Nevertheless, in Sweden as in England the actual volume of legislation was really quite large: the Diet was legislating all the time. Though much of it was of the petty and particular character which would in England have been embodied in Private Acts, a considerable amount of it was of high economic or constitutional importance. It is possible to count not less than twenty-five public Acts, of general application, during the Diet of 1765–6; and at the close of that of 1723 the representatives of Stockholm, reporting to their constituents on their legislative activities, presented a list of more than fifty Acts and Ordinances, most of them with an application which is clearly general.[100] Many of the resolutions of the Diet arose out of the consideration of petitions, of *gravamina*: such *gravamina* (*besvär*), provided they had been classified by the Sifting Deputation (*urskillningsdeputation*) as of general concern, would be sifted again by the Estate to whom they applied, and if approved by them would

[97] Erland Alexandersson, *Bondeståndet i riksdagen 1760–1772* (Lund 1975), p. 28.
[98] Ludvig Stavenow, *Om riksrådsvalen under frihetstiden* (Uppsala 1890), pp. 51–53.
[99] *Sveriges riksdag*, I vi. 254.
[100] *Borgarståndets riksdagsprotokoll*, II. ed. Nils Staf, Uppsala 1951, pp. 648–9. The number of public Acts during the reign of George II is estimated by P. G. H. Thomas at 81 per session, which is certainly more than the Stockholm list of 1723; but half of them were hardly general: they were concerned with petty local matters, not susceptible of being dealt with by a Private Act: P. G. H. Thomas, *The House of Commons in the Eighteenth Century* (Oxford 1971), pp. 45–61.

be adopted as a 'general grievance', in which form they went to the General Grievances Deputation. This body in turn remitted them to the appropriate committee of the Diet, for recommendation or action; their report was sent to all the Estates; and if they, or a majority of them, reached a congruent decision, then the Despatching Committee would formulate it, promulgate it, and the result would be a *law*. The procedure was involved, circular, and time-consuming; but that was the way they did it, and they did a good deal of it. The Stockholm representatives in 1723 reported that the Sifting Deputation received 3308 *gravamina*, which were dealt with 'either by reference to another committee or by resolution'.[101]

Gravamina and petitions, then, were one source of legislation.[102] But they were far from being the only one. Perhaps the most striking thing about Swedish legislation is the very wide dispersal of the initiative. It could come, for instance, from a report of one of the Diet's committees; from an extract from the minutes of one Estate, transmitted to the others; from a proposal by one of the *Collegia* (the central government boards); from the motion of any member, if he carried it in his own Estate; or as arising out of one of those surveys of the state of the nation, misleadingly termed 'Propositions', which the Council of State submitted at the beginning of each Diet. Legislation might then proceed by the normal route of passage by a majority of Estates, and final formulation by the Despatching Committee; but various alternative procedures were available. The Iron Office and the Exchange Control Office were both set up (1747) by secret agreements between the Bank (which was, of course, the Estates' Bank), the relevant business or financial interest, and the Secret Committee: the *plena* of the four Estates were not called upon to debate either issue. Yet these were really major pieces of legislation.[103] Sweden's analogue to the Navigation Act (the *produktplakat* of 1724) was not promulgated as a law in the usual way: it was issued as a regulation by the College of Commerce, the Estates having left the College with discretion to issue it, or not; and in 1748 the same College made what can only be called an attempt to legislate by simple proclamation.[104] The oppressive restriction of the right of public meeting in towns (1752) was

---

[101] *Borgarståndets riksdagsprotokoll*, II 646. Most *gravamina* seem to have come to the Estate of Peasants, and by them were transmitted after endorsement to the other Estates: a great mass of them tended to end up in the Estate of Nobility in the last few days of a Diet, with the Estate working long hours to clear off the business before the session ended: by July 1766 they were sitting from 7 a.m.; on 4 August they met at 6 a.m.

[102] Petitions to parliament were frequent enough in England: 880 of them in the five years ending in 1789: Thomas, *The House of Commons in the Eighteenth Century*, pp. 14–24. But they did not result in Acts of Parliament.

[103] Malmström, *Sveriges politiska historia* III, pp. 395, 397–8.

[104] *Ibid.* pp. 89–90; Per Nyström, *Stadsindustriens arbetare före 1800-talet* (Stockholm 1955), p. 153.

effected by a mere administrative circular; so that in 1765 the member for
Karlshamn could blandly pretend that the circular had never reached his
town.[105] Each Estate was competent to legislate by simple resolution in
matters which were solely its own concern (its *oeconomicum*, as the phrase
went): it could, for instance, expel any member who displeased it, or who
happened to be a person of whom the party that had a majority in the
Estate wished to be quit.[106] In between meetings of the Diet the Council of
State issued such proclamations and ordinances as it thought necessary;
but they had to be submitted to the next Diet for confirmation or
modification. After 1741 the Estates delegated the business of scrutinising
them to one of its committees; but though that committee might duly
report, as time went on the *plena* ceased to debate their observations. Thus
in practice the safeguard almost lapsed, and the Council found itself with a
virtually unchecked ordinance-making power: in 1761 the Estates
admitted that they had been slack about scrutinising ordinances, and
asked the Council to supply them with a list of those issued since the last
Diet, so that they might be incorporated (without scrutiny!) into the
Resolution of this one, and so become unchallengeable law.[107] And finally
there was the very 'modern' procedure which prepared the way for the
Fisheries Statute of 1766, and which amounted more or less to legislation
by consultation: a draft bill was prepared by the Fisheries Committee of
the Diet, was circulated to all local authorities in the coastal regions with
instructions not only to take the draft as a basis for investigation and
report, but also to arrange for local committees of interested parties, who
were to be invited to offer their comments by written memoranda or oral
testimony; and all this evidence was remitted to the Diet of 1765, was
considered by the Fisheries Committee, and was taken into account in
drafting the Statute of the succeeding year.[108]

(iii)

Under the Constitution of 1720 the executive power was formally vested
in the Council of State: a body of some seventeen members. But it was an
executive very different from an English administration. Its share in
legislation, for instance, was marginal, exceptional and on sufferance. It
could hardly be otherwise; for by a development which might seem to be
unfortunate, its members were (with one exception) excluded absolutely

[105] Malmström, *Sveriges politiska historia* IV, pp. 82–3; Gunnar Carlsson, *Enköping under frihetstiden*, pp. 51, 124; Sten Carlsson, *Byråkrati och borgarstånd under frihetstiden*, p. 124.
[106] See, e.g., *Bondeståndets riksdagsprotokoll*, 12, pp. 131–8, 493.
[107] Brusewitz, *Frihetstidens Grundlagar*, p. 209; *SRARP*, XXIII, 370.
[108] S. P. Jacobson, *1766 års allmänna fiskestadga*, pp. 49–60.

from sitting in the Diet.[109] The result was that the Council came to have no
control of the Diet's business, no opportunity to formulate or defend
policies in any of the Estates, no chance of imposing those policies by
force of personality, parliamentary oratory, or irrefutable logic. There
was, indeed, one short period when it seemed possible that Sweden might
escape this consequence. The constitution did not forbid the election of a
member of Council as Marshal of the Diet; and at the Diets of 1726 and
1731 Arvid Horn was both Chancery-President (and as such a member of
the Council) and Marshal, and so was able to present his policies in person
to the first Estate, and above all to the Secret Committee, over which the
Marshal *ex officio* presided. But the strengthening of his political position
which was a consequence of this doubling of parts was precisely the
reason for ending it: men did not want a Walpole. At the Diet of 1734
Horn judged it wiser not to stand for the office of Marshal; and in 1748
members of the Council were finally forbidden to occupy that position.[110]
Thereafter anything like a Chatham, a North or a Pitt became
inconceivable. It was no wonder if the Council became increasingly out of
touch with the Estates: by the end of the period they had almost lost the
capacity for leadership, and seem to have declined in ability.[111]

In practice, however, their divorce from the legislature had less serious
consequences than might have been expected. It did not matter very
much, from the point of view of the conduct of business, that there were
no members of Council in the Estates. For it was not they who
determined policy, nor was it their duty to explain or defend it. That was
the work of the more important committees of the Diet, and above all of
the Secret Committee; and the members of these committees *were* present
on the floor of at least three Estates, able to put the Committee's views
and if necessary to report back on the reactions of the *plena* to what was
proposed. A reading of the debates, admittedly, does not give the
impression that Committee members often felt called upon *ex officio* to do
these things; and in regard to much of the business transacted by the
Secret Committee the question did not arise, for that business was by
definition secret. When the Diet was in session the Council might report,
it might suggest; but it might not determine: its duty was to act on the
decisions of its sovereign masters, the Estates. Between Diets its
members were no doubt invested with a liberty to act within the limits of
the instruction left to them by the Secret Committee; but it was a perilous

[109] The situation had its roots in the *riddarhusordning* of 1626, which for the first time separated
the Council from the House of Nobility.

[110] Carl Hallendorff, *Sveriges Riddarhus. Ridderskapet och Adeln och dess Riddarhus* (Stockholm
1926), pp. 323–4. The essential objection was that since members of the Council were
responsible to the Estates, a Marshal who was a member of the Council would be in the position
of being judge in his own cause.

[111] Ludvig Stavenow, 'Det adertonde århundradets parlamentarism i Sverige', pp. 23–4.

freedom. Their only power of real constitutional importance was their sole right to summon intercalary, extraordinary meetings of the Diet. They must never forget that they were no more than the Diet's fiduciary agents. And they accepted the position, at least after 1739. In 1769 Claes Frietzcky, accused of 'servile obedience' to the Estates, admitted the charge and claimed it as a merit.[112] Tessin at one moment defined the Council's main duty as being to act as a sort of national security-service,[113] and at another as being to serve as a watchdog in the intervals between Diets to prevent the king from violating the constitution[114] – and woe to the Councillor who sought to excuse negligence in that matter by pleading the old maxim that 'the Council must give counsel, but must not govern'. The Estates never forgot the dominant part played by the great Council magnates in the days of Axel Oxenstierna and Magnus Gabriel de la Gardie, and they were determined that those days should not return: even when the Council and the Estates were politically most at one, when the same party had an ascendancy in each, this feeling could cause friction between them serious enough to damage party solidarity – as happened in 1766, 1769 and 1772.

As if this were not disablement enough, the constitution had been at pains to cut off the Council from its natural areas of administrative activity. Though essentially bureaucrats, they were shut out of the central government; for with two exceptions (the Chancery-President and his deputy),[115] they were not permitted to be members of the central government boards (the *Collegia*): the links between Council and *Collegia* which had been forged in 1634 by the Form of Government, and retained in the constitution of 1719, were in 1720 deliberately broken by a Diet which was apprehensive that Absolutism might be followed by 'aristocracy'. The Chancery-President was something like a real Foreign Secretary; but apart from him there were no departmental ministers in the Council: nothing resembling a Secretary of State for war,[116] or even a Chancellor of the Exchequer. In 1765 the Secret Committee tacitly acknowledged the need for a minister of finance, and suggested that a member of the Council be drafted to discharge his functions; but nothing came of it.[117] In a sense the true departmental ministers were the

[112] E. Fahlbeck, 'Studier öfver frihetstidens politiska ideer (1916), pp. 36–7.
[113] 'to dig up matter from where it lies hidden, and counteract its noxious exhalations – that is harder, and dangerous to the digger; but in my view it is the main duty of a member of Council' *Carl Gustaf Tessins dagbok, 1748–52*, p. 6.
[114] F. W. Ehrenheim, ed., *Tessin och Tessiniana*, p. 167. Yet he also believed that their authority was the key to the constitution, and that in this respect the last four years of Frederick I's reign was ideal: *ibid., l.c.*
[115] The *rikskansliråd*. This was the only political office to which the king throughout the period retained the sole right of appointment.
[116] Though one member had always to be a man with at least a semblance of naval experience.
[117] *Sveriges riksdag*, I, vi, 286.

permanent heads of sections in the Chancery, or the officials of the other *Collegia*, who were as a rule men of long tenure and great experience.[118]

The exceptional position of the Chancery-President led to his being conventionally regarded as the Prime Minister; and this no doubt was why the Estates in 1751 resolved to put forward only one nomination at a time for that office instead of the usual three: from their point of view it was essential to have a Chancery-President who was in sympathy with the foreign policy of the Secret Committee, and who could be relied upon to carry it out between Diets. There could certainly be no question of the king's being able to pick a Prime Minister to suit himself. It is significant of the differing political preoccupations of England and Sweden that while in England this position tended to fall to the minister in charge (at last nominally) of the finances, in Sweden it was associated with foreign affairs. But in truth the Chancery-President was not a Prime Minister in the English sense at all. The office of Prime Minister in England evolved partly because of the need for effective management of the House of Commons, partly to supply a regular channel of communication between the two centres of power: king and Commons. In Sweden there was only one centre of power: the Diet; and in so far as it could be managed in the English sense, that must be by the Marshal of the Diet, who was not in the Council at all after 1734. It therefore mattered the less that the Chancery-President had almost none of a Prime Minister's powers. And just as such authority as the Council possessed was submerged by the omnicompetence of a Diet in session, so the leadership of the Chancery-President was eclipsed, once the Estates met, by that of the Marshal of the Diet, who combined the function of Speaker of the Estate of Nobles with that of Leader of the House, and who *ex officio* was chairman of every committee, though he might be too busy to attend them all.[119]

An English minister had a dual responsibility: a responsibility to the king his master, and a responsibility to parliament. The Swedish Council was responsible to the Diet only. Nevertheless, its members were invested with a different duality which entailed awkward constitutional difficulties. On the one hand they were servants and agents of the Diet; on the other they were office-holders for life, removable only upon criminal

---

[118] Elmroth, *Nyrekryteringen till de högre ämbetena 1720–1809* pp. 94–6. The Chancery was divided into four sections with a Secretary of State in charge of each. It prepared all business which came to the Council; hence the importance of the Chancery-President as a link between the one and the other.

[119] The way in which the Chancery-President could be thrust aside, even in a matter which was peculiarly his business, can be seen from an incident in 1743, when the Swedish representatives at a conference with the British minister included the Marshal and three members of the Secret Committee, but neither the Chancery-President nor any other member of the Chancery. Behre, *Underrättelseväsen och diplomati*, p. 10.

conviction. How, then, to get rid of a member of the Council who had
become politically obnoxious to the Estates, or to his colleagues? Such
persons showed no great readiness to retire voluntarily: of the 104
individuals who were members of the Council in the period 1720–1772
only some 15 seem to have done so, and this more often for personal than
for political reasons. More substantial relief could be looked for from
natural causes: about 50 members seem to have died in office.[120] But some
quicker and more certain process than this was required in a political
emergency, and particularly when a victorious party in the Diet found
itself saddled with a Council drawn from the other faction. If Council
members could not be got rid of except upon conviction, or by the hand
of death, how could they be got rid of at all? How bring legislative and
executive into harmony?

This was, of course, one of the central problems of the post-revolution
constitution in England; and in the years after 1715 it was solved on a typically pragmatic basis. Ministers retained office, or fell, in virtue of commanding or losing the confidence of the king, or of the independent
members of parliament, and in virtue too of a general feeling that the
king's minister was entitled to be supported for as long as he did the king's
business, but no longer. But in Sweden it was parliament that made the
ministers – or, more correctly, the Diet that made the Council. By the
end of the period a general election which resulted in a clear change in the
political complexion of the Diet tended to be followed by a corresponding change in the political complexion of the Council: public opinion, in
so far as it was truly expressed by election results, was effective in a way
to which there are few parallels in England between 1715 and 1784.

The device by which the harmony of executive and legislature was
secured was the procedure known as *licentiering*.[121] It was essentially a
judicial proceeding directed against a member of the Council for neglect
or breach of duty; it was initiated by, and conducted in, the Estates and
their committees; and it was followed if successful by forfeiture of
confidence and of office. Its constitutional basis rested firmly on
paragraph 13 of the *riksdagsordning* of 1723,[122] but its origins reach back to
the reign of Charles XI.[123] The charges arose as a rule out of the Secret

---

[120] These figures are based on Malmström, who carefully notes changes in the composition of
the Council, and records deaths or resignations. Some minor figures may have been missed; but
the general picture is clear.

[121] For *licentiering*, see the comprehensive survey by Linnarsson, *Riksrådens licentiering*.

[122] Which directed the Estates to enquire how far the constitution had been complied with, to
scrutinise the Council's conduct since the last Diet, and to judge any delinquencies that might
come to light, if need be in secret, or by a special commission: Brusewitz, *Frihetstidens
Grundlagar*, p. 240.

[123] *Cf.* Fredrik Lagerroth, 'Det svenska statsrådets ansvarighet i rättshistorisk belysning',
Scandia (1939).

Committee's examination of the Council minutes. On the basis of this scrutiny a member might be accused, for instance, of failing to comply with instructions left behind by the previous Diet; or with 'criminally' misinterpreting the constitution; and though the Constitution of 1720 insisted that Council members should not be judged *ex eventu*, ill-success was on occasion used as a convenient indication of bad intentions. Other more intangible grounds of offence might be alleged: notably that the advice of the accused had tended not to advance 'the true welfare of the realm' – a charge which might mean anything or nothing. But whereas under Charles XI members of the Council had been held responsible for what they *did*, after 1720 they were held responsible for what they *advised* – even if no ill consequences could be demonstrated to have resulted; for by giving advice which conflicted with the instructions which the Diet had left behind, or with the true meaning of the constitution (as determined by the exegetical ingenuity of the Secret Committee) they were violating their oath of office.[124] But these were only the necessary and increasingly transparent fictions devised to circumvent the difficulty of getting rid of an enemy who held office *ad vitam aut culpam*; and as the Age of Liberty progressed the essentially political nature of *licentiering* appeared with less and less disguise. C. F. Scheffer, in his guide to the constitution, frankly abandoned the judicial pretext, and accepted *licentiering* as a simple question of confidence:[125] he was himself to be removed a few years later as part of a political deal designed to keep his party in office. Claes Frietzcky in 1769, while maintaining the Council's innocence of the charges brought against them, at the same time asserted the right of the Estates to get rid of them 'even if they have committed no crime, should the welfare of the country require it'.[126] In the same year John Jennings was basing *licentiering* simply on the ground that 'the country needs a new government'.[127] When in 1772 it was the turn of the Hats to face *licentiering*, the 'crimes' with which they were charged rested on such trivialities and strained interpretations that clearly nobody any longer cared much about them.[128] What had begun as an exceptional measure to meet an exceptional political situation became by the end of the period almost a normal consequence of a change in the majority in the Estates: Hats and Caps were coming to see themselves as alternative administrations who would naturally use victory at the polls to turn out

---

[124] Lagerroth, 'Det svenska statsrådets ansvarighet . . .', pp. 40, 45. The most usual accusations concerned the conduct of foreign policy: so in 1739, 1761, 1765–6.

[125] Lagerroth, 'En frihetstidens lärobok . . .', p. 209.

[126] *Den svenska fatburen*, sjette öppningen, Den 1 augusti 1769, no. 20, p. 154.

[127] *SRARP*, XXVII, 70.

[128] *Cf.* Georg Landberg's remark that the *licentieringar* of 1772 were done in a way 'which again shows a total inability to approach the principles of a real parliamentary system': *Sveriges riksdag*, I, vii. 10.

their rivals – and especially those two efficient men in the Council, the Chancery-President and his deputy.

It would be a mistake to think of some of these later *licentieringar* – those of 1769 and 1772, for instance – in terms of the 'fall of a ministry'; for this is to import nineteenth-century concepts and terminology into a totally different political arrangement. It implies that Councils were governments in the sense that Peel's or Melbourne's ministries were; that they 'fell' as a result of adverse votes in the Estates; that they had some sort of programme, and were liable to 'fall' if the Estates rejected it. But none of these assumptions is true.[129] To apply the term 'ministry' to the Council is an unacceptable abuse of language. It did not occur to any member of the Council to resign because he differed from the majority of his colleagues on a point of policy, however important. Before 1769 the Council always contained a fair number of members who were not of the ruling party – or, perhaps, of any party: men who had acquired the habit of political and corporeal survival, and had been fixtures in the Council for more years than men could remember. J. A. Meijerfelt was a Council member for more than thirty years; G. A. von Rosen for more than a quarter of a century. No *licentiering* before that of 1769 really affected this position, or secured the removal of a majority of members: when 'Horn's ministry fell' in 1738–9, what happened was that Horn and Taube resigned, and five members were *licentierade* – that is, a total of some seven out of seventeen. Even in 1769, when the introduction of ten Hats into the places of the extruded Caps gave them complete control, it would never have entered anybody's head to talk about an 'Ekeblad administration', though Ekeblad was Chancery-President; for the effective leader of the Hats was the Marshal of the Diet, Axel von Fersen. The responsibility of the Council's members was personal and individual; and the idea that they might have a collective responsibility was long suspect, as probably unconstitutional. It is only from 1769 that *licentiering* brings anything like a clean sweep: ten Caps evicted in that year; six Hats (out of a Council from which three others had already been persuaded to resign) evicted in 1772. Nevertheless, the idea that the Council ought to consist of members drawn all from one party had even then by no means finally established itself: the debates in the House of Nobility in 1772 show a strong body of opinion in favour of maintaining a balance of parties within it.[130] In 1751, at a time when the Council was more homogeneous than at any previous period, and more closely linked to the party from which it was drawn, Carl Gustaf Tessin had tried to extort something like a vote of confidence

[129] Contrast Michael Metcalf, 'Structuring Party Politics: Party Organization in Eighteenth-Century Sweden': *Parliaments, Estates and Representation*, I (1981), pp. 35, 37.
[130] *SRARP*, xxx, 491–569.

in the Council by the threat of a collective resignation.[131] The attempt failed for lack of support from his colleagues; and it had no successor. Members of the Council faced with the threat of *licentiering* managed their defence on a *sauve qui peut* basis, and often without making a serious defence at all. If they offered resignations in good time, judicial proceedings against them were usually dropped, and the threat of a penal sentence was transformed into permission to retire – with or without a pension, according to the level of party animus; sometimes with an intimation that they had forfeited the confidence of the Estates, sometimes without. But as the Estates could withdraw their confidence, so too they could miraculously restore it when the balance of parties should change; as happened, for instance, in the case of C. F. Scheffer in 1761: as good an indication as any of the unreality of the judicial forms in which the whole business was involved. As the historian LagerBring tartly commented: 'To lose the confidence of society by reason of one's advice in Council, and after the lapse of only a few months to recover it, without anything's occurring in the interval, might seem unexpected, and indeed astonishing, if that age had not exhausted one's capacity for being astonished.'[132]

Though *licentiering* might change the composition of the Council, it was not a procedure which was applicable to the civil servants of the *Collegia*. It could remove the splendid figureheads – members of the Council took rank of all except reigning princes – but it did not touch the permanent, effective administrators of the central boards. And those boards might be at odds not only with each other (as the Chancery and the College of Commerce were in the 1730s) but – much more serious – with the ruling party in the Council and the Estates. For the *Collegia* had all the passive strength of an entrenched bureaucracy, and all its skill in obscuring issues and covering its tracks.[133] The experiment of challenging them was only once attempted. In 1768 the Cap Council (between Diets) attempted to indict the entire College of Commerce for misdemeanours and insubordination. The result was a political disaster. The civil service strike which ensued forced the extraordinary general election of 1769; and that election resulted in a Hat triumph, and the *licentiering* of the defeated Caps.

Thus the effect of the anomalous character of the Council, with its

---

[131] *Tessin och Tessiniana* pp. 147–8; Sven-Ulric Palme, 'Vom Absolutismus zum Parlamentarismus in Schweden', in *Ständische Vertretungen in Europa im 17. und 18 Jahrhundert*, ed. Dietrich Gerhardt (Göttingen 1969), p. 371. He had vainly tried this gambit already in 1747: Arne Remgård, *Carl Gustaf Tessin och 1746–7 års riksdag* (Lund 1968), p. 174.

[132] LagerBring, *Sammandrag af Swea-Rikes Historia*, v, iii. 17.

[133] As A. J. von Höpken wrote: 'Therefore they manage things *propriis arcanis*, contrive to complicate and expand the issues, in order to escape prosecution by prevarication and obscurity': *Skrifter*, I, pp. 24–6.

built-in security of tenure, was that changes to bring it into conformity with the Estates could be effected only by legal fictions, supported by means which were often questionable or violent; that differences of opinion, errors of judgment, were perforce treated as crimes; that every major change in the political allegiance of the Diet might entail violent political consequences. Something of this sort had happened in seventeenth-century England, where the device of impeachment had been ruthlessly used in the same way: Clarendon, for instance, was impeached in order to get rid of him, rather than for real criminality.[134] The events of 1701, when the Commons addressed the king to remove four ministers or ex-ministers for advising the signing of the Partition Treaties, bear some resemblance, in motive and method, to a typical *licentiering*; and perhaps if that clause in the Act of Settlement requiring Privy Councillors to sign their advice had not been repealed in 1706 England might have seen developments along this line. However that may be, it was well into the eighteenth century before Members of Parliament felt happy about agitating for the removal of a minister simply because they disliked his policy: the feeling persisted that in order to justify such an infringement of the king's right of choice they must be able to show some sort of criminality. The attack on Walpole in 1742, which in many respects resembled a *licentiering*, shows this clearly: Walpole himself reflected the general feeling when in response to Sandys' motion to address the king to remove him 'from H.M.'s presence and counsels for ever', he protested that 'an address to His Majesty to remove one of his servants, *without so much as alleging any particular crime against him*,[135] is one of the greatest encroachments that was ever made upon the prerogative of the Crown'.[136] But the attempt to impeach Walpole broke down; and though Shelburne in 1780 was talking rather wildly of impeaching North, the events of 1742 really mark the last occasion when impeachment was resorted to simply in order to displace a minister whose policies had become unpopular. Thereafter, policies and ministers in England contrived to get themselves changed by other means: withdrawal of support in the Commons, withdrawal of support by the king. It was just as well; for *licentiering* was an unpleasant device, and it did not become less so when men no longer took it seriously. Nevertheless, it served a useful purpose, in that by the end of the period it enabled the Diet – indeed, one might almost say, the electorate – to decide who might *not* be in the Council; and as a consequence to give a broad indication of who might be

[134] See the remarks in John Miller, 'Charles II and his Parliaments', *Transactions of the Royal Historical Society*, 5th Series, 32 (1982), pp. 11–12.

[135] My italics.

[136] For the unsavoury proceedings against Walpole, see William Coxe, *Memoirs of the Life and Administration of Sir Robert Walpole*, I (1798), pp. 710–14, 719, 732; and A. S. Foord, *His Majesty's Opposition 1714–1830* (Oxford 1964), p. 140.

in it. And this was a position which in the years between 1715 and 1830 was attained by the English electorate only on the quite exceptional occasion of 1784.

(iv)

It should by now be clear that in some important respects Swedish parliamentarism in the Age of Liberty had progressed further than parliamentarism in Hanoverian England. But the test of any liberal constitution is, first of all, does it work well?; and secondly, does it secure those liberties of the subject which it must be presumed to have been designed to preserve? To neither of these questions did the Constitution of 1720 provide a reassuring answer.

It is obvious that a Diet of four Estates was a more difficult instrument to handle than a parliament of two Houses. In principle, decisions were reached by a majority of Estates; but to this principle there were important exceptions, for each of the three upper Estates claimed the right to veto proposals which it deemed to be an infringement of its privileges.[137] The Nobility, as the largest, most privileged, and most powerful Estate, did not hesitate to use that veto; but in addition they might try to persuade or constrain the other Estates to alter resolutions which were not to their liking. When in the sixties they began to find themselves sometimes outvoted by the three lower Estates, they felt that the natural order of things was being subverted. But the slowness of their proceedings, which was partly a consequence of their being so numerous a body, meant that the three lower Estates might reach congruent resolutions before the Nobility took a vote, so that their debates became otiose, and they were in danger of 'merely saying *amen* like the clerk in a country church'.[138] However, the deadlock-situation of two Estates against two occurred pretty frequently; and even where there was substantial agreement, the resolution of one Estate in favour of a measure might differ in terms from those taken by the others: a special standing committee of the Diet – the Despatching Committee – existed in order to determine what the Diet's decision had really been, and to formulate it; and this committee did not usually complete its business until some weeks or months after the members had gone home. Moreover the Despatching Committee needed to have the resolutions of all four Estates before it could proceed to formulate the Diet's decision; and an Estate which saw itself certain to be outvoted could in effect nullify the decision of the other three by simply refraining from taking a decision at all. It was the

[137] Brusewitz, *Frihetstidens Grundlagar*, pp. 236–7. It is perhaps worth recalling that in England all bills affecting the rights of the peerage had to originate in the Lords, and could not be amended in the Commons: Blackstone, I. 168.
[138] *Sveriges riksdag*, I, vi, 141.

unwieldliness of the Estate structure that provided the practical justification for the concentration of power in the Secret Committee, which at the
height of its influence really functioned as a unicameral parliament. As in
the Diet itself, voting in the Secret Committee was by a majority of
Estates, and not by head; but there no deadlock could occur, since only
the three upper Estates were represented in it.

   Though the Secret Committee thus solved some difficulties, it could
also be productive of others. It was elected at the beginning of each Diet,
and its membership remained unchanged for the duration of the session,
apart from the filling of casual vacancies. It thus reflected the party
position as it stood immediately after the elections, and indeed
exaggerated the ascendancy of the victors. In the course of a protracted
Diet, however, the strength of parties could change, and a situation might
arise in which the all-powerful Committee was no longer of the same
political colour as the majorities in the Estates, and might pursue policies
unacceptable to them: this happened, for instance, in 1743, when the Hats
had a plurality in the Estates, but the Caps controlled the Secret
Committee.[139] The secrecy of the Committee's proceedings, moreover,
meant that at least two matters of prime importance were (or could be)
withdrawn from the knowledge and participation of the mass of the
Estates. One of these was finance; the other was foreign policy. There
was, no doubt, some justification for secrecy over foreign policy: when
during the negotiations for the peace of Åbo in 1743 the Secret
Committee for particular reasons insisted that the *plena* should read the
diplomatic correspondence and debate the answer to be sent to the
Swedish negotiators, the absurdity of the move became evident.[140] But
secrecy over finance was intolerable.

   Throughout the period estimates of revenue and expenditure were
based on the normal year 1696, the budget for which served as a kind of
unchanging Civil List. There was therefore always a deficit, and taxation
was always necessary. Until 1761 the Secret Committee, through its
sub-committee the Estimates Deputation, acted as the equivalent of the
English Committee of Supply, and decided upon the amount of fresh
revenue that would be required. How it was to be raised, what taxes were
to be imposed, was the business of the Grants Deputation, which thus
corresponded to the English Committee of Ways and Means; and on this
Deputation the Peasants were represented along with the other Estates.
The Grants Deputation's task was an unenviable one, for it was often
condemned to work very much in the dark, or at any rate by such light as
the Secret Committee allowed to filter down to it. Demands for
information on the size of the deficit, or the yield of taxation, or the way

[139] Fersen, *Historiska skrifter*, I, p. 114.   [140] *Ibid.*, I pp. 120–1.

the grants were spent, tended to be evaded or refused: so in 1727, 1746–7,
1751–2, 1755–6, 1761–2.[141] The Council's concern with finance was
mainly consultative: three of its members always attended the Estimates
Commission (which continued in being between Diets), and when the
Diet was in session one member was often present by invitation in the
Estimates Deputation; but that was all. In the financial crisis of 1771 the
Council informed the Estates that they did not know what the country's
financial position was.[142] For most of the period even the sovereign
Estates were permitted to know only the method by which it was hoped
to balance the budget and the nature of the taxes to be levied; and
sometimes that information came too late to permit any real debate: in
1752 the Secret Committee did not present its report until two days before
the end of the session.[143] This secrecy was defended on the ground that
Swedish finances, unlike English, could not afford publicity if public
confidence was to be maintained.[144] The *riksdagsordning* of 1723 gave the
Estates a general right of audit; but the Secret Committee declared that
they had divested themselves of that right in its favour.[145] When under
pressure the Secret Committee did consent to provide information it was
sometimes deliberately misleading: in 1746–7 it stated the size of the
deficit at one-third of its true amount.[146] Though it was an accepted
principle that grants of taxes must be unanimous, since no Estate was to
be taxed without its own consent, when in 1723 the Estate of Peasants
refused to agree to what was proposed they were simply ignored; and
other attempts on their part to assert the principle of 'no supply without
redress' had no success.[147] During the Hats' ascendancy in the fifties the
Secret Committee had no scruple about applying the nation's finances to
party ends: pensions, premiums, gratifications, could be given under
cover of secrecy without the Estates' knowing anything of the matter; and
no possibility existed of bringing these abuses to light. It is hardly
surprising that when the Caps came in at the election of 1764 they came in
on a popular demand for reform, and that one of their first measures was
to deprive the Secret Committee of the sole management of the
finances.[148] But though the control of finance now passed out of the hands
of the Committee and into those of the *plena*, it does not seem that the
situation was noticeably improved. Abuses might no longer be covered
by a privileged secrecy, but they remained abuses for all that. The *plena*

[141] Nils Bergsten, *Bevillningsutskott vid frihetstidens riksdagar* (Uppsala 1906), pp. 36, 66–80, 90,
98–9.
[142] *Sveriges riksdag*, I, vi, 283–7. The Secret Committee likewise tried to evade responsibility:
SRARP, xxx, 469.
[143] Malmström, *Sveriges politiska historia* IV, p. 61.
[144] Bergsten, *Bevillningsutskott vid frihetstidens riskdagar*, p. 72.
[145] *Ibid.*, p. 82.   [146] *Ibid.*, p. 80.   [147] *Ibid.*, pp. 30–32, 36–43, 66
[148] Brusewitz, *Frihetstiden Grundlagar*, p. 268. The Hats in 1769 issued a similar instruction.

carried frivolous or irresponsible financial motions without prior warning to the Estimates Office, and in bland indifference as to whether the budget would bear the expenditure:[149] this was precisely the type of abuse which the English Standing Order of 1713 made impossible. The proposals of the Grants Deputation still tended to come so near to the end of the session that serious criticism was almost impossible;[150] financial information appeared to be still as difficult to obtain;[151] the Peasants, in particular, felt that they were being kept in the dark.[152] To the end of the chapter, as Lagerroth sadly admitted, there was no financial planning worth the name.[153] In this area the constitution can hardly be said to have been working well.

Yet the fact remains that without the Secret Committee the government of the Estates must probably have broken down. For they took on far too much administration to do all of it well. When in 1765 the Caps curtailed the Secret Committee's powers, the effect was to slow down the pace of business.[154] They were so overworked as a result of their own jealousy of power, so eager in the pursuit of trivialities, that they defeated their own purpose: by the end of the sixties this was clearly seen by the more discerning friends of the constitution.[155] The Diet floundered in tides of paper. The shelves of Riksarkivet groan under the weight of hundreds of volumes, scores of yards, of parliamentary proceedings: over 150 volumes for the Diet of 1755–6 alone. Compared with this overwhelming mass of material, the records of parliament appear humiliatingly meagre.[156]

---

[149] In 1770, for instance, the Estate of Nobility voted, for political reasons, to pay pensions to former members of the Council, despite the special vote of the Estimates Deputation that the budget could not stand it: *SRARP*, xxviii, 368.

[150] *Ibid.*, xxvi, 198, where the Nobility show irritation at this state of affairs.

[151] In 1769 the Estates were still trying to get the Secret Committee to explain its financial policies in 1761 and 1765: *ibid.*, xxviii, 229. Ridderstolpe compared the situation in this regard unfavourably with that existing in England: *ibid.*, xxvii, 238.

[152] *Bondeståndets riksdagsprotokoll*, 12, pp. 269, 338, 372; But there had been some improvement: in 1765 the Grants Deputation extorted information by suspending work until they got it: Bergsten, p. 118; and in 1771–2 the Estates insisted on being informed before they would appoint a Grants Deputation at all: *ibid.*, p. 132.

[153] *Sveriges riksdag*, I, vi, 291.

[154] *Sveriges riksdag*, I, vi, 290. It is significant that in 1771 the Caps were planning to increase the Secret Committee's powers once again: Kjellin, *Rikshistoriografen Anders Schönberg*, p. 235.

[155] Kjellin, *Rikshistoriografen Anders Schönberg*, p. 94; Axel Brusewitz, 'Ett konstitutionsprojekt från frihetstiden', *Statsvetenskaplig tidskrift* (1913), pp. 12–13; Georg Landberg, 'En svensk författningshistoria från krisåret 1768. Bidrag till den gustavianska rojalismens idéhistoria', *Statsvetenskaplig tidskrift* (1937), pp. 17–18.

[156] Sven Ulric Palme once provided an example of what could happen. He found that the question of what title was to be given to the Duke of Holstein – admittedly an important and highly controversial question – was considered five times by the king, five times by the Council, twice by the Chancery, four times in a *plenum plenorum* of all four Estates, three times in the Secret Committee, four times in the Greater Secret Deputation, twice in the Lesser Secret Deputation, and once in the Despatching Committee; and of every one of these stages a record seems to have

A general disposition to make heavy weather of things was compounded by an attention to detail which at times seems excessive, and a tendency
to use sledge-hammers to crack nuts. However important the principle at
stake, one feels that for the Secret Committee to reserve to itself the
appointment of the crown princess's cooks was an exercise of power
which might have been forgone in favour of some less august body without immediately imperilling the constitution.[157] One may doubt whether
the Minutes Committee was making the best use of its time when in
1770 it debated a proposal to prescribe the number of lines to a page in
judicial judgments, with the stipulation that each line should contain at
least seven syllables, on pain of loss of office for judges who neglected to
comply.[158] The Estate of Nobility spent many hours in deciding
genealogical questions, and the right of families to be accepted as
members. They likewise gave their full attention to such important
problems as whether Växjö town, or the chapter of Växjö cathedral,
should be entitled to take firewood from a local coppice.[159] They delivered
solomonic judgments in disputes over the boundaries of landed property.
They debated, with concentrated attention, all those complaints of
'prejudice', all those demands for promotion, which monopolised the
interest of members of the armed forces, and of the civil service. And they
turned their minds, off and on over a period of seven years and three
Diets, to the offer of Captain Hallonqvist to disclose (in return for a
suitable reward) his secret of 'the art of floating upon water' – an art
which, as was remarked on one occasion, 'could hardly fail to be useful to
one and all' – especially in view of the fact that the Royal Swedish
Academy of Science had warranted it to be scientifically sound.[160]

Even in matters of a more serious sort, the method of government
which had been laid down in the constitution, or had evolved from it,
imposed claims upon the attention of the Estates which were really too
heavy for them to bear. A major portion of their time was necessarily
devoted to the consideration of the reports and recommendations of their
standing committees, which formed, indeed, the basis for most of the

---

been preserved: Sven Ulric Palme, 'Vom Absolutismus zum Parlamentarismus in Schweden',
p. 386, n. 19. The clearest guide to the intricate course of business through the Diet is *Schematiska
framställningar av några riksdagsärendens gång vid frihetstidens riksdagar* (unpubl., Stockholm 1968), a
collaborative work by members of Professor Palme's *seminarium*.

[157] Fersen, *Historiska skrifter*, III, 33.

[158] Johan von Engeström, *Historiska anteckningar*, p. 17: the point being presumably that fees
were charged at so much a page.

[159] *SRARP*, XXIV, 227.

[160] The ludicrous and pathetic case of Hallonquist may be followed in *SRARP*, XXIV, 327;
XXV, 5, 210; XXVI, 345; XXVII, 516; XXIX, 378; *Bondeståndets riksdagsprotokoll*, 10, pp. 339, 413,
434, 645, 665, 760; 11, p. 528; 12, p. 445. The sharp-eyed Daniel Tilas, who with many thousand
other spectators observed Hallonqvist's demonstration on 10 August 1765, decided that the trick
was done with an aid of an (undetected) inflatable life-jacket: Tilas, *Anteckningar*, p. 111

more important pieces of legislation. The committees generally did their business thoroughly and well; they were satisfactorily representative; and as a rule their recommendations were accepted without much amendment. What took the time of the Diet was not so much the debate on their proposals as the method by which they were communicated to the Estates. It was plainly impossible to distribute some twelve or thirteen hundred manuscript copies of each of these reports in order to provide one for each member (and not all of the Peasants would have been able to read them): the only resort was to read them aloud.[161] One has only to open any volume of the minutes of one of the Estates to see what this meant when the Diet was in full activity: item after item of the minutes begins 'Was read the report of . . .'; and so for page after page. So too with those 'extracts from the minutes' (which might be quite lengthy) which all the Estates sent to each other with great frequency, and which were, indeed, the normal method of communication between them: these, too, were read aloud. As if this were not enough, members had an almost unlimited liberty of presenting and reading substantial *Memorials* which were in fact undelivered speeches. An extreme case occurred during the Nobility's consideration of the *Act of Security* on 15 November 1769: the proceedings opened with the reading of no less than nineteen *Memorials*, which took up so much time that before it was completed most members had gone off to lunch. After they returned they found themselves confronted with nineteen more; but when only two of these had been read the Marshal persuaded them to agree that it would be sufficient if the remaining seventeen were simply inserted in the minutes.[162] There must have been many days on which the average member might have felt that his main duty as a legislator was to listen to some official eternally reading aloud, relieved only by the maddeningly frequent interruption of proceedings by deputations from one Estate to another. In view of all this one is the less surprised that affairs moved at a somewhat leisurely pace, and that there was often a considerable hiatus between the Diet's decision and the appropriate administrative action. By the late sixties the parliamentary-administrative machine was already under strain; by 1771 the scrutiny of the minutes and reports of provincial governors and county-court judges, for example, had become little better than a farce.[163] An English parliament might in law be omnicompetent;

---

[161] After the *Ordinance for the Liberty of Printing* (1766) printed copies were sometimes available (e.g. the draft *Act of Security*, 1769).

[162] *SRARP*, xxviii, 64. A majority of these *Memorials* had in fact been printed, on their authors' initiative, and were available to members; but this did not stop them from being read aloud.

[163] See debate in *SRARP*, xxix, 317–24, and Johan von Engeström, *Historiska Anteckningar*, pp. 13–14. In 1766 the Judicial Deputation reported that Judge Carl Engelbrekt Grefvesmohlen had returned none of his records for the previous twenty years, and had employed indecent

but it made little attempt to be so in practice. The total control which the Diet tried to exercise was scarcely feasible even in so moderately complex a society as that of eighteenth-century Sweden. The omnicompetence of a legislature ran up against its effective practical limitation: lack of time.

The difficulty was not lessened by some of the forms that governed the Diet's proceedings. At first sight, they might seem simpler and more clear-cut than those of the House of Commons: a succinct general guide to them was available in the *riksdagsordning* of 1723. It was the duty of the Speaker to see to it that debates were properly conducted, to determine the order of speaking, and to decide the order of business; and increasingly the Marshal tended to consult with the Speakers of the other three Estates in order that business in each might proceed more or less in step with the others.[164] But the Speakers in Sweden had far more influence on the course of debate than was the case at Westminster, for they alone might formulate every motion that came up for decision. That motion must however reflect, fairly and fully, the general trend of the debate. This sometimes resulted in complicated motions embodying different and essentially separate questions; and that meant that the decision of the Estate might be taken on a rather different issue from that which had been raised originally: one could not always be sure, when a debate started, what one would end by voting on. This was particularly the case as a consequence of the duty of the Speaker also to formulate the 'counter-proposition': that is, to define precisely what the implications would be if the motion were rejected; and sometimes this 'counter-proposition' by no means represented the obvious or logical consequence of the defeat of the motion that was under consideration. Not surprisingly, much parliamentary time was devoted to preliminary wrangling about what exactly the terms of the motion and the 'counter-proposition' ought to be. Thus when an Estate could not agree, it did not vote on an *amendment*; it had to choose between what were in fact alternative motions, and it might well be that neither really corresponded with the views of some of the members. If a successful counter-proposition had afterwards been put as a substantive motion (which it never was) one may well doubt if it would always have been carried.[165] It was no wonder that Fersen remarked in

expressions in a letter to the Estates: Bexell, *Riksdags-historiska anteckningar*, p. 146: a sharp circular to officials now threatened a fine for non-compliance – half the proceeds to go to schools in Lappland: Brusewitz, p. 447. The yield was probably small: one county-court judge, after repeated orders to return the records of the cases tried before him, is said to have hired a hearse, loaded the records on to it, and marched in derision behind as chief mourner: Kenneth Awebro, *Gustaf III:s räfst med ämbetsmännen 1772–1779*, Uppsala 1977, p. 50.

[164] But the Speaker's right to determine the order of business could conflict with the right of a member who had jumped the gun and begun to speak on a different matter, to be heard out to the end: this was a main issue in the tumultuous and chaotic debate of 2 November 1769: *SRARP.*, XXVIII, 1–23.

[165] E.g. *Bondeståndets riksdagsprotokoll*, 12, p. 136, where the Speaker, having defined the

1765 that 'It seemed to him deplorable and strange, that forty years after the *riksdagsordning* . . . we still on every occasion wrangle about the basis and form of the Marshal's proposition.'[166]

It seems that in the Diet divisions were much less frequent than in the House of Commons.[167] The reason may partly be in the state of parties: in the Clergy and the Burghers one side might be so dominant that it was scarcely worth while to divide the House. In the Nobility, parties tended to be more evenly balanced, and there the number of divisions was higher. But it was still notably low by English standards, and for this there may be another explanation, namely as arising from the manner of voting. Each member was summoned, individually and in due order of precedence (absent members being summoned twice) to come up and deliver his sealed, but unsigned, ballot at the Table of the House. The result was that while it took the Tellers in the House of Commons about half an hour to count a division in which 350–400 members voted, in the House of Nobility it took them five and a half hours to count a division of 327–394: a daunting prospect to face at the end of a long day of violent parliamentary strife.[168] One reason for the slow pace of parliamentary business was that they lacked those useful devices which were available in England to cut short debates:[169] for intance, a motion for the Order of the Day; or a motion to adjourn; or a motion 'that the Question be now put' – any one of which put an end to the debate without further argument. In theory a debate could not continue if the Speaker left the Chair; but when on 2 November 1769 the Marshal tried to terminate a tumultuous sitting by doing so, he was prevented by force from leaving the chamber, and had no option but to resume it.[170] The Speaker's authority was in principle acknowledged, and his person entitled to all respect – the Peasants on occasion alluded to their Speaker as 'Father' – but debates seem to have

---

motion as being to expel a member for the duration of the Diet, defined the counter-proposition as being that he make a public apology, be fined 10 copper *daler*, and be excluded for six weeks: of this everything except the apology was the Speaker's suggestion, and did not arise from the debate.

[166] *SRARP*, XXIV, 517.

[167] In the Commons they averaged about 50 in each session during the period 1768–80: in the Estate of Clergy in 1734 there were only 7; in the Estate of Burghers in 1740–1 only 7; in the Estate of Peasants in 1771–2 only 7. In the Estate of Nobility there were 26 in 1765–6, 17 in 1769–70, and 21 in 1771–2: Thomas, *The House of Commons in the Eighteenth Century*, p. 262.

[168] *SRARP*, XXIV, 398; cf. ibid. XXVIII, 61 (five hours for 431–421).

[169] They also lacked any rules about a *quorum*: a situation which the Hats exploited at Christmas 1746 to carry out a notorious political *coup* in the Clergy. See below, p. 120: L. A. Cederbom, *Serenius*, pp. 78–85. But it was only in the small Estate of the Clergy that such a *coup* was possible: in the other Estates there was never any lack of numbers. And hence there were no provisions for a call of the House.

[170] *SRARP*, XXVIII, 1–23. it may be noted that Speakers in Sweden had no casting-vote: on the only recorded occasion when the votes were equal in the Estate of Nobility the question was deemed to have fallen away: *ibid.*, XXIV, 184–217.

escaped the control of the Chair much more often than in England; and
the sustained shouting, and even physical violence, which from time to
time disgraced the debates of the Nobility or the Peasants, were
sometimes uncomfortably reminiscent of a Polish Diet.[171]

On the other hand the Estates tolerated less licence of language than the
opposition to Lord North habitually permitted itself; and they punished
speeches that offended with exemplary rigour: in 1766 Baron Josias
Cederhielm was expelled from the Nobility for *life* for an insult to the
Marshal; and the same sentence was pronounced on Carl Estenberg for
what seems to have been no more than a habitually provocative and
impertinent language, and a talent for getting himself disliked.[172] So too in
other Estates: in 1771 the Peasants declared Nils Jeremiaesson incapable of
election *for ever* because in his lodgings he had said to a fellow-member
'You are a Cap, and you shall die like a dog'.[173] All these cases involved the
annulment by mere resolution of a statutory right (the stiffest penalty
permitted by the *riksdagsordning* of 1723 was exclusion for the remainder
of the Diet); they illegally purported to change the law; and they were
thus strictly comparable with the resolution of the House of Commons
which declared John Wilkes 'incapable of being elected'. But just as the
House of Commons thought better of it in the end, and let Wilkes in a few
years later, so these fulminating condemnations proved less terrible than
they sounded: either the Estate in question later changed its mind (or its
party majority), or the culprit waited until the next Diet, or the next but
one, and came back as though nothing had happened. The unpopular
Estenberg, it is true, disappears from the scene (except as a solicitant); but
Josias Cederhielm turned up at the Diet of 1771–2, as irrepressible as ever,
and not discernibly abashed by his experience.

The length of the sessions, which was a result of the amount of business
the Estates undertook, and their complex methods of transacting it,
entailed some unfortunate consequences. One of them was to hamper the
ordinary work of the executive. The central offices of government were
on the whole in the hands of competent professionals who had been
admitted to the service only after an examination, and had entered it

[171] *SRARP*, XXVIII, 63–90; Tilas, *Anteckningar* pp. 159–61; *Dagboks–Anteckningar of Johan Gabriel Oxenstierna åren 1769–1771*, ed. Gustaf Stjernström (Uppsala 1881), p. 58. For the outrageous incident in the Estate of Burghers in 1743, see below, p. 118. And there was a regular battle in the Peasants in 1755: Fersen, *Historiska skrifter*, II. 70–77.
[172] For Cederhielm, *SRARP*, XXV, 540. He had the unusual distinction of being expelled for life twice in the same Diet (though for different reasons): *ibid.*, XXVI, 416–19; for Estenberg, *ibid.*, XXVI, 388, 429–33. For a delightful account of Cederhielm (and the slightly eccentric Cederhielm family in general) see Oscar Levertin, 'En aristokratisk tidningsskrivare och hans familj', in *Svenska Gestalter* (new edn. Stockholm 1958), pp. 141–77.
[173] *Bondeståndets riksdagsprotokoll*, 12, pp. 131–8. Not the least part of his offence seems to have been his use of the word 'Cap': even in 1771 speakers could profess (hypocritically?) that they knew nothing of such party-terms.

(nobles included) at the bottom.[174] Their performance of their duties was probably not improved by erratic parliamentary interference. It might be disorganised also in a more serious way. For those members of the civil service who were nobles attended the Diet as a matter of right, and they attended it in such numbers that when the Diet was sitting the ordinary work of the courts and the administration suffered through lack of staff: in 1734 the Nobility expressly resolved that attendance was an obligation which took precedence over all other duties.[175] It could therefore happen that junior officials who sat in the first Estate took advantage of their membership to criticise and harass their official superiors; or, conversely, senior officials might use a party majority to persecute subordinates whom they happened to dislike.[176] This was not good for discipline. It was still worse in regard to the armed forces: in 1760 members of the Nobility serving with the army in Pomerania flocked back home to the Diet at a critical moment of the war, indifferent to the effect of their absence upon military operations.

That such abuses could occur was due to the fact that – apart from a few years under Tessin's leadership – all Swedish Councils of State after 1739 were far too weak to exercise the authority required to curb them. Most members of the Council were as a rule looking apprehensively over their shoulders at their masters the Estates. Even Tessin, who was not afraid of independent initiatives, could write that a member of the Council was

infinitely vulnerable; his enemies rend him, calumny as a rule sticks; the multitude becomes his judge; the misery of the times and the run of events become his accusers; and he may consider himself favoured if no more is demanded of him than humiliating explanations in reply to captious criticism formulated by his enemies.[177]

More and more the Council became only the dignified façade of a party: the real party leaders such as Fersen took care not to accept election to it. The strength of the Secret Committee entailed the enervation of the Council even when the Diet was not sitting; and when in 1765 the powers of the Secret Committee were abridged, it was the *plena*, not the Council, who were the beneficiaries of the change. To the very end the problem of devising an effective executive was bedevilled by the Estates' fear lest it become too formidable.

[174] Elmroth, *Nyrekryteringen till de högre ämbetena*, pp. 94–6, 124, 133. Examinations, conducted by the universities, were introduced in 1750; but the standard was so low that the *Collegia* instituted supplementary examinations of their own: Martin Weibull, *Lunds Universitets historia*, I, 242–3, 266.

[175] C. F. Malmström, 'Om ämbetsmännens ställning till riksdagen under Frihetstiden', *Smärre skrifter*, pp. 159–67. In 1774 Bishop Filenius of Linköping excused himself for having held only one diocesan synod in twelve years by pleading that he had been too busy attending Diets: Awebro, *Gustaf III:s räfst med ämbetsmännen 1772–1779*, pp. 80, 158.

[176] Daniel Tilas, *Curriculum vitae 1712–1757* (Stockholm 1966), pp. 319ff.

[177] *Carl Gustaf Tessins dagbok*, (Stockholm 1915), p. 18

Finally, it was to the excessive length of the sessions that was due, in some measure, the most notorious abuse of the age: parliamentary corruption. For most of the Nobility, nearly all the Peasants, and many of the Clergy were more or less poor by English standards; and the expense of a long Diet was more than they (or their constituents, if they had any) could afford. This opened the way for corruption: corruption by well-organised party funds, distributed through 'operators' and usually drawing heavily on foreign money. Already in 1725 the English minister, Poyntz, was writing that 'a Swedish Diet is always corruptible';[178] and thereafter foreign corruption, by France, Russia, England, and even Denmark, became a normal feature of politics. Swedes of the eighteenth century – and Lagerroth in the twentieth – considered that the House of Commons was far more corrupt than the Diet;[179] but this view was probably based on a misunderstanding of how English politics really worked. The difference between England and Sweden lay in the fact that whereas corruption *alone* could never assure a majority in the Commons, it usually could, and sometimes did, secure one in the Diet. It was not that there was any essential difference in the personal integrity of politicians in the two countries; it arose rather from disparities in international standing and domestic affluence. For a relatively weak country such as Sweden then was, foreign policy was of crucial importance, and it was one of the main points that divided Hats from Caps. Foreign powers, anxious for their own purposes to secure Sweden's alliance, or to deny it to their enemies, naturally sought to bribe politicians – as politicians had been bribed in England, in a somewhat similar case, in the 1670s. Members of the Diet might take the money because they really needed it; and often enough they were bribed to vote as they would have voted in any case. The Swedish nobleman or burgher who accepted Russian or French money was perhaps less often paid to change his vote than to cast it – to come up to Stockholm for a critical division, or to stay there (with free meals) when otherwise he would have been forced to go home because he could not pay for board and lodging any longer.[180] And just as in England there were occasions when the ties of dependence snapped, when the inducements of a minister, or the threats of a patron, were swept aside by strong spontaneous waves of feeling, so in Sweden it could happen that quite lavish supplies of foreign gold proved unavailing, and the parties

[178] H. Valentin, *Frihetstidens riddarhus*, p. 76. The charge of introducing 'Walpolean corruption' was made by Hats against Arvid Horn, and by Horn's friends against the Hats: Fersen, *Historiska skrifter*, I, 45; Linnarsson, *Riksrådens licentiering*, p. 75.
[179] Lagerroth, *Frihetstidens författning*, p. 316.
[180] In 1755 numbers of aged or impoverished noblemen who had never attended a Diet in their lives were thus whipped in: Olsson, *Hattar och mössor*, pp. 196, 237. In 1746 the Russian minister had a list of 300 nobles who were too poor to live in Stockholm without support: Ludvig Stavenow, *Frihetstiden. Dess epoker och kulturif* (Göteborg 1907), p. 121.

they had supported broke loose and went their own way – as occurred for instance in 1766 and 1772, when the Russian and English ministers lost control of their Cap clients. It is true, too, that foreign pensions were often *honoraria* for past services, or payments for compiling Journals of the Diet, or pretexts for foreign ministers to ask their courts for more money: Anders Schönberg wrote in 1769 that if there had been no possibility of bribing with jobs, economic advantages, and so forth, foreign gold would never have sufficed to keep the strife of parties going.[181] But it remains true that the attempts of apologists to shrug off the corruption of the Diet as not of major importance cannot be accepted: the period can show numerous occasions when changes of party allegiance were effected by corruption, sometimes decisively so.[182] Baron von Korff, the Russian minister, was only voicing a general opinion among foreign diplomats when he wrote (in 1747) 'The Swedish youth is so totally corrupted and devoid of all finer feelings that with money you can get them to do anything at all'.[183] The swarming mass of penurious nobles – military officers on half-pay, civil servants waiting for an established post, Finnish members far from home, indigent gentlemen herded by the party-bosses to Stockholm to make up a majority – had little in common with the substantial men who formed a majority of the English House of Commons. Even the poorest nobleman, however, brought with him one highly marketable article: his proxy. The sale of proxies became a regular trade, with regular offices in Stockholm; proxies were made out in blank; they might change hands (at enhanced prices) several times in a single day; they were not infrequently spurious – proxies made out in the name of families which had become extinct. In the course of the period their price rose as spectacularly as that of pocket boroughs in England: in 1727 the rate for a proxy was 300 *daler*; in 1772 it had risen to 12 000.[184]

At the root of many of the difficulties in the way of making the constitution work smoothly was the basic fact of the Diet's division into four Estates. There were cogent historical reasons for this, potent enough to preserve the Estate-structure until 1865; but already in the Age of Liberty it had become an anomaly and a nuisance; for it corresponded less and less satisfactorily to social realities. Yet only on three occasions, it

---

[181] Kjellin, *Rikshistoriografen Anders Schönberg*, p. 202.

[182] See, e.g., Roberts, *British Diplomacy and Swedish Politics*, pp. 173–4.

[183] Quoted in Ladislaus Konopczyński, 'Polen och Sverige i det adertonde århundradet', *Historisk tidskrift* (1925), p. 115.

[184] For the abuses connected with proxies, see Valentin, *op. cit.*, pp. 151–62; for the rise in prices, Hallendorf, *Sveriges riddarhus*, p. 308; for proxy-buying campaigns in the months before a Diet, Olsson, *Hattar och mössor*, p.195 (for 1751), or Roberts, *British Diplomacy and Swedish Politics*, p. 342 (for 1770–1). The Estate made a serious effort to stop the scandal, but without real success.

seems, were any proposals for changing it put forward, and none of them received serious consideration. In 1719–20 the non-noble civil servants demanded the vote, and representation for themselves in the Diet, on the surprising principle of universal suffrage; in 1744 the forge-owners of northern Sweden claimed recognition as a separate Estate. And in 1765 Anders Nordencrantz was advocating the admission to the franchise of non-noble landowners, and the replacement of the Estates by a unicameral Diet.[185] The Estate-structure shut out from participation in politics categories of men whose absence from the Diet weakened it: all those whom contemporary parlance denominated as 'persons of Estate' (ståndspersoner). It was a perverse way to describe them, since it was precisely the fact that they belonged to no Estate that distinguished them, and that ensured their political impotence; but we may perhaps translate ståndspersoner as 'persons of standing', or 'persons of quality', though these terms are appropriate only to the upper strata of a very heterogeneous collection of people. They included all the professions (unless an individual happened to have been ennobled), many substantial landowners, most forge-owners, merchants who had not acquired burgage-rights, more than three-quarters of the lower civil service, all non-noble officers and subalterns. By the mid-century these 'persons of quality' were more numerous than the Clergy and the Burghers combined, and they included perhaps two-fifths of the upper classes in Stockholm.[186] Their absence deprived the Diet of that weight of property which was the regulator of politics in eighteenth-century England. This was a point fastened on by critics of the constitution, and by none more tenaciously than by that committed anglophile Anders Nordencrantz, who believed that the relatively high property qualification for M.P.s guaranteed their independence, and who pointed out that it was precisely 'persons of quality' that formed the backbone of the House of Commons, and gave it its peculiar strength.[187] The Swedish constitution may have been designed, as Isak Faggott contended, to safeguard property; but Nordencrantz would have retorted that the Diet lacked the property to safeguard the constitution.

---

[185] Sveriges riksdag, I, v, 52, 181–3; Sten Carlsson, Ståndssamhälle och ståndspersoner 1700–1865 (Lund 1949), p. 247; Brolin, Hattar och mössor, p. 336.

[186] Carlsson, Ståndssamhälle och ståndspersoner, pp. 7–13; Tom Söderberg, Den namnlösa medelklassen. Socialgrupp två i det gamla svenska samhället (Stockholm 1956), p. 203. Many of the big iron-masters were of course nobles or burghers, and perhaps those who were not were less concerned at their exclusion than might be supposed: they had other organs for voicing their views – the College of Mines, for instance, and (after 1747) the Iron Office.

[187] Anders Nordencrantz, Undersökning om de rätta orsakerna til den Blandning som skedt af Lagstiftande och Lagskipande, Redofordrande och Redoskyldige Magternas Gjöromål (Stockholm 1770), pp. 13, 32–3, 83.

(v)

The constitution thus suffered from serious defects, in principle and still more in practice; and by no means all of them were recognised by the men who had to work it. The most serious of all still remains to be mentioned. Of all the criticisms that can be directed against the Constitution of 1720, much the most damaging is that it came to present as grave a threat to the liberty of the subject as the Absolutism which had been overthrown in 1719, or the constitutional monarchy which followed it in 1772. Charles Sheridan was exaggerating only a little when he wrote that 'while they paid so much attention to political liberty . . . they totally forgot that an equal attention was due to civil liberty, or the freedom of individuals considered in their private capacity'.[188] It was no accident that Isak Faggott should have reached the end of his treatise before he came to discuss the position of the subject, and that he should have been far more concerned with the citizen's duties than with his rights. The duty of the subject, he insisted, was simply to obey the law; the duty of the government was to keep a constant watch on him to make sure that he did so, and a wise government would 'purge those who are unserviceable, and put the rest within such bounds, that even if not all can be punished, yet most can be kept upon a tight reign'.[189] In eighteenth-century Sweden the rights of the citizen were imperilled by the very constitution which, one might suppose, was designed to safeguard them; or at least by the interpretations and theories which were erected upon it. Arbitrary action by the Estates was a constant possibility and a frequent reality. Blackstone had predicted that the 'total disjunction' of executive and legislative would in the end produce a tyranny:[190] 'The legislative would soon become tyrannical, by making continual encroachments, and gradually assuming to itself the right of the executive power'. The Swedish experience proved his prediction correct in every particular. The Diet intervened from party motives to upset judicial decisions: its members used their parliamentary privilege to delay judgments against them, or to evade them.[191] In 1752 they severely restricted the right of public meeting in towns.[192] The extraordinary tribunals which they set up used torture in political cases. They voted money for spies and *agents provocateurs*.[193]

---

[188] Sheridan, *History of the Late Revolution in Sweden*, p. 163.

[189] Faggott, *Swea Rikes Styrelse efter Gundlagarne*, p. 176.

[190] Blackstone, *Commentaries on the Laws of England*, I, 153. Nordencrantz quoted this passage in his *Undersökning om de rätta Orsakerna . . .* , at p. 32.

[191] Johan von Engeström, *Historiska Anteckningar och Bref från åren 1771–1805*, p. 22.

[192] Malmström, *Sveriges politiska historia*, IV, pp. 83.

[193] *Ibid.*, 160: A. J. von Höpken was a strong advocate of this: von Höpken, *Skrifter*, II, pp. 134–5, 150–1.

Freedom of speech within the legislature was precarious: members who vented unpopular opinions might find themselves voted out of the house and disqualified for future election, as in the cases of Cederhielm and Estenberg, noticed above.[194] Political persecution disguised under judicial forms was among the most odious feature of the age. The period opened with the judicial murder of Görtz; the execution of Erik Brahe and seven others in 1756 was no better, and that of Alexander Blackwell in 1747 a great deal worse.[195] Lewenhaupt and Buddenbrock, the incompetent or unfortunate commanders in the disastrous war of 1741, were sent to their deaths (presumably, as in the case of Admiral Byng, *pour encourager les autres*) by an extraordinary tribunal set up by the Estates, and it was small consolation to Buddenbrock's heir to be told later that though there had been an admitted miscarriage of justice in his case, still the Estates could not err.[196] The last time the House of Commons acted as a court of first instance for a political offence (as against a contempt) seems to be *Mist's Case*, 1721; and perhaps the best that can be said for some of these Swedish cases is that they occurred in more or less analogous circumstances of hysteria. Mist's crime was to be a Jacobite; Blackwell was accused of plotting to disturb the succession. In the years around the mid-century it is clear that the Hat Secret Committee was exploiting a dynastic panic to carry out an inquisitorial reign of terror. But long after the succession was secure the excesses continued: the exploits of the Palmstierna Commission after 1758 were quite as bad as anything that had gone before. The Caps, despite their loud denunciations of extraordinary parliamentary tribunals, proved no better than the Hats – except that they gave their proceedings full publicity. The Hats had sentenced Christopher Springer to life-imprisonment for contending that members were responsible to their constituents; the Caps condemned Kierman to the same penalty for allegedly manipulating the operations of the Exchange Office to his own advantage; but in each case the proceedings were a mockery of justice: in effect, they were Acts of Attainder, expressions of the Diet's determination to punish, no matter what the law might say.

Until the sixties, the Estates considered themselves totally self-sufficient, raised by the constitution high above public opinion, protected against the blasphemy of criticism, and happily infallible. The publication of any discussion or criticism of the constitution, or of the actions of the Diet, was forbidden; on the characteristic ground that 'Ignorance is better than wrong ideas'.[197] The only apparent exception to this rule in fact

[194] *Supra*, p. 99.
[195] For Blackwell's case, see Arne Remgård, *Carl Gustaf Tessin och 1746–67 års riksdag* (Lund 1968), pp. 206–77 and p. 121, below.
[196] Lagerroth, *Frihetstidens författning*, p. 372; *Fredrik Axel von Fersens historiska skrifter*, I, p. 111.
[197] Bishop Browallius, in his *Memorial on false and erroneous ideas*, Malmström, IV. 436.

confirmed it; for the weekly periodical *En Ärlig Swensk* (1755) was permitted to discuss these matters because it was in fact the Hat party-organ. Members of the Estates were free to publish; but this was only another indication that they were subject to other laws than those which applied to the ordinary citizen: Anders Nordencrantz, for instance, was vastly indignant when a member of the public published a reply to a book of his which had been sanctioned by the Estates, saying that 'it was a culpable impudence for a private individual to dispute with a member of parliament in print'.[198] For the nation at large there was no liberty of printing; no public discussion of finance or foreign policy; no public exposure of abuses. As Malmström put it: 'Every doubt about the excellence of the fundamental laws, every criticism directed against government or Estates, every scrutinizing of their actions, every illustration of any weak point in the government's direction of the economy or the defences, was considered a crime, or prevented from coming to the notice of the public.'[199] Only the existence of a flourishing crop of manuscript pamphlets provided a vent for views which could not otherwise be expressed.[200] For the censorship extended to all printed publications: on one occasion the censor asked the Chancery (to whom he was responsible) whether books ought to be banned which contained such words as 'liberty', 'law', 'patriot', 'slave'.[201] One might be tempted to think that he had his tongue in his cheek when he put the question; but perhaps in prudence he could do no less. For these words (or most of them) were heavily laden with special applications deriving from party warfare.[202] After 1766 the situation greatly improved; for in that year the Young Caps, who had consistently opposed secrecy, carried their *Ordinance for the Liberty of Printing*,[203] which abolished preliminary censorship except for religious books.[204] But it still left the heart of the system rigorously protected: any criticism of the constitution might bring a heavy fine; any attack upon the Estates was to be punishable with death – or if there were mitigating circumstances, with hard labour. The

---

Resolutions of the Diet were published from 1739; journals from 1755. Division-lists were never published: *Sveriges riksdag*, I, vi, pp. 161–4.

[198] Malmström, *Sveriges politiska historia*, V, p. 73.

[199] *Ibid.*, IV, pp. 433–4.

[200] See Ingemar Carlsson, *Frihetstidens handskrivna politiska litteratur. En bibliografi.* (Göteborg 1967), and *idem, Olof Dalin och den politiska propagandan inför 'lilla ofreden'* (Lund 1966).

[201] H. Eek, *Om tryckfriheten* (Uppsala 1942), p. 160. One is reminded of the Emperor Francis I, who is said to have forbidden his physician to allude to his constitution.

[202] Carlsson, *Olof Dalin*, pp. 47, 49–50, 73, 75, 77.

[203] Printed in Brusewitz, pp. 451–7: See below, p. 166. See also Olle Stridsberg, 'Hattarnas och mössornas ställningstagande till tryckfrihetsfrågan på riksdagarna 1760–2 och 1765–66' *Historisk tidskrift* (1953).

[204] They continued to be subject to preliminary censorship by the chapter of the diocese: for a survey of the continuing intolerance of the Swedish church, see Carl Arvid Hessler, *Stat och religion i upplysningstidens Sverige* (Uppsala 1956).

savagery of the penalty reveals the crucial importance attached to the Diet by the champions of the constitution: it was the keystone of the constitutional arch, and anything that might undermine its stability was the ultimate betrayal, the first step on a road which led inevitably back to the Absolutism from which they had escaped.

One serious attempt, and one only, was made to check the abuses which had gradually disfigured the constitution. In 1769 the Estates set up a Grand Committee (the so-called 'United Deputations') to draft necessary reforms; and in due course that Committee produced a draft statute to which they gave the name of the *Act of Security*. Most of the members of the Grand Committee had come to realise that if the constitution were to be saved from the effects of the excesses for which it had been made the excuse, or had provided the shield, a serious reform must take a proper care of the liberty of the subject. Anders Schönberg, who played a main part in framing the *Act of Security*, said bluntly that 'a member of the Estates in an absolute Diet can be a worse tyrant than an absolute king'; and he could even risk the suggestion that the Estates might be 'misled'.[205] The *Act of Security* sheds some light on how much liberty needed to be safeguarded.[206] It would have prohibited arbitrary arrest and imprisonment without trial, the use of informers and of torture, and above all, of all kinds of special parliamentary tribunals and commissions. In what was probably an echo of Wilkes, it forbade the seizure of papers of persons not properly charged with an offence. The confounding of the legislative and executive functions it denounced as 'precisely what produces despotism and sovereignty . . . for whoever can both create law and administer it is thereby above the law, and not bound by any law whatever'. There must therefore be a clear separation of powers: the Estates must no longer interfere with the ordinary work of the executive; king, Council and officials must 'discharge their important duties undisturbed, as the constitution enjoins'. Though it was of course the duty of the Estates to take care of the economy, they must not try to run it themselves. They must not bestow offices or rewards, pensions or gratifications; nor decide disputed claims to promotion; nor conclude contracts with private individuals – and afterwards alter them. It was none of their business to enter into private disputes, under the pretext of including them in the Estates' 'general grievances'; and in no case must they concern themselves with the administration of the law: the whole business of appeals to the Estates by disgruntled private litigants must come to an end.

It was a comprehensive conspectus of the abuses and distortions of

[205] R. Kjellin, *Anders Schönberg*, p. 186; K. O. Rudelius, 'Författningsfrågan i de förenade deputationerna 1769', *Statsvetenskaplig tidskrift* (1935), p. 339.
[206] Printed in *SRARP*, xxviii, Appendix, pp. 50–58.

Swedish parliamentarism, and it could hardly have had weightier sponsorship: the United Deputations comprised the Secret Committee, the Secret Deputation and the Judicial Deputation. Schönberg and his friends thought of reform mainly as a corrective within the framework of the Constitution of 1720, and they believed that it would be sufficient to remove the accretions and excrescences which had grown up as the Age of Liberty settled into its stride. They professed to want no more than to return to the Constitution of 1720 *simpliciter* (and so were called 'Simplicists'); for they thought that the constitution itself had contained the checks and balances which were essential to a stable polity. It was essentially a conservative approach; but as a matter of practical politics it was as little capable of realisation as Bolingbroke's dream of wiping out the distortions of Walpole and going back to 1689. The opponents of the *Act of Security* were not a bit impressed by allusions to *Magna Carta* and *Habeas Corpus*.[207] They saw the question in terms of power, and with jealous vehemence defended the sovereignty which in practice inhered in themselves. Only the Clergy accepted it; the Burghers refused even to discuss it; the Peasants rejected it without a vote; and it was defeated in the Estate of Nobility by 26 votes in a house of 888.[208] At no time were its provisions the subject of serious parliamentary debate: the evils and abuses which the *Act* condemned were neither defended nor denied; they were simply ignored. The views of the majority were probably succinctly embodied in Grönhagen's comment that 'Security at the expense of the Estates, and with the loss of their rights, is bought too dear.'[209] And so what may well have been the last chance of saving Swedish parliamentarism from itself was lost. As Daniel Tilas ruefully commented, 'the future will show whether we ever get such another moment to put our liberty on a permanent, secure and reasonable footing'. Such a moment never arrived. The Estates learned nothing and forgot nothing as a result of the episode. Despite their own resolutions they continued to meddle in appointments and promotions; they did not hesitate to violate the newly won liberty of the press if their measures were criticised; and when the revolution came three years later, it came at a moment when the Cap majority was on the point of setting up an extraordinary commission equipped with powers quite as objectionable as those which had been given to any of its predecessors.

Whether such an outcome was inherent in the very nature of the constitution is another question. Experience had shown that the

---

[207] Rudelius, *Författningsfrågan i de förenade deputationerna 1769*, pp. 176–7.
[208] *SRARP* xxviii, 15, 20, 68–9; Daniel Tilas, *Anteckningar från riksdagen 1769–1770*, ed. Olof Jägerskiöld (Stockholm 1977), pp. 165–8; *Dagboks-Anteckningar af Johan Gabriel Oxenstierna åren 1769–1771*, ed. Gustaf Stjernström (Uppsala 1888), pp. 58–61; Roberts, *British Diplomacy and Swedish Politics*, pp. 313–14.
[209] *SRARP*, xxviii, 79.

constitution was less rigid than it seemed to be, was susceptible of interpretations which were really amendments and even improvements, and that it left room for useful innovations. The device of legislation-by-consultation;[210] the remarkable meeting of the three non-noble Estates of Österbotten at Gamla Karleby in 1763 – which amounted in fact to an *ad hoc* local parliament assembled on local initiative to discuss local interests:[211] these were neither of them provided for in the constitution. And the very letter of the constitution provided for a much more widely-disseminated participation in policy- and decision-making, and therefore a much more broadly-spread process of political education, than in any other system in Europe. This was one effect of the highly developed committee-system: a list from July 1760 gives 172 members of the Nobility and 430 from the three lower Estates as members of Deputations, to which must be added another hundred for the Secret Committee, and as many more for the Sifting Committee and the Despatching Committee, which were not included in the list. Apart from the Estate of Clergy, whose members necessarily took on a wide variety of committee work, relatively few members seem to have served on more than one. The back-bencher was made to work: of the members of the Nobility listed, there were many who are never recorded as opening their mouths in the *plena*.[212]

Moreover, in the last years of the Age of Liberty some of the worst abuses did begin to be tackled: the obsessive concern for secrecy which had marked the rule of the Hats was no longer so evident;[213] after the abolition of the preliminary censorship it was almost possible to speak of 'open government'; the *Ordinance for the Better Execution of the Laws* (1766) was (among other things) an attempt to prevent tinkering with the constitution for party purposes.[214] When the Hats returned to power in 1769 they showed (at first) a decent restraint in the distribution of premiums and rewards: they had at least learned something since the days of their long tenure of power. It might be considered a hopeful sign that in 1769 the vices and malpractices which disgraced the Diet were being called by their proper names and openly denounced, and that the *Act of Security* was at least a beginning: after all, it took thirty years to complete the process of 'economical reform' in England, and over fifty to carry the great Reform Bill. And as to the exclusion of 'persons of quality' from

---

[210] See above p. 82.

[211] Gunnar Sundberg, *Partipolitik och regionala intressen*, pp. 79–83.

[212] *SRARP*, xxvii, 173–4, 176–82: cf. *Bondeståndets riksdagsprotokoll*, 12, pp. 58–62.

[213] But there were some who feared that when foreign affairs and finance came to be discussed in the *plena* as a matter of course, there was a real risk of Sweden's becoming a *democracy*: *SRARP*, xxviii, 153–4.

[214] For the *Ordinance* see below, pp. 168.

political life, an apologist might perhaps urge that it was England that was the home of the doctrine of 'virtual representation'.

Nevertheless, when all this has been conceded, the uncomfortable fact remains that the *Act of Security* was thrown out. The only really serious attempt at reform was defeated. The 'Age of Liberty', by a bitter irony, ended with the liberty of the individual as precarious as it had been for fifty years. Absolutism had brought its temptations, and to those temptations the Estates had succumbed: soon it would bring its retribution also. 'Liberty' in the end fell victim to the corroding poisons of Swedish politics: suspicion of the executive, constitutional hair-splitting, the selfishness of vested interests, foreign corruption. And, not least, to the rage of party.

III

The rise of party 1734–1746; the Hat ascendancy, 1747–1764

(i)

The emergence of parliamentary parties, and their swift maturing after 1740, was one of the most remarkable features of the Age of Liberty. Nowhere else in Europe, save in England, did a comparable development occur. It proved, indeed, but a short-lived episode; it left no permanent traces behind it; but while it lasted it imparted to the age a hectic quality which grew more intense as the régime neared the final catastrophe.

It has been said that the emergence of parties is an inevitable consequence of parliamentary government; that as soon as a legislature begins to decide important questions by voting, parties will be organised in order to secure a majority.[1] But there was nothing inevitable in the appearance of parties in Sweden; and the Constitution of 1720 had been in operation for almost twenty years before they can be said to have begun to take shape. Swedish parties were born of personal ambitions and personal rancours: with differences of opinion on high political questions, with clashes arising from issues of principle, they had – at first – very little to do. No ancient controversies, constitutional or religious, provided them with historic roots; and though they came fairly soon to appeal to persons of differing types of temperament, they were not in origin the vehicle or expression of such differences. The first Swedish party was rather an artefact, a device imposed from above to forward the ends of its devisers.

In the mid-twenties the most conspicuous conflict of opinion, inside the Council as well as out of it, had been upon the claim of Charles Frederick of Holstein, if not to the throne, then at least to the succession.[2] The Holsteiners can be seen as Legitimists, and Charles Frederick as a Swedish Pretender. But they did not constitute a party any more than the Jacobites did. Nevertheless, when Arvid Horn set about manoeuvring Sweden into adherence to the Alliance of Hanover they were sufficiently formidable to compel him to use strong measures to surmount their

[1] Ludvig Stavenow, *Frihetstiden. Dess epoker och kulturlif*, (Göteborg 1907), pp. 32, 42.; Björn Ryman, *Eric Benzelius d.y. En frihetstida politiker*, (Motala 1978), p. 11
[2] See chapter 1, above.

opposition: two of the leading members suffered *licentiering*, and the Council of State was afforced beyond the number permitted in the constitution, in order to assure him a safe majority there. Thereafter the Holstein faction declined; and its leading members made no overt challenge to Horn's authority. For the moment they collaborated in the administration, awaiting the day when circumstances should once more offer the prospect of successful opposition. Arvid Horn for his part was no party man. He liked to have his friends around him, tried to enlist former adversaries in their ranks, and once secure was strong enough to bear no grudges.[3] That he exercised patronage to reward his friends or attract supporters was a device of government which had no necessary connexion with the formation of a party, and the charge of parliamentary corruption levelled at him by his enemies seems to rest on their testimony alone.[4] It would be difficult to establish that he had any notion – as Walpole, perhaps, had – of constructing a monolithic political arrangement. But his cumulation of the offices of Chancery-President and Marshal of the Diet (until 1734), which gave him a concentration of power unparalleled thereafter, excited unease in some and jealousy in more; his caution and deliberation caused impatience in others; his long monopoly of power seemed to bar the way to the ambitious and the young; and though his hold on the Diet remained strong, there were men in the Council of State who were his enemies, and senior civil servants in the central offices of government who intrigued against him and tried to thwart his policies.[5]

These men provided the nucleus of what was afterwards to be the party of the Hats; and many of them had strong personal links with the former Holsteiners. They found a leader, first in D. N. von Höpken,[6] and after his death in Carl Gyllenborg. Gyllenborg had been Swedish minister in London. In 1717, in a notorious international incident, he had been imprisoned by the British government for his involvement in a Jacobite conspiracy; he had married a Jacobite wife; and he returned to Sweden a violent anglophobe. To this he added a personal hatred of Arvid Horn which may have been related to Horn's supposedly pro-English orientation, but more probably represented a desire for revenge for the *licentieringar* of 1727. From about 1731 he and his friends began to

[3] E.g. in regard to Carl Gustaf Tessin: Walfrid Holst, *Carl Gustaf Tessin* (Stockholm 1936), pp. 68, 73.

[4] It was his adversary, Carl Gustaf Sparre, who was accused of introducing 'Walpolean corruption' into Sweden in order to evict Horn's colleagues from the Council: Linnarsson, *Riksrådens licentiering* (Uppsala 1943), p. 75.

[5] Malmström, *Sveriges politiska historia*, II, p. 245; Carlsson, *Parti – partiväsen – partipolitiker 1731–1743*, p. 168.

[6] For the unattractive D. N. von Höpken, see Abel Helander, *Daniel Niklas von Höpken, 1669–1727* (Stockholm 1927).

organise; by 1734 he had established Sweden's first political club for the Stockholm members of the Estate of Burghers; he had recruited agents and lieutenants to manage votes in the Diet; and he had established something like party Whips.[7] In his brother Fredrik he was fortunate enough to find a first-rate party manager. Carl Gyllenborg was a man of some literary gifts, and in 1737 his play *Den svenska sprätthöken* (*The Swedish Petit-Maître*) – which contained a satire upon that old aristocracy of which Horn was considered to be the representative – provided Sweden with its first political comedy.[8] As the general election of 1738 approached, his paid pamphleteers opened an organised campaign of manuscript pamphlet warfare directed against Horn's policies and person; and we hear of agents touring the provinces to buy up proxies from needy members of the nobility.[9] When the Diet met, every Gyllenborg supporter was furnished with lists indicating for whom he was to vote when it came to the election of the Diet's committees;[10] and a consortium of six generals – the so-called *lilla generalitetet* – clubbed together to maintain a common table for such thirsty members as might care to avail themselves of it. Thus in a surprisingly short space of time a faction was structured into a party; managed, maintained, and to some extent disciplined. The Holstein faction was dead; the Hat party had been born.

The main thrust of their attack upon Horn in 1738 – the charge which at last led him to resign – concerned his acceptance of the Russian offer of alliance in 1735, and the loss of the French alliance which was alleged to have been the consequence of that acceptance.[11] Thereby the Hats provided themselves with an intelligible political stance: they stood forth before the country as the champions of the French connexion and the patriot advocates of war against Russia. This programme, with the clear distinction which it was designed to draw between themselves and their adversaries, was as much a matter of tactics as of conviction. The Holsteiners in the twenties had naturally looked for support to St Petersburg, and Gyllenborg himself had been accounted a friend of Russia until as late as 1734. But he needed a cry, and he needed money, if his purpose of ousting Horn was to be realised. The charge of compromising

---

[7] Malmström, *Sveriges politiska historia*, II, pp. 132, 172–3, 178, 245–7; Carlsson, *Parti. . .* pp. 95–108. Some contemporaries thought that Gyllenborg (and also Carl Sparre) picked up tips from their experience of English parties: *ibid.*, pp. 95–6, 151. Göran Nilzén, unlike Ingemar Carlsson, can see no real sign of party-formation until after 1734: Nilzén, *Studier i 1730-talets partiväsen, passim*; *idem*, 'Näringsfrågor och partipolitik 1734', *Historisk tidskrift* (1972), pp. 15–41.

[8] Ingemar Carlsson, *Olof Dalin och den politiska propagandan inför 'lilla ofreden'* (Lund 1966), p. 44.

[9] *Ur Axel Reuterholms dagbok. Några kulturbilder från frihetstiden*, ed. Henrik Schück (Stockholm 1921), p. 40; Malmström, *Sveriges politiska historia*, II, p. 257.

[10] Carlsson, *Parti . . .*, p. 120.

[11] See above, chapter I.

the chance of recovering the lost provinces provided the one; alliance with
the French ambassador ensured the other. Miscellaneous discontents
could now be welded together under the guise of a patriot cause, and
French gold would defray the cost of the operation. All this made a strong
appeal to middle-aged officers on half-pay, with no chance of active
service; to subalterns who waited in vain for promotion; to ingenious
enterprisers on whose behalf the government's purse-strings had not been
loosened sufficiently generously; to that lesser nobility, the so-called
'*riddarhus* democracy'; which was now challenging the 'aristocracy' of the
titled nobility and the old Council families;[12] to the reckless and the
thoughtless, for whom the whole style of Horn's rule was outmoded, his
authority resented, his solid ability an irritation, his old-fashioned piety
mere hypocrisy, and himself a relic from a dead epoch.[13] On foreign
policy the difference between Horn and his critics was more apparent than
real; for most Swedes at that time (Horn included) hoped for the reversal
of the verdict of 1721: what divided them was the question of timing and
feasibility. But the Hats contrived to make it appear that they had a
monopoly of patriotism and energy; and they branded those who
opposed them as inert and somnolent: hence the epithet 'Night-Caps', or
as it soon became, 'Caps', in contradistinction to themselves, who had
already assumed the name of 'Hats' for their party.[14]

Despite their novel political machine the Hats did not have it all their
own way at the Diet of 1738–9. The Estate of Peasants, now as always,
was for peace, economy, and no increase in taxes; the Clergy were for the
most part supporters of Horn. The real battles came in the Estate of
Nobility. However, the Hats had no difficulty in carrying the election of
Carl Gustaf Tessin – later to be their most successful Chancery-President
– as Marshal of the Diet; and the machine had worked well in regard to the
Diet's committees: the Secret Committee, in particular, had a safe Hat
majority, and this was what really mattered. For the resignation of Horn
and Taube marked the starting-point, and not the limit, of the Hats'
attack, and in that attack the Secret Committee was their indispensable

[12] For the '*riddarhus*-democracy', and the changes in voting procedure in the Estate of Nobility
in 1734, see below, p. 129, n. 57.
[13] It was once thought that the Hats were essentially a party of men who had never
experienced the wars of Charles XII; or that the political upheaval of 1738 coincided with a clash
of generations, and was perhaps caused by it: see Sven Ulric Palme, 'Befolkningsutvecklingen
som bakgrund till partiomvälvningen 1738. Ett social-historiskt försök', *Scandia*, 1960. But it
has become clear from the researches of Göran Nilzén and Ingemar Carlsson that this was not so.
Carlsson in his sample of members of the Estate of Nobility for 1731–43 found no difference in
age-profile for the two parties; an equal number of the high nobility in each; and *more* friends of
Count Horn in the lower nobility and inferior officers than among his opponents: Carlsson: *Parti
. . .*, pp. 166–7, 179–81; Nilzén, *Studier i 1730-talets partiväsen*, pp. 201–3.
[14] From the French *tricorne*, much affected by the dashing young sparks to whom
Gyllenborg's policies appealed.

instrument. They purged the Chancery of Horn's most prominent supporters; they forced the *licentiering* of no less than five members of the Council of State. The Clergy and the Peasants would have blocked the *licentieringar* if they could; but they were precluded from doing so by the decision that the Secret Committee's verdicts, being based on considerations of foreign policy which were themselves secret, were for information only, and not for debate; they were overawed by imperious deputations from the Nobility; the Burghers meanwhile were secured by heavy bribery; and the Nobility itself was terrorised by a group of young officers who shouted down opposition, disrupted debate, and employed threats and physical violence against members who had the courage to resist them.[15] When it was all over, thanks to four opportune deaths, two resignations and five *licentieringar*, the Hats emerged with a clear majority in the Council of State to match their majority in the Secret Committee.

The *licentieringar* of 1739 were a baleful presage. Based on a constitutional juggle, forced through by moral blackmail and by violence, inspired by a thirst for revenge which the wiser Hats deplored as injudicious, they established a pattern of tyranny which the Hats would follow (when they could) for nearly twenty years; and they tainted the struggle of Swedish parties from its earliest days with a spirit of persecution which inevitably communicated itself to their defeated opponents, and which did not fade until it was effaced by the extinction of parties after the revolution of 1772. Axel Reuterholm, commenting on the events of 1739, prophesied the evil consequences of what had happened:

the seed is now sown which will either be the destruction and ruin of our country, or at least – once we get a king who has the will and courage for it – will, as a consequence of our having used so ill the liberty we won, put us again under the yoke which we have felt so severely, and have so painfully cast off. And yet this may be the ultimate remedy, if we are to be saved from destruction.[16]

The event was to verify the prediction in every particular.

(ii)

The Hat victory of 1738–9 was anything but final. The violence of their proceedings disgusted many; the Clergy were shocked by their alliance with the Turks; their despatch of troops to Finland alienated some of their warmest supporters – including three of the *lilla generalitetet* and (more important) Samuel Åkerhielm, who was to emerge in the forties as the

[15] Linnarsson, *Riksrådens licentiering*, pp. 81–149; Malmström, *Sveriges politiska historia*, II, pp. 297–310; Gustaf Bonde, *Historiska Uplysningar om Tillståndet i Swerige under Konung Frederic den Förstes Regering* (Stockholm 1779), pp. 51–2.
[16] *Ur Axel Reuterholms dagbok*, p. 152.

strong man of the Caps, and the inheritor of many of Horn's policies.[17] The materials for an opposition were certainly there, if anyone cared to organise it; and the work was taken in hand not least because there were many who felt it to be necessary to their own preservation: the proscriptions of 1738–9 might well be repeated. And so there arose what was to be the party of the Caps, as a simple measure of self-defence. Almost of necessity they copied the examples which the Hats had set them: attempts to arrange an election campaign before the next Diet; the appointment of 'chiefs' and 'recruiters' to manage the Estate of Nobility; plans designed to secure favourable elections to the Diet's committees; preliminary decisions on tactics; reliance on support from the Russian minister, to match that which the Hats received from the French.[18] But it was all an improvisation, inferior in effectiveness to the organisation of their adversaries. They lacked forceful, acknowledged leadership; they lacked the Hats' precocious sophistication in parliamentary manoeuvre. When the Diet met in 1740 the Hat General Lewenhaupt was almost unanimously elected Marshal; and the Secret Committee was firmly Hat.

Nevertheless, the Hats' command of the situation was by no means assured: two Estates – the Clergy and the Peasants – were hostile; and the Peasants, in particular, absolutely refused to agree to the transfer of more troops to Finland. In the Estate of Nobility passions ran high, and on occasion erupted into near riot. The Hats were rescued from a position which looked like becoming untenable only by two unforeseen accidents. The one was the deaths of Charles VI and the Empress Anna of Russia, which for the first time offered something like the favourable 'conjuncture' upon which their calculations had been based; the other was the detection of a certain Gyllenstierna in the act of sneaking away from the house of the Russian ambassador. The Hats made the discovery the occasion for a political witch-hunt, designed to demonstrate the treasonable activities of their opponents. The Caps were silenced by patriotic bombast and by terror.[19] They might privately condemn the war, but this was no moment for saying so.

That moment came, soon enough, in 1742–3, when the Diet was summoned in extraordinary session to take stock of the disaster in Finland. On any ordinary calculation the outcome might have been expected to be the crushing of the Hat party. The composition of the Diet

---

[17] Birger Sallnäs, *Samuel Åkerhielm d.y. En statsmannabiografi* (Lund 1947), pp. 95 ff.; Malmström, *Sveriges politiska historia*, II, p. 387.

[18] Carlsson, *Parti . . .*, pp. 122–6; Nilzén, *Studier i 1730-talets partiväsen*, pp. 196–200, 235–6; Malmström, *Sveriges politiska historia*, II, pp. 385–7.

[19] The prominent Hat Burgher Thomas Plomgren considered that 'It was better to chop off the heads of people that deserved it; if they had made a start with this at the last Diet things would have gone a great deal better': Malmström, *Sveriges politiska historia*, III, pp. 449–52; Ryman, *Eric Benzelius*, p. 181.

reflected the anger of the country and its desire to bring the Hats to book; the new Marshal, Ungern-Sternberg, was a Cap; the Secret Committee – to which, as an exceptional measure in the country's critical situation, the Peasants were on this occasion admitted – was solidly Cap also: only the Estate of Burghers remained reliably Hat. But though the Cap leaders professed themselves to be for 'a just retribution'[20] they did not succeed in obtaining it. Adversity had not made them an effective party; success seemed to lessen their ambition to become one. Their Secret Committee was almost unique among the Secret Committees after 1738 in its moderation and its respect for law. Their leaders were blundering and negligent, to the exasperation of some of their more zealous supporters;[21] and some of them – including Ungern-Sternberg – seemed more anxious to eliminate party than to lead a party campaign. The Hats did not hesitate to divert attack from themselves by shuffling off all the responsibility for the Finnish fiasco upon Generals Lewenhaupt and Buddenbrock; and it was these two who had the privilege of expiating on the scaffold the sanguine expectations and incompetent planning of the party leaders: in the end, only the obstinate opposition of Clergy and Peasants blocked an audacious Hat attempt to have their war policy actually approved.

What really saved them in 1743 was the question of the succession, adroitly tossed into the debate as an apple of discord to distract attention from their own delinquencies. The Estate of Peasants, desperate to end the war, had clamoured for the young prince of Holstein, naively believing that the choice would induce the Empress Elizabeth to give Sweden a quick and lenient peace. And when that hope had been dashed by Elizabeth's adoption of him as her own successor, they rushed precipitately into a unilateral election of the Danish crown prince. By March 1743 they were threatening to break the Diet and go home, if the other Estates did not concur in his election. Their demands were backed by a rising of the peasants of Dalarna – that traditional nursery of rebellion – which brought an insurrectionary army into Stockholm itself, and was put down only after the arrival at the very last moment of the news that peace with Russia had been concluded at Åbo: then, and only then, the Estate of Peasants agreed to concur with the other Estates in the election of Adolf Frederick. Thus the raising of the issue of the succession had served the purpose that the Hats intended it to serve: with the Estate of Peasants almost uncontrollable, with a peasant army in the heart of Stockholm, men had other things to think of than the wrongs of 1739 or the follies of 1741. With the crushing of the rising of the Dalesmen the most dangerous threat to the Hats was removed.[22] It had caused panic in

---

[20] Ryman, *Eric Benzelius*, p. 117.   [21] Carlsson, *Parti . . .*, pp. 122, 126.

[22] For the rising of the Dalesmen, see Bjarne Beckman, *Dalupproret 1743 och andra samtida rörelser inom allmogen och bondeståndet* (Göteborg 1930).

Stockholm; and it left behind it among the upper Estates a fear of 'peasant government' which was still lively as late as 1766. And it presented the Hats with a political weapon which during the next few years they would know how to wield with formidable effect: the idea that behind differences of opinion and party divisions there lay concealed a sinister design to upset the succession.[23] The Hats would recover from disaster and ride to victory on a dynastic panic which was – at least to a great extent – factitious, the creation of their own propaganda. Already at this Diet it formed an important element in the great controversy over whether members of the three lower Estates were to be considered as their own 'principals', or whether they were responsible to their constituents. This was, no doubt, a dispute about political theory and constitutional law; but it was also a straight party question: most of the Caps, and especially Samuel Åkerhielm, who was now providing them with the resolute leadership which they had hitherto lacked, believed in the principle of responsibility, and argued that when the constitution spoke of 'the Estates' it intended not only the members assembled at the Diet, but the political nation which had elected them.[24] But if this principle were accepted, was it not possible to challenge the title of a successor who had been chosen by the Diet without reference to the nation? Neither Christopher Springer, who first enunciated the principle of responsibility, nor the Caps in general who supported him, had in fact any such intention; but the Hats insisted that the 'doctrine of principalship' (*principalatsläran*) was a device to cast doubt upon Adolf Frederick's title to succeed. It was a suspicion which Adolf Frederick's wife, Lovisa Ulrika, adopted wholeheartedly; and for the next four or five years it helped to make her and her husband zealous Hat partisans.[25]

By the time the Diet came to an end it was clear that the Caps had lost the advantage with which they began it. Moderation and a respect for the forms of law had proved unrewarding. When it met again in 1746 they were no longer in a conciliating temper; and they had money at their disposal on a larger scale than ever before. It came from Korff, the Russian

---

[23] The idea could be used as a pretext for violence: Gustaf Kierman, one of the Hat leaders in the Estate of Burghers, confronted with a resolution on the succession which displeased him, dealt with the situation by tearing up the minutes and the voting-papers. No one ventured to stop him; for outside the chamber stood a collection of young officers ready to interfere forcibly if he were prevented. The whole affair had been planned in advance in the *conciliabulum* which determined the Hats' tactics: Ingemar Carlsson, *Parti. . .*, pp. 10, 109, 119.

[24] For Springer and *principalatsstriden* see Torgny Höjer, 'Christopher Springer och principalatsstriden vid 1742–43 års riksdag', *Studier och handlingar rörande Stockholms historia*, I (Uppsala 1938); Bertil Boëthius, *Magistraten och borgerskapet i Stockholm 1719–1815* (Stockholm 1943), pp. 220–225; Malmström, *Sveriges politiska historia*, III, pp. 133, 185–6, 189, 222–3, 235; Sallnäs, *Åkerhielm*, pp. 177–9.

[25] Fritz Arnheim ed.: *Luise Ulrike, die schwedische Schwester Friedrichs des Grossen. Ungedruckte Briefe an Mitglieder des preussischen Königshause* (Gotha 1910), II, 25, 33, 41.

ambassador, but also from the English minister Melchior Guy-Dickens, who between them brought organisation and method into the business of Cap corruption. Korff, indeed, acted almost as leader of the party, as in the years before 1738 the French ambassador Casteja had supplied the pabulum on which the embryo Hats could batten:[26] here begins that foreign leadership of domestic parties which in the last two decades of 'Liberty' was to be a consistent feature of the Swedish political scene. At the beginning of the Diet the parties were fairly evenly balanced: heavy Anglo-Russian bribery carried the re-election of Ungern-Sternberg as Marshal, but the Hats made a clean sweep of the more important committees, and in particular they dominated the Secret Committee. It was this that presented the most serious threat to the Caps; for a situation in which the Council (irremovable except by *licentiering*) favoured one party, while the Secret Committee was controlled by the other, was in the long run constitutionally intolerable.

Though it might appear that by this time the idea of party had become a normal and accepted feature of political life, there were still many who did not think so: many, even, who still hoped that the trend to party-division might be halted by some measure of reconciliation. The Caps' nominal leader, Ungern-Sternberg, was one of these; Count Bonde, one of the victims of the purge of 1739, was another. And so, for particular reasons, was that prominent Hat, Carl Gustaf Tessin.[27] Tessin feared that party quarrels might precipitate a serious clash between the Estates; but he feared still more that they offered far too tempting a field for foreign intrigue: if the danger from Russia was to be averted, the best and perhaps the only method was by the restoration of national unity and the ending of party strife. He tried therefore to effect a reconciliation with Count Bonde, and with other members of the Cap Council whom he had been instrumental in displacing in 1739.[28] Bonde was willing enough; the others were not. It was already too late. Too many Caps still hoped for revenge, too many Hats desired total victory. The day of men like Ungern-Sternberg was passing: the leadership of the Caps in the Council of State passed to the tough and able Samuel Åkerhielm, and in the Estate of Clergy to the bitter-tongued and formidable Serenius. Men such as these now formed the hard core of the Caps, just as men such as Nils Palmstierna, Anders Johan von Höpken and Claes Ekeblad formed the hard core of the Hats; and Tessin, once disabused of his irenical ideas,

---

[26] Malmström estimated that Russia and England between them provided 818,000 copper *daler*; France, more than a million: *Sveriges politiska historia*, III, pp. 419–20.

[27] By this time Carl Gyllenborg, the Chancery-President, was incapacitated by illness, and responsibility for foreign affairs devolved upon his deputy (*rikskansliråd*), Tessin.

[28] Arne Remgård, *Carl Gustaf Tessin och 1746–7 års riksdag* (Lund 1968), pp. 25, 29 *n.* 31, 84, 102, 112.

would soon engage this group's support, and emerge as his party's unquestioned leader.

Meanwhile the struggle for control of the Council could not long be postponed, if only because there were six vacancies, which meant that the other members were overburdened with work. When it came to drawing up lists of candidates it was reasonably certain that the electors chosen by the Nobility, and by the Burghers, would propose sound Hats for the vacancies. For the Hats, therefore, it remained only to make sure of the Clergy. This they effected by a ruse which was probably unconstitutional and certainly dishonest. In mid-December 1746 the Marshal of the Diet announced that there would be no more meetings of the *plena* until after Christmas. The Clergy and the Peasants took him at his word, and most of them hurried home for the holidays. But the Nobility and the Burghers, ignoring the Marshal's announcement, continued their sittings. A rump of the Clergy had lingered on in Stockholm. Under pressure from the other Estates, their deputy Speaker was induced to summon them to a meeting. The hard-core Caps were taken completely by surprise. Led by Serenius they protested again and again at the irregularity of the meeting, and denied the validity of its decisions. But the Estate was now subjected to heavy pressure: badgered by insistent deputations from the Nobility, tempted by their usual desire to avoid any clash with the first Estate, plied with specious pleas of urgent necessity, and at last beset by scarcely-veiled threats, their resistance quickly crumbled. An assembly of a dozen to fifteen persons – less than a third of the Clergy's total membership – at last agreed to what was demanded of them. They duly chose electors; and those electors duly associated themselves with the electors chosen by the other Estates, and put forward a list of candidates almost exclusively Hat. The manoeuvre had succeeded; and the Council found itself, before Christmas, afforced by five Hats and one neutral.[29]

By this piece of sharp practice the aspect of Swedish politics was transformed for more than a decade. Provided that they did not repeat the disastrous error of 1741 the Hats were now in an unassailable position. Höpken's 'National Declaration'[30] – though many Caps had supported it – had reasserted the claim of the Hats to be the party of all patriots, the national party. The insulting provocations of von Korff, and the undoubted fact that many of the leading Caps were in close relations with him, gave the Hats a chance to discredit their adversaries. They proceeded to exploit their capture of the Council of State by a series of trials which were more concerned with party advantage than with a nice respect for

[29] For this episode see L. A. Cederbom, *Jakob Serenius i opposition mot hattpartiet 1738–1766* (Skara 1904), pp. 78–81; Malmström, *Sveriges politiska historia*, III, pp. 285–6, 307, 311–12.
[30] For the 'National Declaration', see chapter 1, p. 18, above.

the law. The threat to the succession which might seem to lie behind Korff's crude attempts to bully Adolf Frederick and displace Tessin was manipulated to produce hysterical alarm: as in 1740–1 the Hats contrived to make their countrymen's blood run cold by hints of plots, half-substantiated accusations, and proceedings cloaked in secrecy on the plea that dangerous or terrible revelations might confound the public mind if they were suffered to be disseminated.

The first victim was Christopher Springer. A special investigating commission, set up to deal with his case, revealed his contacts with Korff and Guy-Dickens (which were, of course, precisely on a level with Hat contacts with the French ambassador), and condemned his doctrine of responsibility to constituents as being (among other things) a dark design to upset the succession. Springer, sentenced for these crimes to imprisonment for life, sought sanctuary in the British Legation, was removed from it (in defiance of international law) by a threat of force, and could count himself lucky to be able to escape from his prison at the second attempt and get away safely to London.[31] His case was soon followed by another. King Frederick's medical attendant, a Scots agronomist by the name of Alexander Blackwell, was detected in private intrigues about the succession, the precise significance of which is obscure: they were certainly wholly unofficial, and the ministry in London had no share in them. He was thrice tortured, and under torture confessed that George II had offered either £100 000 from the Civil List to promote a Danish succession in Sweden, or £1 million if he could obtain the throne for the Duke of Cumberland: revelations sufficient to discredit his testimony in the eyes of anybody who had any knowledge of the state of the Civil List or the character of George II. The English ministers concluded that Blackwell must be out of his mind. However, this did not save him from execution: Tessin was needing a victim, and Blackwell seemed in all respects a suitable candidate.[32]

Springer and Blackwell were after all small fry: the man the Hats were after was Samuel Åkerhielm, the renegade of 1740, and now the leader of last-ditch Cap resistance in the Council. The investigating commission had been empowered to judge not only the case of Springer, but everything *connected* with it also; and the more rabid Hats succeeded in enlarging its powers so that it became in fact a commission of public safety, authorised to imprison without the usual procedures and entitled

---

[31] He lived in London for many years, much esteemed by Swedish residents there, as a pensioner of the British government; to the considerable chagrin of Sweden's diplomatic representatives at the Court of St James's. For the international aspects of the affair, see E. R. Adair, *The Exterritoriality of Ambassadors in the Sixteenth and Seventeenth Centuries* (1925), p. 225.

[32] The Blackwell affair has most recently been subject to exhaustive examination in Remgård, *Carl Gustaf Tessin och 1746–7 års riksdag*, pp. 191–236.

to condemn 'without being so strictly bound by due process of law'.[33] As it happened, they did not need these additional powers: they had no difficulty in 'connecting' Åkerhielm with Springer's case. But his hostility to the French and Prussian alliances, and his advocacy of good relations with Russia; his uncompromising assertion of the doctrine of responsibility to constituents; his opposition to the Hats' policies of paper money and commercial monopolies – these were enough to make Åkerhielm's patriotism suspect, without adding the charge of plotting to disturb the succession. For a long time he offered undaunted resistance; but at last his nerve gave way: he feared for his life, and twice arranged with Guy-Dickens to be smuggled abroad in an English ship. At last he offered his resignation; and he was lucky to have his offer accepted on condition that for the remainder of his life he kept out of politics.[34] With Åkerhielm's removal the victory of the Hats was complete. The Caps were frightened, and for the moment hopeless; their improved organisation, even with Anglo-Russian financial backing, had availed them nothing; their nominal leader, Ungern-Sternberg, was no fighter; and their best hope had been for ever removed from the scene.

Their desperation tempted them into dangerous courses. Many of them now saw no hope of retrieving the disaster of 1747 except through foreign aid. That aid could come only from Russia. It could come, for instance, through Korff's direct attacks on Tessin, and his attempts to drive him from office; or it could come by Panin's successive Declarations. It could come by the ostentatious concentration of Russian troops on the Finnish border, or the passage of Russian naval craft through the Finnish skerries; by more explicit threats of military action; and in the last resort by a Russian invasion of Finland. There is some reason to suppose that Panin's Declarations may have been prompted by his Cap friends. Certainly some of the leaders of the party, and conspicuously Åkerhielm, went pretty far towards treason. Åkerhielm had been educated at Oxford at the expense of the British government, had returned to Sweden a staunch anglophile, and in foreign policy would have preferred an English system, if only England had been prepared to pay for one.[35] But he was no friend of Russia, however ready he might be to use Russian pressure to further the ends of his party.[36] How far he went in provoking or condoning Russian actions has been a matter of

---

[33] Cederbom, *Jakob Serenius i opposition mot Hattpartiet*, p. 91; Malmström, *Sveriges politiska historia*, III, pp. 351–6.

[34] For the attack on Åkerhielm, see Birger Sallnäs, *Åkerhielm*, pp. 187–8, 189–201, 231–305.

[35] His incitements of Russia after 1747 had been matched earlier by his urging of the British government to capture Swedish merchantmen by way of reprisal for alleged injuries, in order to damage the Hat-dominated East India Company: Sallnäs, *Åkerhielm*, pp. 198–9.

[36] In a conversation with Adolf Frederick he admitted that he hoped for the recovery of the lost provinces, 'though', he added, 'one must not go about saying so'; and he conceded that

controversy; but his most recent biographer, though he acquits him of any wish to use Russian arms to alter the succession, comes to the conclusion that in 1748 and 1749 he was ready to contemplate Russian military action in order to overthrow the Hats, even though he was not prepared to go as far as actually to invite it. No doubt he was moved by exceptionally strong personal resentments; but other prominent Caps were likewise compromised – not, however, Ungern-Sternberg, who consistently refused to have anything to do with the Russians, nor (perhaps) Serenius – but sufficient to blast the party's reputation and to provide a measure of justification for the inquisitorial excesses of their opponents. Those survivors from the old order of things who lamented the new age of parties might fairly complain that the effect of the change seemed to be to offer the nation a choice between tyranny and treason.

When the last of Panin's Declarations missed fire in 1750 the Hats attained the summit of their power. They had exploited the dynastic question to crush their opponents; they had defeated attempts to use it as a pretext for foreign intervention; they had rejected Russian pretensions to be the conservators and interpreters of the Constitution of 1720. Yet the fifties, which to begin with seemed to be set fair for a period of internal stability and one-party rule, proved unexpectedly troubled and confused. The Hats had scarcely consolidated their ascendancy before a process of fragmentation and division began to become apparent. No doubt it was in part to be explained by the fact that total success provided them with the luxury of being able to quarrel among themselves. No doubt, too, we are witnessing – for both parties – a split in generations. One important indication of this was the emergence in the Hat ranks of Carl Fredrik Pechlin, an ambitious and unscrupulous intriguer who was to play a major part in politics in 1760–2, and again in 1769–72: disappointed in his hope of succeeding Fredrik Gyllenborg as party manager and distributor of French corruption, he became a bitter enemy of the Chancery-President, A. J. von Höpken, and of Höpken's supporters in the Council.

The schisms among the Hats were largely matters of temperament and personalities: Tessin, their Chancery-President until 1752, was a skilful diplomat and a capable director of foreign policy; but he was morbidly sensitive, inordinately vain and self-righteous, tiresomely inclined to extort personal votes of confidence by threats of resignation too often repeated. Between the Scheffer brothers, on the one hand, and Tessin's successor as Chancery-President, A. J. von Höpken, on the other, were not only serious disagreements on foreign policy, but barely concealed

Elizabeth might well be aiming at a 'Northern Monarchy' which would include Sweden on much the same terms as Poland; but the only means of averting the danger, he believed, was the careful cultivation of good-neighbourly relations, and the avoidance of provocative engagements: Sallnäs, Åkerhielm, pp. 273–4.

personal animosities. These disharmonies produced a situation in which
the French ambassador, d'Havrincour, allowed himself to drift into being
the ally of a faction within the party, rather than the impartial patron of
them all. Despite all this, to outward seeming the position remained
unshaken: at the Diets of 1751–2 and 1755–6 the Hats were in full control.
In 1755 they recruited, in the person of Axel von Fersen, an extremely
able politician and a Marshal of the Diet unequalled since the days of
Arvid Horn.[37] The fissiparous tendencies within the party were indeed
halted, and for a time reversed, by the abortive attempt at a royalist
revolution in 1756,[38] which united them all against the Crown and in
defence of the constitution. Yet within a year Fersen could distinguish at
least three little personal parties among the Hats, all more or less hostile to
one another.[39]

The crisis of 1756 was the most sensational manifestation of a new
factor in politics, destined to have disturbing effects upon Caps and Hats
alike. This was nothing less than the emergence of a political grouping
which would one day qualify for consideration as a party: a Court party.
The group was recruited from a small collection of high aristocrats, some
of them sons or near relatives of the victims of 1739; but it attracted
support also among some younger officers – the same elements as had
been fanatically Hat in 1738–41 – who may possibly have been influenced
by Adolf Frederick's hard work to modernise the army and make it
efficient, and above all by his resistance to Hat violations of the ordinary
rules for promotion in favour of their new man, Axel von Fersen.[40]
Royalist agitators deployed incendiary tactics within the Estate of
Peasants: in 1755 these tactics culminated in a scandalous tumult which
led to the appointment of a special commission (that characteristic Hat
device) whose perquisitions soon extended far beyond the immediate
circumstances which had led to its appointment.[41] And, not least, the rise
of royalism tempted some of the Cap leaders to ally with the Court and
play the royalist game, as once in similar desperate circumstances they
had been ready to play the game of Russia. Some of them sincerely
believed that it was high time that the balance of the constitution was

---

[37] Fersen's Memoirs (*Riksrådet och Fältmarskalken m.m. Grefve Fredrik Axel von Fersens
historiska skrifter* (Stockholm 1867–72, II)), though written some time in the 1780s, are an
indispensable source for the fifties. His reliability was sharply attacked by Malmström; *Smärre
skrifter* (Stockholm 1889), pp. 209–240, and by Fritz Arnheim, *Die Memoiren der Königin von
Schweden, Ulrike Luise, Schwester Friedrichs des Grossen. Ein quellenkritischer Beitrag zur Geschichte
Schwedens in XVIII. Jahrhundert* (Halle 1888). But Malmström's criticisms were directed mainly
at Fersen's account of the period after 1772; and Arnheim's at points of minor importance.

[38] For this see below, ch. V, pp. 180–2.

[39] Fersen, *Historiska skrifter*, II, p. 140.

[40] For this episode, see Malmström, *Sveriges politiska historia*, III, p. 482.

[41] For the riot in the Estate of Peasants, and its consequences, see Gardar Sahlberg, *Mer makt åt
kungen!* (Stockholm 1976), pp. 49 *seqq.*

adjusted to temper the sovereign autocracy of the Estates;[42] and one
leading member of the party, Thure Rudbeck, who was to be their
Marshal in 1765, was at least cognizant of the plans for a revolution in
1756, though he withdrew his support at the crucial moment.[43]
Nevertheless, in view of the past and future record of the party, it seems
unlikely that many of them should have been ready to support Lovisa
Ulrika's absolutist ambitions: it is significant that the relentless enquiries
of the special commission of 1755 never succeeded in pinning any degree
of culpability upon those whom we may call the true Caps. But the
expression 'true Caps' is itself a reflection of the growing confusion of
politics as the decade came to an end. It was a period when men began to
change sides and shift allegiances: for instance, Carl Gustaf Löwenhielm,
hitherto a staunch member of the Hat party, now alienated from his
colleagues by their contempt for legality, and destined in 1765 to become
the Caps' Chancery-President[44] or C. F. Scheffer, who in 1766 began to
tread the path of disillusionment which would lead him to be Gustav III's
coadjutor in the Constitution of 1772. Historians can reach no agreement about the membership of parties when the Diet met in 1760 –
or even about their number. Were the Caps still alive as an independent
party? or had they become absorbed into a party of the Court? Since about
1755 there had been emerging an oppositional group which attracted
allies from Hats, Caps and Court alike, and called themselves the
'Country Party' (lantpartiet), possibly with English terminology in mind:
they would be of decisive importance in 1760–2. But once again there is
no agreement as to whether they are to be considered as a transient
political phenomenon, or as a fraction of the Hats, or as a true
independent party, or merely as the Caps under another name.[45]
    One thing, however, is apparent: that within the once-solid Hat party
there had arisen a clear distinction between those who supported Höpken
and his colleagues in the Council, and those who wished to get rid of them
in order to disburden the party of a liability which it could no longer
afford. In the last resort it was the Pomeranian War, more than any other
single factor, that was responsible for this disintegration. Their Council

---

[42] E.g. C. W. Grönhagen in 1755; for which speech he was expelled from the House of
Nobility: Sveriges ridderskaps och adels riksdagsprotokoll [SRARP] xix, Appendix pp. 119 seqq.
[43] For Rudbeck's involvement, Gardar Sahlberg, Mer makt åt kungen! (Stockholm 1976), pp.
178, 199; Fersen, Historiska skrifter, II, pp. 92, 110.
[44] Löwenhielm had for a short time been the Hats' Attorney-General (justitiekansler). There is
unfortunately no study of him.
[45] For these controversies see Olsson, Hattar och mössor, p. 154; Gunnar Sundberg, 'Lantpartiet
vid riksdagen 1760–62', Historisk tidskrift (1971), pp 352–61; idem, Partipolitik och regionala
intressen 1755–1766 (Uppsala 1978), pp. 23–6; Malmström, Sveriges politiska historia, IV, p. 128;
Arnheim, Luise Ulrike, die schwedische Schwester . . ., II, p. 338 (to August Wilhelm, Dec. 1755);
Ulla Johansson, 'Hattar och mössor i borgarståndet 1755–56', Historisk tidskrift (1973), pp. 490,
515, 518–19, 521.

of State had begun it unconstitutionally; they had carried it on by financial
expedients which were ruinous, and of dubious legality. Above all, they
had failed to win it; and they had been reduced to the final humiliation of
appealing to Lovisa Ulrika to get them out of the mess. All this produced
a situation in which the Hats were divided into 'senatorial' and
'anti-senatorial' camps – that is to say, into those who supported the
Council of State, and those who opposed it. The 'anti-senatorials' would
of course find opportunist support from the Caps and the Court, and this
gave them a reasonable prospect of success when the Diet should meet in
1760.[46] However it might turn out, what was clear was that by 1760 the
long ascendancy of the Hats was over for good. They were now on the
defensive; and after their defeat in the election of 1764, in the remaining
eight years of 'Liberty' they would be in power for less than twelve
months.

(iii)

In 1760–2, then, we are at a parting of the ways; and this seems an
appropriate moment to attempt some analysis of the nature of Swedish
parties, their functioning, and the ideas which may have inspired them.
How far did they conform to, how far fall short of, the modern idea of
party? Is it possible to consider them as true parties in any acceptable
sense? Can they (for instance) be compared with English parties in (say)
the Age of Anne?

In one respect, no doubt, they may be held to have been defective, in
that they did not arise out of any need to give organised expression to
strong currents of popular feeling. Neither had the same deep roots in
popular sentiment as had the Whigs and Tories; neither had the same
emotive slogans to fall back upon as a substitute for argument. Stockholm
elections did not produce the popular excitement and participation which
was to be observed at Westminster; still less could any election in the
countryside show anything to compare with the Oxfordshire election of
1750, or the Yorkshire election of 1784. Nor should we assume without
examination that they performed that function which has been termed
'the aggregation of interests'. It is by no means certain that the members
of the Diet considered that it was that body's function to represent
interests: this is one of the ways in which it differed from parliament in
eighteenth-century England. The historian who writes that 'the national

<hr />

[46] Sir John Goodricke, impatiently awaiting the moment when he could take up his post in
Stockholm, made a clear distinction between the allies of the Court and 'the sensible men of the
anti-senatorial party' – men who did not share the Court's desire for political confusion, but who
did wish to see the power of the Council reduced, and did not desire an absolutism: Roberts,
British Diplomacy and Swedish Politics p. 59, and the references there cited.

parties represented separate aggregations of interests' propounds at best a half-truth.[47] Fredrik Lagerroth put forward the converse of the proposition when he denied that the Hats and Caps were parties of interest, and insisted that they were parties of opinion.[48] But of course they were both. And by 'interests', it should be remembered, we must to a large extent understand the interests of the separate Estates – that is, their sacrosanct *privileges*; and this was not, and could not be, a party question at all. The corporate interests of an Estate in the last resort transcended party, and not vice-versa: throughout the period the interest of the Estate of Peasants (apart from a traditional but mostly latent royalism) was bounded by severely material considerations;[49] and for the Nobility privilege was always more important than party: as they showed in 1771–2. There were certainly interests which historians agree in identifying with one or other of the parties; but there were others, and some of the most important, which neither party could 'aggregate', since they included men from both: the most conspicuous example, perhaps, being the military interest, which might have completely dominated the Estate of Nobles, but which seems only rarely to have been mobilised as an interest, and which certainly had no consistent or solid party-affiliation.[50] Again, if our definition of a party requires that it must 'strive for the implementation of programs based on sets of ideas commonly subscribed to by its adherents',[51] then the Hats and Caps fit the definition only if we are prepared to restrict the meaning of 'programmes' to something very different from that which a modern party would give to it: that is to say, to rid our minds of legislative programmes. The Hat leaders may perhaps be considered to have imposed a programme on the country in 1738, or to have created factitious support for one. The Caps may have come to power in 1765 with a general disposition towards certain sorts of reform; but they probably owed their victory at the election of 1764 more to a wide-spread feeling of discontent and disillusionment with the Hat régime than to any electoral preference for such measures as they may have had in mind.[52] In 1769, similarly, the Hats' only programme seems to have been to capitalise on massive resentment at the effects of the Caps' deflationary policies: for themselves, they appear to have been almost

---

[47] Michael F. Metcalf, 'The first "Modern" party system?' *Scandinavian Journal of History* (1977), p. 295.

[48] Lagerroth, *Frihetstidens författning*, pp. 314ff.

[49] This is a leading theme in Erland Alexandersson, *Bondeståndet i riksdagen 1760–1772* (Lund 1975); but *cf.* Ragnar Olsson, *Riksdagsmannavalen till bondeståndet under den senare delen av frihetstiden* (Lund 1948), pp. 65, 112.

[50] Contrast Gunnar Artéus, *Krigsmakt och samhälle i frihetstidens Sverige* (Stockholm 1982), *passim*; which argues that the military shaped, or influenced, policy.

[51] Metcalf, 'Structuring Party Politics: Party Organization in Eighteenth-Century Sweden', *Parliaments, Estates and Representation* (1981), p. 36.

[52] See below, chapter IV.

bankrupt of ideas. In 1771 there was certainly something like a programme in the minds of the electorate; but it was a social programme which to a great extent transcended party.[53]

All this is no reason for dismissing Hats and Caps as not being parties at all in any real sense: it is neither helpful nor sensible to expect of eighteenth-century parties that they should satisfy the criteria which are appropriate to parties of the present age. The Hats and Caps certainly performed some of the functions of a party: they offered the electorate relatively simple choices at election time (though whether in fact electors voted on that basis is another matter); they made it possible to oppose a government without opposing the régime, so that men could feel that the ills of the day were remediable by parliamentary means: by 1772 the general public did not feel this any longer, hence the success of Gustav III's *coup d'état*. The parties followed recognised leaders, without being dependent on those leaders for survival: just as there was in Sweden little to correspond to those ties of dependence and clientelage which were so important in England, so too there was little resembling the 'proprietary parties' of Bedford or Grenville.[54] Parties had a nucleus of constant members; they could command a respectable measure of party loyalty, and a more than adequate reservoir of party fanaticism. They were (after 1739) permanent organisations continuing from Diet to Diet, rather than transient improvisations provoked by a single issue. They possessed recognised, well-established, elaborately articulated parliamentary machinery; they had caucus meetings of leaders to decide on long-term objectives or day-to-day parliamentary tactics; and they had a general community of ideas, background and personal relationships.[55] Perhaps the strongest force that kept men loyal to their party was the desperate competition for official appointments, however small; for every appointment tended to become a fierce party issue. It is this above all that is responsible for the strong impression that the whole of Swedish life, towards the end of the period, was tainted with party rancour; though in reality this was true mainly in the larger towns (especially Stockholm) and when the Diet was meeting. But it reinforces the point that the parties panted for office, not so much to implement any constructive legislative projects, as to exercise the patronage of power.

It is difficult to make precise estimates of the strength of Swedish

---

[53] See below, chapter v.

[54] A. J. von Höpken was thought to have a fairly solid following for a time in 1764–5: Roberts *British Diplomacy and Swedish Politics*, pp. 69–71; and in January 1765 (but only then) we hear of a group of 60 'followers of Gyllenborg' in the Estate of Nobility: PRO SP 95/106/32–4; but neither of these was more than an ephemeral grouping.

[55] Carlsson, *Parti – partiväsen – partipolitiker, passim*; Björn Ryman, *Erik Benzelius d.y.* – but see Anne-Marie Fällström's review in *Historisk tidskrift* (1979).

parties, or to construct lists of their members: the available material is inadequate for the purpose. But obviously they were not mass parties, any more than Whigs and Tories were. The active element in each party seems to have been relatively small, with a long tail of followers who tended to drift away during the protracted sessions, and had to be retrieved in a hurry for crucial divisions. There were many about whose party allegiance even contemporaries had difficulty in deciding; and for the historian the task becomes extraordinarily difficult. There were no division-lists, scarcely any lists of party members, no poll-books, virtually no newspaper press before 1766. The parliamentary managers – a Fredrik Gyllenborg, a C. F. Pechlin – took care to leave no archive behind them. All the more remarkable, therefore, is the achievement of Ingemar Carlsson, who with the aid of manuscript pamphlets and literary sources has succeeded in establishing the party affiliation of no less than 416 members of the Diet in the period 1731–43, and added a brief biography of each one of them.[56] But when one reflects that his survey covers five meetings of the Estates, at each one of which there might be up to 1200 members present, not necessarily identical from Diet to Diet, it is unfortunately apparent that the area thus mapped and measured bears but a modest relation to the *terra incognita*.

The key to political success lay in a few crucial divisions at the beginning of each Diet: in the election of the Speakers of each of the four Estates, and above all of the Marshal of the Diet (who was the Speaker of the Estate of Nobility); in the choice of electors;[57] and, as a result of these operations, in the choice of the Diet's major committees, and above all of the Secret Committee. This meant that for the first three or four weeks every possible voter must be mustered; the start of the session must see the party organisation in top gear; and the party coffers must be as full of money as could be managed. But the result of these divisions could not be relied upon to have a permanent effect; for once they were over party members, having done what was expected of them, might lose interest and return home, so that a party which might have supposed itself secure could be faced with dramatic swings in the voting, and mortifying defeats.[58] An efficient party-organisation had to foresee all this and take measures against it by inducing members to remain in Stockholm, or by sending urgent expeditions into the country to bring them back if they

---

[56] Carlsson, *Parti . . .*, pp. 187–302.

[57] Election to committees was in three stages in the House of Nobility: those sitting on the same bench elected benchmen, who elected electors, who elected to the committees. In 1734 this procedure was altered so that voting by benchmen became secret rather than open: a change which was a deliberate blow against the old aristocracy of birth; and a victory for the so-called '*riddarhus*-democracy'.

[58] As for instance in 1761–2, and (a conspicuous example) in the Estate of Clergy in August 1765: Roberts, *British Diplomacy and Swedish Politics*, pp. 172–4.

had gone away. Members of the three lower Estates were paid a subsistence allowance by their constituents; members of the first Estate, who were their own constituents, had no such resource, and this made them particularly accessible to bribes or retainers in cash or kind (or to the purchase of their proxies), since so many of them were in fact poor rather than rich. Erik Wrangel (a royalist, however) in 1756 described this impoverished provincial nobility, whose function was really to provide brute votes and party cannon-fodder, and for whom a meeting of the Diet represented a much-appreciated financial opportunity, as men

living a life of poverty far from Stockholm, in ignorance of everything that goes on outside their own parish, brought up to the Diet by the load in dung-carts, provided on arrival with clothes, and especially with an abundance of food and drink, and then taken to the House of Nobility under the supervision of some bear-leader, to shout, roar and vote according to orders.[59]

One convenient method of keeping some sort of check upon members, and at the same time of providing them with the sustenance they needed, was the party club. From small beginnings in 1734 the clubs very soon became an essential element in parliamentary life. Each Estate would have at least one for each of the two parties: clubs with membership from more than one Estate do not seem to have occurred.[60] The clubs were useful centres of control: here the 'operators' (sc. Whips), the 'recruiters', the 'scouts', the proxy-buyers, could do much of their business. But the clubs were also social centres, much needed by men uprooted from their homes and ill-lodged in a strange environment for months at a time. Men frequented them not only for instruction on the tactics to be followed in the next debate, but also as places where one could smoke and drink in an atmosphere of conviviality.[61]

[59] Valentin, Frihetstidens riddarhus, p. 135.
[60] Though something that looks like a unique example from 1769 is reported: Brolin, p. 303. It was typical of the basically non-party attitude of the Estate of Peasants that in 1765 its Speaker should have tried (though in vain) to persuade members that henceforward there should be only one club for the Estate, and not, as hitherto, two: Erland Alexandersson: Bondeståndet i riksdagen 1760–1772 (Lund 1975), pp. 181–2.
[61] The poet Johan Gabriel Oxenstierna confided to his journal a famous description of a meeting of the Hat club of the Nobility one evening in June 1769:
Numbers of men sitting round tables, gambling and swearing. . . Thick clouds of black tobacco-smoke arising from them, as from the cone of a volcano. On the floor, smashed fragments of tobacco-pipes, with liquor from an overturned bottle running over them. Glasses shivered against the walls; the floor littered with torn-up playing-cards . . . A little further off, mutterings about politics or parliamentary disputes. This is the home of all futile motions, rickety laws, bribes, false rumours, and scribblers who write libels for anyone that is prepared to pay their price . . . Folly and tippling here go hand in hand, and the little sense a nobleman may be possessed of is drowned in floods of punch. One man thinks he has defended liberty because no one can stop him from drinking as many glasses as he chooses; another pledges his faith and honour with his right hand, but behind his back takes a bribe with his left for his vote in the next division . . . A party leader comes in, climbs on a table and begins to speak; his raucous voice is reason enough to trust him;

Diets were supposed to meet every third year; but as time went on the intervals between party activity at the close of one Diet and party activity in preparation for the next tended to get shorter, and eventually to disappear altogether; though the party clubs in Stockholm (and it was only in Stockholm that they existed) shut their doors as soon as the session was over, if only because it was so costly to maintain them. But the most notable difference between Hats and Caps on the one hand, and the Whigs and Tories of Queen Anne's reign on the other, was in fact that the Swedish parties were essentially parliamentary and metropolitan parties, and did not until the very end of the Age of Liberty show much sign of evolving into national parties. The party leadership, for instance, did not interfere to suggest candidates, nor did they go down to the constituencies at election time to give a hand to the candidate whom they sponsored. It has been suggested that in some of the larger towns there may have been more or less permanent party groupings who prosecuted their domestic or municipal quarrels under party names; but before 1764 there seems in fact to have been little or no connexion between these essentially local rivalries and a national party organisation. If the Hats dominated the south Swedish towns in the 1750s, that was because in those towns political and party interests were almost wholly absent: they normally returned their burgomasters as members, as a matter of custom and routine, and the burgomasters happened to be Hats[62] – naturally enough when for more than a decade the Hats had been in power, and had taken care to appoint their friends to any vacancy. The more we know of borough elections in the fifties and sixties (and these are the only borough elections we know much about at present) the less they appear to be concerned with party issues, or fought on party lines. In many towns, such as Hudiksvall or Enköping, parties in the national sense simply did not exist, and in Nyköping a recent study found no link before 1765 between the opposing groups and any national party organisation.[63]

In 1768, however there are signs that the situation had begun to alter. In that year – two years before the next election was due – the Caps drew up a comprehensive list of party agents covering the whole country, whose task it was to be to fish for noble proxies, lobby the clergy, and nurse the

he is believed in proportion to the strength of his bellowing, and is answered by a roar of 'Ay!' After which they pledge themselves, glass in hand, to vote straight and not desert; healths are drunk to the king, the law, and liberty, and they stagger about reeling, out of pure love of the fatherland.
J.G. Oxenstierna, *Dagboksanteckningar af Johan Gabriel Oxenstierna åren 1769–1771* (Uppsala 1881), pp. 34–5.
    [62] Ulla Johansson, 'Hattar och mössor i borgarståndet', *Historisk tidskrift* (1973), pp. 497–9, 511.
    [63] Anne-Marie Petersson, 'Nyköping under 1700-talet', in *Nyköpings stads historia*, ed. Stellan Dahlgren, (Nyköping 1973), II, 459–70.

borough constituencies.[64] It is inconceivable that the plan may have existed mainly on paper, and may have been designed to impress the foreign ministers to whom the Caps looked for financial support;[65] but it is reasonable to suppose that this elaborate network of agents was at least to some extent operative when, unexpectedly, the election occurred in 1769. If so, the outcome – which was a Cap disaster – suggests that they can hardly be said to have justified the expenditure upon them. Nevertheless, the experiment seems to have been repeated in 1771. In that year the Cap estimates for corruption made provision for election expenses in every one of the boroughs; and a central office in Stockholm, run by the master-tanner John Westin, maintained an extensive election correspondence.[66] And among Westin's papers is one letter which for the first time seems to indicate a measure of party activity among the leading peasants in one area. But there seems to have been no general attempt to involve the Estate of Peasants in electioneering: in their case the means of persuasion were husbanded until after their arrival in Stockholm. Still, in 1769 and 1771 we do get the impression of a party fighting an election on a basis of careful, centrally directed planning, in a style not matched in Hanoverian England before the Foxite campaign of 1790.[67] But when so much has been conceded, it remains true that even in 1771, and certainly until then, party feeling at the constituency level (where it existed at all) went to sleep between elections, and even at election time lacked the emotive appeal and the rabble-rousing slogans which made English party politics such a satisfying outlet for the brute passions of a turbulent populace. Dr Rutström, after all, was but a poor substitute for Dr Sacheverell.[68]

(iii)

Despite their differences, Hats and Caps had at least one thing in common: namely, that both were for the maintenance of the constitution as established in church and state. The dynastic difficulty of 1743 was not essentially a party matter at the time, and never became so afterwards:

[64] Printed in Michael F. Metcalf, 'Structuring Parliamentary Politics: Party Organization in Eighteenth-Century Sweden', *Parliaments, Estates and Representation* (1981).
[65] The list appears to have survived only in the despatches of the Danish minister to Sweden.
[66] PRO SP 95/118/103–6, Goodricke to Halifax, 2 April 1771, for the corruption estimates; Uppsala University Library, W-n 978, Bref till Ålderman John Westin den äldre angående riksdagsmanna valen 1771.
[67] D. E. Ginter, *Whig Organization in the General Election of 1790: selections from the Blair Adam Papers* (Berkeley, Calif., 1971).
[68] Rutström was a Pietist divine who became the centre of acrimonious party strife. For the Rutström controversy, and its importance for the Church, see Carl-E. Normann, *Enhetskyrka och upplysningsideer. Studier i religionspolitik vid 1700-talets mitt* (Lund 1963), chapters VI–VII.

despite their intrigues with Korff and Panin, the Caps were not really concerned to expel Adolf Frederick. Though Hats and Caps might from time to time engage in temporary alliances with the Court, these dalliances were no more than tactical manoeuvres, or moves by party leaders which had neither the support nor sometimes the knowledge of the bulk of their followers. Even in the final years of the Age of Liberty it was only a small and unrepresentative section of either party that was really interested in constitutional reform. Nevertheless, though there was thus a large area of solid common ground between them, it is clear that Hats differed from Caps in important, and in some respects fundamental, ways; and an attempt must be made to analyse the nature of those differences. First, then, what were the marks of a Hat?

With a very generous margin for exceptions, the Hats by the mid-century had come to stand for an active and enterprising foreign policy – as, for instance, the Whigs stood for a 'continental' foreign policy. They thought of themselves as progressive, in contrast to the temperamental conservatism of the Caps. They stood for industry, finance and the big exporters: they were the party responsible for the creation and lavish support of new industries designed to lessen the country's dependence on foreign imports, create employment, and discourage emigration. For many years their control of the Diet meant that they controlled the Estates' Bank, whose Board of Governors they filled with their own men: this, and their policy of loans on easy terms to entrepreneurs, their paper-money inflation which made loans from the Bank or the Iron Office an attractive proposition (since the borrower could count on being able in due time to acquit his debt in a depreciated currency) – all this meant that the very abuses and errors of Hat finance attracted to the party those who were doing well out of them: not without justice did Anders Nordencrantz stigmatise the Hats as a party of debtors. But they were also a party of plutocrats, tightly interrelated. Their majority in the Diet ensured that the irregularities, abuses and mistakes of the Bank would always escape without censure. Their institution of the Exchange Office (*växelkontoret*), whereby a consortium of financiers was empowered, on very advantageous terms, to gamble on the exchanges with the object of restoring Sweden's depreciated currency to parity, drew still closer their links with the great capitalists. In the Bank, in the Exchange Office, in the Iron Office, in the Stockholm magistracy, the same handful of Hat politicians found rich opportunities to exploit their position.

In general, then, the Hats were in one aspect the party of the speculators on a grand scale; but also of the solid commercial houses which were strong enough to weather the post-war crash of 1763: firms whose leading members in Stockholm were referred to as 'the Skeppsbro nobility';[69] men whose life-style compared with that of the aristocracy, and who not seldom married their daughters into the nobility, to whom they brought a much needed injection of capital. All this made the Hats, almost from the beginning, something of an urban party, and in particular a metropolitan party. Until 1762 they dominated the Estate of Burghers, not only because so many towns were content to be represented by Hat-appointed burgomasters, but also because the Hats stood firm for gild-regulations, town privileges, and protectionist policies. But it was just the growing hostility of the ordinary burgher to the municipal magistracy, and the outports' jealousy of the specially privileged position of Stockholm and the staple towns, which would eventually lead the municipal oppositions to think of themselves as Caps: a transformation which first becomes important in the general election of 1764.

By 1764 the Hats had been effectively in power for a quarter of a century. For a quarter of a century they had dominated the committees and exercised an influence on appointments which grew stronger and more unscrupulous as time went on. The immortal bureaucracy, which had emerged triumphant from the ruins of the Absolutism, had now passed into their hands: it had sunk to being the party's administrative front. Vacancies on the episcopal bench had been filled by Hat bishops, and by the mid-century the political complexion of the Estate of Clergy, which had once been Arvid Horn's staunchest support, had been modified in much the same way as Bishop Gibson transformed the Church of England in the thirties: among the portents which fore-shadowed the fall of the Hats, not the least ominous was the election of their arch-enemy Serenius to the see of Strängnäs.[70] Lastly, the Hats might count on the grateful support of at least some of the beneficiaries of the scandalous outpouring of pensions, premiums, rewards for highly questionable services, *solatia* for equally questionable disappointments, which reached a peak at the Diet of 1760–2. The Hat régime was in one important aspect a vast edifice of patronage, financial irresponsibility, corrupt bargains for party friends, ill-considered magnificence, and indiscriminate generosity: it was a disillusioned Hat – A. J. von Höpken – who summed it up as 'un pillage des fonds publics qui ne connaissait ni bornes ni décence'.[71] It was, in fact, a system; and only an attack on the whole system, as a system, could really hope to bring any amendment: to this cause Anders Nordencrantz was to address himself, with mono-maniac virulence, for the last decade of his long life.

[69] So called because many of their great houses lined the Skeppsbro quay: for them see Kurt Samuelsson, *De stora köpmanshusen i Stockholm 1730–1815* (Stockholm 1951).

[70] Lars Hagberg, *Jacob Serenius' kyrkliga insats* (Lund 1952), p. 144.

[71] Höpken, *Riksrådet Anders Johan von Höpkens skrifter*, I, p. 124.

It was a system also in a quite different sense: a system of ideas and principles which may or may not have been mistaken, but which were at least honestly believed in and long adhered to. The first of these articles of belief was the French alliance: it was this that the Hats (and their enemies) meant, when they spoke of 'the System'. On it depended the hope, never abandoned, of recovering the lost provinces; on it depended their ability to furbish up their armed forces and begin work on the country's defences, while at the same time conveying the illusion that they were balancing the budget. In France they had no need to see, as they saw in England, a potential industrial and commercial rival. France was the historic ally, the friend of Sweden since the days of Axel Oxenstierna – whose caustic remarks about the French they conveniently forgot. But the relationship with France was based also on strong cultural sympathies. Such sympathies may not have been very potent in middle-class Hats such as Kierman and Plomgren, Renhorn and Bishop Browallius, but they were part of the intellectual habits, aesthetic sensibilities, and view of life, of men such as Tessin, or the Scheffer brothers, or Höpken, or Fersen. For such men, French was almost their native language; French drama, French literature, French art, formed their taste, and was felt to be an essential component of civilised existence: as ambassador in Paris, C. F. Scheffer spent a good deal of his time keeping Tessin supplied with notices and criticisms of the latest manifestations of the French genius.[72] Tessin was, in fact, the greatest connoisseur of the arts that Sweden had hitherto known, comparable with but excelling Magnus Gabriel de la Gardie in the previous century: a man whose taste and knowledge made him the arbiter of a whole generation; a collector whose discriminating extravagance ended by ruining himself and enriching his country: Sweden's national collections are in no small measure based upon the treasures which he was forced, by financial embarrassments, to sell to Lovisa Ulrika and to the future Gustav III, and which in due course became the nation's property. He was the generous patron of rising talent. It was under his supervision that the superb royal palace in Stockholm, planned by his grandfather, begun by his father, was at last completed. He was indefatigable in attracting to Sweden men who were to become some of the country's most celebrated artists and craftsmen.[73] But Tessin was only the most brilliant example of an eminence in the arts which was common to many of the Hats' leading politicians: to Carl Hårleman, who was to dominate the architecture and decoration of the mid-century; to A. J. von Höpken, scholar, *littérateur*, orator of classical purity in an age

---

[72] Carl Fredrik Scheffer, *Lettres particulières à Carl Gustaf Tessin 1744–1752*, ed. Jan Heidner (Stockholm 1983).

[73] For the cultural circle round Tessin, see Sigrid Leijonhufvud, *Carl Gustaf Tessin och hans Åkerökrets* I–II. (Stockholm 1931, 1933).

when oratory was still cultivated among the arts, the first secretary of the Royal Academy of Science, the first man to be nominated to Lovisa Ulrika's Academy of Literature, History and Antiquities.[74] For such men as these Paris was really their spiritual home; it offered the revelation of a new world of experience, the world of the *Encyclopédie*, the world of Voltaire, the world of the Rococo, with its grace, its arcadian diversions, its aim to charm rather than to impress: a world far removed from the sober piety and the massive and dramatic assertions of the Swedish Baroque. And if we turn to the greatest literary genius that the age produced, a poet whose reputation and popularity has endured and strengthened as that of no other literary work of the age has done – if we turn to Carl Michael Bellman in search of such foreign models as may have influenced him, once again they turn out to be French: the French *vaudevillles*, and the French popular melodies which he borrowed, and to which he fitted his verses.[75] But here the influence scarcely matters. When we look at the leading Swedish painters of the period the French provenance is usually immediately apparent. When we hear Bellman's *Epistles* or *Songs* they convey no French suggestion at all: the influence has been transmuted and hence obscured; and what we hear is wholly and immortally Swedish.

The French connexion was one aspect of that idealism which was the Hats' most positive quality. They were the party of national revival; they were born of the astonishing resurgence of national energy that had marked the twenties and thirties; and their youthful optimism was the obverse of their follies and of their inflated notions of themselves and their country. No doubt they expected to reap where they had not sown; no doubt they were intoxicated by their own rhetoric. But they believed that there were things that could be done about their country's situation; and they tried to do them. It was this spirit that underlay their economic policies. In the seventeenth century Sweden had emerged as a major metal-producing and metal-working country: the copper mine at Falun had dominated the European market for half a century, the foundries and forges of Uppland and Värmland had established the international prestige of Swedish iron. These results had been made possible by the importation of foreign workmen and the investment of foreign capital. No development on an equal scale had occurred in other fields; but the Hats saw no reason why it should not be attempted. They were, most of them, orthodox mercantilists: they believed in protecting home industries against foreign competition; they believed that the value of Swedish

---

[74] And with him Carl Fredrik Scheffer and Claes Ekeblad. But not Tessin, who by that time had quarrelled too bitterly with Lovisa Ulrika to be included.

[75] See Carl Fehrman, *Vin och flickor och Fredmans stråk* (Stockholm 1977), especially chapters I–II.

currency on the international market depended upon whether the balance of trade showed a visible surplus or a deficit. They bitterly grudged the presence of English textiles in the Swedish market. Their objective was 'Swedish men in Swedish cloth', and they pursued it resolutely, even though Swedish cloth might be more expensive, poorer in quality, and in short supply. The necessary techniques existed already, or could be acquired by Swedes who learned them abroad, or if need be by industrial espionage; water-power was abundant, fuel likewise, labour was cheap. All that was required was capital and encouragement during the initial years of an enterprise. This the Hats provided. The pioneer undertaking was Jacob Alströmer's 'factory' at Alingsås, a thoroughly inefficient business upon which the Hats lavished premiums, concessions and exemptions, and which came – rather unfairly – to stand as the type of the whole system.[76] But there were numbers of others, less favoured, and as it proved more viable, which managed to survive to the end of the century,[77] though they did not really thrive. Nevertheless, the example of Alingsås was followed in regard to other industries. Factories for tobacco 'spinning' were established; Rörstrand china attempted, with some success, to vindicate Swedish craftsmanship and taste in competition with Dresden and Meissen; silk was to be produced to compete with the silks of France and the imports of the Swedish East India Company, and the mulberry was enthusiastically cultivated in a climate for which Nature had scarcely intended it. It is obvious that some of these enterprises might seem to accord ill with the activities of the Swedish East India Company: in regard to silk, for instance, and in regard to china, now imported from the East on a massive scale. But the contradiction was not absolute, for since the export of silver from Sweden was prohibited, they could drive their trade with the East only by exporting Swedish products (mainly to Cadiz) and there obtaining in exchange the silver they required. The Hats were strong supporters of the Company, for to them it appeared as the grandest example of another economic principle in which they believed – that Swedish goods (and foreign goods too, as far as possible) should be shipped in Swedish bottoms: a principle which had lain behind the *produktplakat* of 1724, which was the Swedish equivalent of a Navigation Act.

One of the criticisms levelled against the Hats by their opponents was

[76] The adverse judgment on these ventures – *e.g.* in Heckscher, *Sveriges ekonomiska historia från Gustav Vasa*, II: 2, pp. 585–642, has been somewhat modified by Kurt Samuelsson, *Från stormakt till välfärdsstat* (Stockholm 1969), pp. 93–7. For a good account of Alströmer and his wide-ranging interests, see Birger Planting, *Baroner och patroner. Porträtt ur Sveriges jordbrukshistoria* (Stockholm 1944), pp. 51–83. But the best general account of Swedish industry in this century is now Nyström, *Stadsindustriens arbetare före 1800-talet*.

[77] They were not really factories at all, in the nineteenth-century sense: they were rather examples of a concentrated putting-out system under the central direction of one or more *entrepreneurs*: in no sense the ancestors of the later Swedish factory-system.

that they concentrated their interest upon industry and took too little account of agriculture, despite the fact that agriculture gave employment to a far larger percentage of the population than any other activity.[78] It might seem therefore ironical that it fell to the Hats to promulgate Ordinances which marked the beginning of a revolution in Swedish farming. These were the Ordinances of 1749 and 1757 concerning enclosures. But in fact they were in no sense party measures, and they enjoyed wide support. Land in the villages had hitherto been repartitioned among owners on the strip-system, familiar from English agricultural history. In Sweden, however, the division into strips had proceeded to lengths unknown in England: holdings, in any case never very large, had been partitioned and repartitioned in successive generations in order that a farmer might provide farms for as many of his sons as possible; and in extreme cases this had resulted in strips which might be no more than one or two metres broad.[79] There had been demands for reform of the system for more than a decade, and among the peasants themselves there were those who wished it to be altered in order to make possible a rational rotation of crops. But the main credit for the reforms of 1749 and 1757 is due to the initiative of Jacob Faggot, from 1749 the director of the Survey Office. In 1746 he published his famous essay on *Obstacles and Aids to Swedish Agriculture*, which first developed the argument for the consolidation of strips. Faggot started from the generally accepted view that the wealth of any state was a function of the size of its population. Sweden, he considered (and in this thinkers of both parties agreed with him) was under-populated. A more rational arrangement of holdings would lead to increased productivity and the creation of smaller, but still viable, farms; and this would facilitate marriage at an earlier age, and so lead to an increase in population.[80] Faggot's arguments convinced his readers; and the two Ordinances were the direct result. They differed essentially from the enclosure procedure in England; for they were no more than permissive measures: reallocation of strips could take place only on the initiative of an individual farmer (no matter how small his holding might be); and when permission to consolidate had been granted, and when the surveyors had completed their work, those who objected might appeal to the county court for its

---

[78] Around the mid-century some 20,000 persons are estimated to have been employed in manufactures; 49,000 as country craftsmen; 57,000 in the iron industry and the mines; 1,287,000 as peasants or cottars: Per Nyström, *Stadsindustriens arbetare före 1800-talet*, p. 141.

[79] Heckscher, *Sveriges ekonomiska historia från Gustav Vasa*, II, i, pp. 245–64.

[80] It has however been argued that it was the already existing increase of population, necessitating an increase in food-production, which was the real reason for the pressure for enclosure, and that the Ordinances were thus not simply reforms imposed from above by economic theorists: for an example of this line of argument see Birgitta Olai, *Storskiftet i Ekebyborna. Svensk jordbruksutveckling avspeglad i en östgötasocken* (Uppsala 1983).

cancellation or revision. It was thus not a question of large landowners of 'progressive' views imposing consolidation upon a peasantry that did not desire it: it was a question of a peasantry becoming gradually convinced that consolidation was in their own interest; and though the Minutes of the Estate of Peasants contain many complaints about the qualifications of surveyors, about delays, about anomalies, they reveal no real objection to the general principle. Moreover, consolidation was relatively cheap; for the necessary surveying, being undertaken by state-paid surveyors, imposed no burden on the peasant. Nevertheless, the process of consolidation after 1757 progressed fairly slowly, and at different rates in different parts of the country. It was not until the 1790s that a dictatorial reforming landowner, Rutger Maclean, *enforced* consolidation upon the peasants on his own estates; and the whole process was not completed until the middle of the next century: as late as 1865 there was a village in Dalarna where twenty peasants owned 5600 strips between them.[81] At all events the extinction of the strip-system in Sweden was carried through without oppression, and in many cases was genuinely popular; and it is probably true that no piece of legislation during the Age of Liberty had such far-reaching and beneficial consequences as this.

Making allowances for obvious points of difference, the Hats may be said in many ways to resemble the Whigs of the age of the Pelhams: the preference for an active rather than a passive foreign policy, the deliberate alliance with the commercial classes, the relatively tolerant attitude in matters of religion, the alliance of political families which provided their leadership. And not least in their typically Whiggish attitude to the monarchy: an attitude which contemporaries thought of as 'republican'. It did not have its roots, as English Whiggism had, in great historic memories – the Interregnum, the Exclusion Crisis, the Revolution; but the great magnates could not forget what they had lost by Charles XI's *reduktion*, nor the civil servants recall without a shudder the last days of the reign of Charles XII. As a defence against such dangers they erected the sovereignty of the Estates; and to the Hats the doctrine of a representative's responsibility to his constituents was naturally intolerable because it implied that the sovereign body was something less than sovereign. It was entirely appropriate that it should have been the Hats, through the mouth of Bishop Browallius and in the pages of *En Ärlig Swensk*,[82] who produced the classic formulations of the extreme 'republican' creed, as it had been evolved out of the letter of the Constitution of 1720. The sovereignty of the state necessarily implied the denial of legitimacy to any independent and autonomous corporation within the state. And, not least, to the universities and *gymnasia*, whose clear duty it was to produce

---

[81] Heckscher, *Sveriges economiska historia från Gustav Vasa*, II, i, pp. 245–64.
[82] For *En Ärlig Swensk* see above, p. 109.

the kind of human material of which the state stood in need; and of the nature and extent of that need the state, and not the universities, must be the judge. Their ancient rights and semi-autonomies might indeed be founded upon hitherto unchallenged privileges; but the Estates could revoke any privileges – except their own. And such a revocation became imperative if the universities were to be what every citizen must be; that is, 'useful' to the community as a whole. It followed that the state must dictate curricula, that it ought to insist on a switch from such 'useless' subjects as Greek or Hebrew to more 'practical' studies such as economics, science, and applied science. The Hats did not hesitate to create new chairs at Uppsala – economics in 1740, physics in 1760, constitutional law in 1761 – though having imposed these new departments (and their first professors) upon the university they were content to leave it to the university somehow to find the money to support them: the state had a right to call the tune, but felt no obligation to pay the piper. The Hats interfered with the regular procedures for appointments to university posts; they would have limited the intake of medical students, on the ground that Sweden had medicos enough already; by prohibiting the printing of Swedish works abroad they did what might have had the effect of isolating their scholars from the European learned community – a measure which provoked the fury even of that loyal Hat, Linnaeus, who on one occasion confessed that if it had not been for his family he would have accepted an appointment at Oxford, where at least there was academic freedom. They did not hesitate to supervise and where necessary correct a university's teaching. Anders Berch, the first holder of the Chair of Economics at Uppsala, aroused the suspicion of the Estates that his views on economic policy did not square with Hat orthodoxy: he was instructed to submit his lectures for scrutiny.[83] Nils Palmstierna, appointed Chancellor of the University of Lund in 1751, pursued a policy of political indoctrination in the Hat interest, personally censored its disputations, and forced the Professor of Law to read extracts from En Ärlig Swensk as part of his lectures.[84] Yet in spite of it all, the Hats' educational policies were in some important ways typically progressive. The Swedish universities were as much in need of thorough reform as even Oxford and Cambridge; and it was disquieting that their undergraduate population was falling all the time.[85] They had

---

[83] Yet Berch had been appointed to the Chair precisely because he was supposed to be a champion of Hat economic theories.

[84] Lars-Arne Norborg, 'Universitetet som indoktrineringsinstrument. Statsmakt och studium politicum under Nils Palmstiernas kanslerstid', in Historia och samhälle. Studier tillägnade Jerker Rosén (Malmö 1975); Martin Weibull, Lunds Universitets Historia (Lund 1918), I, pp. 224–31.

[85] The number of students at Uppsala, for instance, has been estimated at around 1000 in 1730; 800 in 1748; 600 in the 1760s; around 500 in the 1790s: Torgny T. Segerstedt, Den akademiska

come to be considered (unjustly) as backwaters of learning; supplanted, to some extent, by such institutions as the Royal Academy of Science (founded 1739), and Lovisa Ulrika's Academy of Literature, History and Antiquities (1753). Naturally, the universities deployed all the well-practised academic tactics to avert or delay the changes which threatened them. Passive resistance found a solid base in indolence, prejudice, interest and conservatism. But it rested too on more respectable foundations. There was a deep and rational belief that the intention of transforming the universities into mere tools of the state was a threat to true scholarship and the betrayal of a trust. This feeling united academics of both parties; and it made the Cap Professor Ihre as firm in resistance to 'progress' as his Hat colleague Linnaeus.[86]

The community of the learned might resent these applications of the Hats' political theories, but they had in fact already to a large extent accepted them. For, like the Hats, they believed that scientific research had an obligation to the community to be useful, and was deserving of support especially for its practical applications: so with chemistry, metallurgy, botany. The famous travels of Linnaeus over the length and breadth of Sweden were not merely designed to furnish material for the new taxonomy of which he was the begetter, nor to charm the reader by an appreciation of nature free from the outworn literary *clichés* or the tiresome 'sensibility' which had hitherto burdened such descriptions, but also to benefit the community by the identification of plants which might have value for medicine, for industry, or for agriculture. The pursuit of 'utility' was indeed common to both parties, and agronomy became something of a hobby with improving landlords,[87] but it was necessarily more closely associated with the Hats, since as the party in power it fell to them to pursue it most conspicuously. It was Jacob Alströmer who first cultivated the potato in Sweden;[88] but it was Claes Ekeblad, the Hats' Chancery-President from 1752 to 1765, whose experiments on his

friheten under frihetstiden (Uppsala 1971), p. 93, quoting Wilhelm Sjöstrand. But it is fair to note that there was a general view (not confined to the Hats) that there were too many students, and that many of them might be more usefully occupied. In 1749, for instance, Anders Berch calculated that the universities were producing twice as many graduates as could be absorbed into suitable employments: Sven-Erik Åström, 'Studentfrekvensen vid de svenska universiteten under 1700-talet', *Historisk tidskrift* (1949), pp. 5–7.

[86] Segerstedt, *Den akademiska friheten under frihetstiden*, pp. 18, 24, 37–8, 63–8, 101, 123. Segerstedt is a liberal of international stature, and an undaunted champion of academic freedom and academic standards against the authoritarianism and utilitarianism of the state's educational policies.

[87] See Linnaeus' enthusiastic description of David Gustav Hamilton's improvements (which included consolidation of strips) on his Barsebäck estate in Skåne: Linnaeus, *Skånska resa år 1749* (new edn. Stockholm 1977), p. 332. Tessin thought that agronomy had become a mania: *Tessin och Tessiniana*, pp. 223–4.

[88] Birger Planting, *Baroner och patroner. Porträtt ur Sveriges jordbruks-historia, 1700-talet.* (Stockholm 1944).

Västergötland estates really began to persuade the sceptical Swedish farmer of the value of potatoes as a food, and it was his wife Eva who provided the clinching argument by her discovery that potatoes could be used for the distillation of that national necessity *brännvin* (snapps) – a service which was appropriately rewarded by her election to the Royal Academy of Science: the only woman to receive that honour until 1945.

Whatever we may think of Hat political theory, the party cannot be denied the merit of facing and accepting the logical implications: secrecy as a device of government; censorship of the written and spoken word; spies, delation and torture to break resistance; political trials; extraordinary commissions whose proceedings trampled upon the laws of the land. If they appeared to sacrifice liberty, it was because they believed (or, at least, professed to believe) that the sacrifice was necessary in order to preserve it. To some extent their belief was understandable; though whether what was preserved by such means was worth the preserving is perhaps another question. It is difficult not to come to the conclusion that the Hats came to embody many of those vices and malpractices which make the Age of Liberty, despite its cultural and scientific achievements, painful reading to a liberal historian. But their services to the arts and sciences are a handsome memorial to them. They transformed their country and made it – far more than the Age of Greatness had ever done – a participant in the taste and intellectual movements of the age. Their discriminating patronage could on occasion show a laudable ability to rise above considerations of party: no political differences prevented them from paying tribute to the achievements of Dalin, of Serenius, of Ihre. If they came to be attacked as an 'aristocracy', in the pejorative sense in which Swedish contemporaries used that term, they were an aristocracy also in another and more honourable signification.

(iv)

What, then, did the Caps embody? What, except the circumstances of opposition, marked them off from the Hats? To these questions there is no single and simple answer, if only because – like all parties everywhere – they presented a rather different appearance in office from that which they had borne in opposition. The Old Caps (as distinct from the Young Caps who came to power in 1765) were the heirs of the men who in the thirties had called themselves 'the friends of Count Horn', as in England men called themselves friends of Lord Bute, or of Mr Pitt. They comprised representatives of that aristocracy of counts and barons against which the '*riddarhus*-democracy' had asserted itself in 1734, together with the upper *échelons* of the bureaucracy, many of whom the Hats displaced in the purge of 1739. Thus they too were an aristocracy, but an aristocracy whose outlook had become old-fashioned and was certainly conservative. This temperamental conservatism won the support of many of the provincial nobility: men not much exposed to French intellectual influences, often in modest circumstances, in general the friends of peace. It was natural also that the Estate of Clergy, always the firm supporters of Arvid Horn, (who to some extent shared their orthodox intolerance)[89] should be a bastion of the Caps; and though they might on occasion capitulate to pressure from the Nobility, since they felt it to be an obligation to avoid any 'strife of Estates', they could be remarkably firm when deeply stirred: it was their stubborn opposition (together with that of the Peasants) that saved Åkerhielm in 1747 from a harder fate than that which overtook him. Till 1739 they usually followed the lead of their bishops;[90] but when the Hats began to put men of their own party on the episcopal bench a rift in the Estate became apparent, for the lower clergy did not deviate from their Cap allegiance. The Finnish members of the Diet tended in general to be Caps: they had most to lose by a war with Russia, and their catastrophic experiences under Charles XII were repeated in 1741–3; moreover, Arvid Horn was himself of the Finnish nobility. The Estate of Peasants could usually be relied upon to support the Caps also. They had as yet little sense of party; and their turbulent attempts to assert their full political equality with the other Estates, and the ease with which they could be manipulated by unscrupulous incitements from outside, made them at times an embarrassing ally; but an ally they remained. In their support, and in that of the lower clergy (whose circumstances did not differ greatly from their own) may perhaps be detected something of those 'Country' attitudes (in the English sense) from which after 1764 would grow that popular radicalism which to a limited extent was parallel to contemporary currents in the England of the sixties.[91]

The Caps, no less than the Hats, had attitudes and reactions which remained reasonably constant. From the beginning they were 'English', as the Hats were 'French'. In the sixteen years during which England had no diplomatic representative in Stockholm, the Caps took care to maintain their English contacts through the fugitive Christopher

[89] For the rigid orthodoxy of the Estate of Clergy, see Carl Arvid Hessler, *Stat och religion i upplysningstidens Sverige* (Uppsala 1956).

[90] Though in the first few years after 1719 the Estate made it very clear that they were prepared to overrule the archbishop if they suspected him of trying to restore the primate's hierarchical authority, and to revert to conditions that had prevailed before the 1680s: on this see Otto S. Holmdahl, *Studier öfver Prästeståndets kyrkopolitik under den tidigare frihetstiden.* I (Lund 1912), pp. 203–10, 222, 226–50, 256.

[91] Compare the way in which the 'tactical' radicalism of the Tories under George II was in some cases transmuted into a genuine, if limited, radicalism after 1760: see Linda Colley, 'Eighteenth-Century English Radicalism before Wilkes', *Transactions of the Royal Historical Society*, 5th series, 31 (1981).

Springer in London; and also through the English pensioner Carl Gedda
in Stockholm, who furnished the British government with journals of the
Diet, and acted as its private agent and intermediary with Swedish
politicians. But the English cultural influence was less pervasive than the
French, and of a different nature. It was most obvious in science,
technology and economics. Christopher Polhem, the inventor of
water-powered machinery for mining, a rolling-mill, mechanical shears
for ironworks, and many other devices, Mårten Triewald, who built the
first Swedish steam-engine as an improvement on Newcomen, the
polymath Emmanuel Swedenborg, whose contributions to science have
been unjustly obscured by his religious interests – all learned much from
their stays in England. Swedish mining-engineers made pilgrimages to
England to take note of the advances they were making there.[92] Anders
Nordencrantz drew much of his political and economic theory from
English sources, and was deeply read in English political literature; Claes
Frietzcky was an enthusiastic admirer of English business methods. But
this kind of influence was not necessarily indicative of party allegiance,
nor was that allegiance necessarily determined by economic interests. The
Swedish iron industry might be heavily dependent upon the British
market, and upon British finance, but a majority of the owners of forges
and foundries was probably Hat, though they also included such
prominent Caps as de Geer, Rudbeck, Frietzcky and Nordencrantz. So
too with big business. A fair sprinkling of the most important names were
actually men from the United Kingdom who had settled in Sweden: so
the Ulsterman John Jennings; so his Scottish partner Robert Finlay; so
Colin Campbell, to whom more than to anyone else was due the
successful launching in 1731 of the Swedish East India Company. It might
have been expected that their British birth would make them Caps in
politics; but in fact for these businessmen exactly the opposite was the
case. With a few minor minor exceptions such as John Fenwick they were
Hats to a man: Hat economic policies coincided with their interests, and
considerations of business rather than of party or nationality were for
them decisive – as they were also for the archetype of the Hats'
manufacturing enterprises, Jacob Alströmer, who started his factory at
Alingsås only after some years of running a firm in England. If the Caps as
a party were consistently 'English' it was not for reasons such as these.
Confronted with a Hat party which was consistently 'French', they
became 'English' because the only alternative was to become 'Russian';
and even when they were most dependent on Russian money for their
support they would have sacrificed it all if only they could have got
English money to replace it. They had a general feeling that British

[92] See Sven Rydberg, *Svenska studierosorna till England under Frihetstiden* (Stockholm 1951), an
invaluable and comprehensive study, with a long and excellent English summary.

politicians were men of a temperament similar to their own: pragmatic, sensible, careful of the finances, inaccessible to cloudy notions of glory or quixotic ideas of chivalry. If they had been Englishmen, they would probably have been followers of Walpole; being Swedes, it was natural to them to have been the supporters of Arvid Horn, and to strive, as Horn's successors, to follow the lines he had chalked out.

In the arts, the English influence, though not negligible, was much less apparent than the French. Johan Helmich Roman, the leading Swedish composer of the age, a pupil of Pepusch, learnt his craft in England; the painters Michael Dahl and Elias Martin likewise; but these isolated instances were nothing in comparison with the numerous examples of men who earned a reputation in Paris, or were influenced by French masters. In literature also, the English influence was discernible only within narrow limits; and some of it, indeed, was operative only at second hand, through French translations. The numerous Swedish travellers who visited England – either on business, or attracted by the magnet of the Royal Society, and who sometimes, as in the case of Bengt Ferrner, combined the learned convivialities of the Mitre Tavern with diligent industrial espionage[93] – necessarily mastered English, if only because Englishmen seemed to know no modern language save their own, and the English pronunciation of Latin made that universal tongue a barrier rather than an aid to learned conversation; and many of them brought back to Sweden quite large libraries of contemporary English literature. Even for those who stayed at home, Locke was one of the fundamental texts of Swedish liberty, Shaftesbury was well-known also, and towards the end of the period Bolingbroke and Hume were important influences. Most men of letters knew something of Pope – at least to the extent of the *Essay on Man*, though Swedish verse-forms did not favour the heroic couplet. James Thomson's *Seasons* influenced Gustaf Fredrik Gyllenborg's *Song of Winter* and *Song of Spring*. The most important prose writer of the age was Olof von Dalin, who is credited with being the real founder of modern literary Swedish prose, besides being responsible for a vast epic poem, *Swedish Liberty*: in its own day esteemed a classic masterpiece, now read only by the historians of literature. Dalin had little patience with Hat ideas and ideals; basically Cap in sympathy, though he became an active royalist later, he was a curious mixture of French and English influences: a cynical and sceptical Voltairean, and thus exactly suited to Lovisa Ulrika's taste, a master of long-dead epigrams and *vers de société*, he survives as the author of that attractive parable of Swedish history, *The Tale of a Horse*, and above all of the periodical *Then Swenska Argus*: essays light or serious, moralising or

---

[93] See Bengt Ferrner, *Resa i Europa, 1758–1762* (Stockholm 1956), *passim*.

satirical (not least of French fashions), which plainly reflect (and are sometimes directly lifted from) the writings of Addison, Steele, Swift and other prose luminaries of the Augustan Age. Yet on the other hand his serious and scholarly *History of Sweden*, which first applied modern critical criteria to the legends which had done duty hitherto as Sweden's early history, was probably mainly influenced by Voltaire;[94] though before the end of the period Robertson's European reputation had firmly established itself in Sweden also.[95] What is truly remarkable is that a society which was familiar with many aspects of English literature failed altogether to produce any equivalent to the contemporary English novel.[96] Not even Richardson, let alone Fielding and Smollett, found an imitator. In the genial good-humour of Jacob Wallenberg's travel-book *Min son på galejan* we catch the feeling of a relationship to the travel journals of Sterne and Fielding (not to mention a fairly strong dose of Smollett in his more scatological moments); and Wallenberg was sufficiently well-read in English literature to be able to quote Milton as well as Pope when occasion served. But the emergence of the realistic Swedish novel had to await the appearance of Fredrik Cederborgh's *Ottar von Tralling* in the second decade of the next century.

The Caps until 1760 were for the most part as firm mercantilists as their opponents; but they disapproved of luxury imports (especially if they came from France) not less on moral than on economic principles; and they disliked the Swedish East India Company, among other reasons, because it drew off the wealth of the country for unnecessary luxuries. But in regard to the constitution, the experiences of 1738–9, reinforced by similar experiences in the forties, produced an attitude which differed radically from that of the Hats. If the central Hat commitment was to Liberty, that of the Old Caps was to Law. They consistently opposed special commissions, extrajudicial proceedings, and the violation of the rights of the citizen in the name of security. They resisted and deplored the increasing usurpation of power by the Secret Committee, insisting that the Committee was no more than the representative of the *plena* who were its principals, and was accountable to them. They believed too that the Estates themselves were similarly accountable to the nation: the 'doctrine of principalship' was Cap in origin, and had the support of the Cap party; and though that doctrine was condemned as a constitutional heresy, the Caps did not forget it: it remained a half-submerged element in their thinking, and it lay behind their emancipation of the press in 1766.

[94] Erik Bollerup, 'Om franska inflytelser på svensk historieskrivning under frihetstiden', *Scandia* (1968).

[95] For Robertson's influence on Jonas Hallenberg, see Nils Ahnlund, *Jonas Hallenberg* (Stockholm 1957), pp. 60–1.

[96] Though the marriage of the future Gustav III and Sophia Magdalena in 1766 was celebrated by the performance of an opera based on *Tom Jones*.

In opposition to the Hat orthodoxy as enunciated by Bishop Browallius, they believed in some sort of balance in the constitution, and imagined that the Constitution of 1720 had secured it. Some of them did not hesitate to speak of the relationship between king and Estates as a contract. But though many of them would have conceded that the king had rights, they were never more than tepid supporters of the prerogative, and that only for reasons of party expediency; and when those reasons fell away (as they did, after 1765) the Caps would become as 'republican' as the Hats, if not more so.

Much of all this remained Cap policy after 1762; and already within the Old Caps could be discerned some of the special elements which were to characterise the party of the next generation. The link between the two was undoubtedly Jacob Serenius, whose long political career extended from 1738 to 1772. Serenius was born in 1700. In 1723 he was appointed chaplain to the Swedish congregation in London, and rapidly became an enthusiastic anglophile. His admiration for things English comprehended the English language, English agriculture, the Church of England, and the British constitution. In 1727 he published *The English Farmer and Shepherd*, which for the first time introduced Sweden to the new English use of clover and lucerne; in 1741 he produced the first English–Swedish pronouncing dictionary. He was a Fellow of the Royal Society. The accident that the Bishop of London was responsible for the spiritual welfare of the Swedish-speaking congregations on the Delaware brought Serenius into contact with Edmund Gibson; and he took back to Sweden the Anglican rite of confirmation. He eventually made an exemplary bishop – except in matters that trenched on party politics; but he had the distinction of being more cordially hated than any other man of his party – a distinction to which the bitterness of his tongue and his tenacity in opposition fully entitled him.[97]

As early as 1738 Serenius denounced the supplanting of the ordinary courts by commissions, and asserted the supremacy of law; he was the enemy of all encroachments by the Secret Committee upon the rights of the *plena*; a champion of the doctrine of principalship; suspicious of artificially fostered industries. If the state must intervene, agriculture, he thought, was better deserving of its assistance. He believed in a government open to inspection and criticism, and in particular attacked the intolerable secrecy in which the Hats shrouded the finances of the state: there must be strict accounting and full publicity. He protested

[97] For Serenius, see Lars Hagberg, *Jacob Serenius' kyrkliga insats* (Lund 1952); L. A. Cederbom, *Jacob Serenius i opposition mot Hattpartiet*; for an example of the hatred he inspired see J. G. Oxenstierna, *Ljuva ungdomstid. Dagbok 1766–1768* (Uppsala 1965), p. 126. Yet it is typical of one of the better aspects of the Age of Liberty that a Diet dominated by his enemies should have voted him three gold medals in recognition of the publication of his Dictionary: Cederbom, *Jacob Serenius i opposition mot Hattpartiet*, p. 50.

against the paper-fuelled inflation, and bitterly attacked the Exchange Office; demanded that the state should cut its financial coat according to its cloth; and waged harassing war against premiums, rewards, gifts, jobbery and graft. In short he was what the Younger Caps were so notably to be – an 'economical reformer', in the English sense of that expression. There were other Old Caps who thought on similar lines: Åkerhielm was one; Claes Frietzcky – one of the men of the future – was another; and from 1760 there was Anders Nordencrantz, in his prime the most powerful mind that the Caps had at their disposal: admirer of the British constitution, well acquainted with Locke and with other English publicists (large chunks of whose works he was in the habit of inserting into his pitilessly verbose books), financial oracle, the hammer of the bureaucrats. From such men came the principles which were to be the driving force behind the party after 1764. But in the period 1747–60 these principles mostly lay dormant, adumbrated only by a few, and obscured by the manoeuvrings of that troubled and confused decade.

(iv)

When the Diet met in the autumn of 1760, Höpken and his colleagues faced – in the words of no less a person than Tessin – 'a war which they had not expected, an immeasurable financial disorder, an intolerable rate of exchange, scandalous extravagance, and a crushing cost of living'.[98] In these circumstances they soon found themselves confronted with the most formidable opposition any Hat government had encountered since 1747. No matter that it was a conglomerate of elements which lacked unity of principle: that defect was supplied by the emergence of a leader of this ragged army in the person of Carl Fredrik Pechlin. Pechlin was a Holsteiner by birth, but he was connected by marriage with prominent figures in the Hat plutocracy: brother-in-law to John Jennings, and likewise to Robert Finlay; son-in-law to Thomas Plomgren. Though his command of Swedish was imperfect, that did not prevent his being an inflammatory parliamentary orator, and among the Hats he was clearly a rising man. His skill as a parliamentary manager was matched by a total lack of scruple. Corrupt, treacherous, ambitious, notorious for his cruel treatment of his peasants, he was no good advertisement for Swedish 'Liberty'. He was always ready to snatch a temporary and tactical advantage by collaboration with politicians who were prepared to subserve his purposes – including Lovisa Ulrika herself, against whom he had advocated the harshest measures in 1756. Yet in a career marked by shifts and treacheries which even contemporaries found uniquely

---

[98] *Tessin och Tessiniana*, p. 190.

repugnant he was nevertheless true to two principles: the maintenance of the constitution in its integrity, and the subordination of the executive to the legislature. It was this consistency which made him something of a hero in the eyes of those who in the first decade of the twentieth century were fighting to obtain a truly representative parliamentary system, and for whom he stood out as the most striking forerunner of real democracy that the Age of Liberty produced. It was in line with the logic of his politics that he should have been one of the only two men (Rudbeck was the other) who attempted resistance to Gustav III's *coup* on 19 August 1772, and that he should have ended his life a state prisoner for his share in organising that king's assassination, twenty years later.[99]

Pechlin's object in 1760 was not to change the system, but to remove the members of the Council who had mismanaged it, who had usurped the authority of the Diet, and who seemed disposed to constitute themselves an 'aristocracy'. The Marshal of the Diet, Axel von Fersen, concurred in some of these ideas: his experience as one of the Swedish generals in Pomerania had convinced him that Höpken was a liability; the parliamentary situation was labile and disquieting: already before Christmas the Hats could no longer be sure of a majority in the Estate of Nobles. Fersen was therefore ready for a bargain with Pechlin, and Pechlin was not the man to decline one. On 5 January 1761 a secret pact was concluded (to which the French ambassador was an accessory), whereby Pechlin agreed to intensify his attacks on the Council and to secure the *licentiering* of Höpken, C. F. Scheffer and Nils Palmstierna, on the understanding that when they were disposed of he would forbear further attacks on their colleagues. In terms of this bargain Scheffer and Palmstierna were duly driven from office; Höpken averted *licentiering* by a timely resignation. The innocuous Claes Ekeblad succeeded him as Chancery-President; and Fersen might hope that the worst of the danger was over. Within a month or two Pechlin, to the fury of his former allies, openly changed sides, and completed the bargain by declaring himself once more a loyal Hat. The comedy was over.[100] But there were limits to what even a Swedish Diet was prepared to tolerate; and what had appeared to be an adroit manoeuvre turned out to be the prelude to disaster. Court, Caps, Country Party were now united in one common aim: to avenge Pechlin's treachery. Their combined strength in the Estate of Nobility was growing every day; in July 1761 they not only invited

[99] A modern study of Pechlin is much needed: the only general book about him seems to be Hj. Lindeberg, *En ränksmidare. Strödda blad ur 1700-talets partistrider* (Stockholm 1928), though the final phase of his career receives full attention in Lolo Krusius-Ahrenberg, *Tyrannmördaren C. F. Ehrensvärd. Samhällssyn och politiskt testament* (Stockholm 1947), chapter III.

[100] See Gunnar Olsson, 'Krisuppgörelsen mellan hattpartiet och Carl Fredrik Pechlin 1760', *Scandia* (1959); and Gunnar Sundberg, 'Lantpartiet vid riksdagen 1970–2', *Historisk tidskrift* (1971).

Höpken to resume his seat in the Council (an invitation which he prudently declined), but they restored to membership of that body Counts Bonde and Bielke, victims of the great purge of 1739; now old and feeble, but living symbols of Cap principles and Cap rancours, presages of a Cap resurrection. And at last, on 24 August 1761, after six weeks of bitter debates and by a majority of *one*, they voted Pechlin out of the House, not for this Diet only, but for the next also.[101]

To Fersen only one means of saving something from the wreck now seemed conceivable: a reconciliation with the queen and a bargain with the Caps; a compromise, in short: in the language of the day, a 'Composition'. Lovisa Ulrika was very willing to act as broker. Her little group of Court supporters held the balance of power in the Estates; she had money for corruption at her disposal provided by Prussia and England; and she could afford to set a high price on her services[102] at a moment when the conclusion of peace with Prussia seemed to depend upon her good offices. By the spring of 1762 the Composition had been drafted, and it assumed its final form two years later. The Hats found themselves making far-reaching concessions: the *Act of State* of 1756[103] and all the papers concerning the investigation into the attempted royalist *coup* of that year were destroyed; the Crown's debts were to be paid; discussions were to take place, once the Diet had ended, about reasonable extensions of the prerogative. The queen insisted that the opportunity be taken to put an end to party strife: thenceforward the Council was to be bipartisan in composition; there was to be no more party persecution; Hats and Caps were to forswear corruption for the future. Lovisa Ulrika could appear not only as the bringer of peace in Pomerania, but as the beneficent composer of domestic strife. Hats and Caps were welcomed at Court with even-handed graciousness, and astonished observers saw the leaders of each party fraternising with a cordiality which would have seemed inconceivable in 1760.[104] The Composition, it appeared, had extinguished party.[105]

As the event proved, it had done no such thing; but it is certainly true that from 1761 to 1763 considerations of party advantage were

---

[101] The result was affected by the accident that one of Pechlin's supporters attempted to vote twice, and was detected.

[102] For other motives which may probably have influenced her, see chapter v, below, p. 182.

[103] For the *Act of State* of 1756 (which was in effect a conditional threat of deposition if the royal pair did not behave themselves) see below, p. 182.

[104] So, at least, it seemed to Fredrik Sparre: the entry in his journal is quoted in M. J. Crusenstolpe, *Portefeuille*, I (Stockholm 1837), 108.

[105] For the intricate (and contentious) history of the Composition see, [S. Piper], 'Pro Memoria, 1771' in RA Stavsundsarkivet, Smärre enskilda arkiv, fos. 7–9; Olof Jägerskiöld, *Hovet och författningsfrågan 1760–1766* (Uppsala 1943), pp. 64–72, 102–15, 118, 125–6, 141, 151–7; Fersen, *Historiska skrifter*, III, 29, 305–15; Michael Metcalf, *Russia, England and Swedish Party Politics 1762–1766* (Stockholm and Totowa, N.J., 1977), pp. 103, 119.

transcended by larger issues. It was not merely that the Hats, as a party, were now fighting for survival. What was at stake was their whole system of government, and many of the fundamental presuppositions of politics which had prevailed for the last generation. The storm had been gathering since 1756, at a time when the Hats had appeared inexpugnable: after 1760 it raged with a violence which for a time seemed likely to sweep all before it. The hand which launched the thunderbolts and unloosed the whirlwind was that of Anders Nordencrantz; who in 1756 and 1760 published a succession of voluminous attacks, some of them directed at abuses, but others at the basic principles of the constitution: above all, at the idea that office was a property, to be forfeited only on legal conviction; at the election of office-holders to the Diet's committees; and at the consequent confusion of administrative responsibility with legislative sovereignty: this, he thought, was the great evil of the constitution.[106] Nordencrantz's pamphlets of 1756 were the first blast of the trumpet against the monstrous regiment of office-holders; they were to be basic to Cap policy after 1764; and for Nordencrantz personally they assumed the character of a vendetta which ended only with his death in 1772. In 1760 his offensive was broadened to include economic no less than constitutional issues. He denounced the Exchange Office as fallacious in theory and probably corrupt in practice; identified the cause of the alarming inflation, not – as orthodox Hat economists usually contended – as an effect of the country's adverse balance of trade, but as the result of the Bank's readiness to make loans (not least to men like Pechlin) on inadequate security,[107] with a consequent disastrous increase in the money-supply. The Bank, the Iron Office, the Exchange Office – all of them effectively dominated by the same narrow ring of Hat plutocrats – were, he thought, combining to ruin the economy.

The proceedings of the Diet of 1760–2 made it clear that Nordencrantz was to be the herald of a new era and the oracle of a new generation. Members of the Diet ploughed their way though his interminable volumes, to emerge shaken or converted: notably Thure Rubeck, who declared (to Lovisa Ulrika's indignation) that Nordencrantz's demonstrations were themselves sufficient to dish the Hats.[108] Their industrial policy now came under heavy attack;[109] in April 1761 the contract with the consortium which managed the Exchange Office was abrogated, and the

---

[106] Malmström, *Sveriges politiska historia*, IV, pp. 442–6.

[107] In 1762 it became clear that the Bank had even been making advances against the security of lottery-tickets: *SRARP*, XXIII, 107, 321; and see in general Malmström, *Sveriges politiska historia*, V, pp. 13–14, 46–9, 53.

[108] Which caused Lovisa Ulrika to cut off financial aid to the Caps, and really marks the moment when there can be no question but that they were an independent party again: Lovisa Ulrika's *Journal*, in Fersen, *Historiska skrifter*, III, pp. 263, 291–3.

[109] See, *e.g.*, *SRARP*, XXIII, 16–17, 289.

Office declared to be not merely useless but positively injurious.[110] A year later the Diet carried a demand that the Bank publish full information as to its loans to the government; forbade it to make any more loans unless authorised by the Estates to do so – which was in effect to condemn the method by which the Hat Council had financed the Pomeranian war;[111] and ordered the Bank to produce full accounts for the inspection of the Secret Committee. That Committee was still firmly under Hat control, and the Bank could therefore risk presenting figures which concealed the worst of the truth; but even so they looked bad enough, and there could be no mistaking the dissatisfaction of members of the Diet, especially the Nobility.[112] An era had come to an end: henceforward the old secrecy would be impossible.

That this was so was obvious from the operations of the censorship. It had been the Hats themselves who first made a crack in the dyke by encouraging the publication of *En Ärlig Swensk* in 1755; which, even though its object was to make propaganda for their party, brought into the open topics of discussion which had hitherto been forbidden ground. The censor, Nils von Oelreich, thereafter increasingly passed for publication matter of this character. It was Oelreich whom the country had to thank for the licensing of Nordencrantz's writings, and for Rudbeck's memorandum on the principles that determined the rate of exchange: it is significant that by 1764 he had become an avowed Cap. But the Estates themselves bore much responsibility for what was happening: they authorised the publication of the arguments for and against Pechlin's expulsion; and in the sharp controversies which arose between (for instance) the Nobility and the Burghers, each Estate published extracts from their minutes, designed to justify their respective points of view. They were doing what no Diet had ever done before: they were appealing to the country; they were submitting arguments to the judgment of the nation at large. It is true that a motion in the Estate of Nobility to publish their minutes *in extenso* found no support;[113] but they were nevertheless coming dangerously near in practice to that doctrine of principalship which they had so firmly condemned, a generation before. Above all, the availability to the general public of Nordencrantz's and Rudbeck's exposures of the fallacies and abuses of Hat economic policy really made any return to the old censorship impossible. When the Caps abolished the preliminary censorship in 1766 they were completing, not initiating, a process which was really a symptom of the decay and ruin of the Hats. And when a member suggested that pensions granted when the state could afford to pay them should now be cancelled, it is clear that the

[110] *Ibid.*, 143, 146, 387.   [111] *Ibid.*, 107.
[112] *Ibid.*, 274, 329.   [113] *SRARP*, XXIII, 42–5, 51.

spirit which was to animate the Diet of 1765–6, and was then to be ruthlessly translated into action, had already found expression.[114]

Meanwhile, no change in the political climate could avert the state bankruptcy which by the summer of 1764 seemed imminent. In September of that year the Council was reluctantly driven to the desperate decision to summon an Extraordinary Diet for January 1765. And that decision, as it turned out, led directly to the collapse of the Composition. For the Hats, the Composition had been a lifebelt, the last hope of survival, a necessary sacrifice. Not so for the Cap negotiators, of whom Rudbeck was the chief. At a time when they seemed already to have the Hats on the run, the best that could be said for the Composition, from their point of view, was that without it they might lose the alliance of the Court; and even so the constitutional concessions to the Crown which they were prepared to contemplate were less ample and less precise than those which the Hats apparently were ready to swallow.[115] It had been agreed that the Composition was to be considered as a wholly domestic matter: considerations of foreign policy were explicitly excluded from it. This was all very well in 1762, when both sides were equally anxious for peace with Prussia; but the case would be altered if once again there should be a British minister in Stockholm round whom an 'English' party could rally. With the arrival of Sir John Goodricke in the spring of 1764 that possibility became a reality. Lovisa Ulrika might do her best to preserve the Composition intact, and to keep the Court above party, but circumstances were too strong for her. Goodricke's arrival meant the end of the party truce, and the resumption of foreign corruption – sooner or later. And when a mere seven weeks before the Extraordinary Diet was due to meet, the Council rashly accepted an ensnaring French offer to pay off arrears of subsidy on terms which would bind Sweden to France until 1772, the Court was forced to abandon its posture of neutrality; for Adolf Frederick prudently calculated that he had no option but to cast his two votes against the agreement, or expose himself to awkward consequences when the Diet should meet. The resolution to accept the French offer was carried by a single vote; but the king's votes with the minority finally shattered the Composition.[116] For another year Lovisa Ulrika would attempt, by irreconcilable negotiations with both sides, to maintain a position of neutrality and keep the spirit of the Composition alive, in the belief (which was after all justified) that any reform of the constitution

---

[114] *SRARP*, XXIII, 21.

[115] The Caps later professed that they entered the Composition reluctantly, and for tactical reasons: Metcalf argues that they did so simply as 'clients of the Court': Metcalf, *Russia, England and Swedish Party Politics*, pp. 103, 119.

[116] Roberts, *British Diplomacy and Swedish Politics*, pp. 94–6; Jägerskiöld, *Lovisa Ulrika* (Stockholm 1945), pp. 237–8.

could come only as a non-partisan measure. But the attempt failed: party
feeling was too embittered; and for the remainder of Adolf Frederick's
reign the Court would be forced to become the ally, or the coadjutor, of
one party or the other.

IV

The Caps in power, 1765–1769

(i)

The general election of 1764 differed in character from any that had preceded it. It revealed a popular reaction against notorious abuses; and that reaction had been made possible by increasing laxness of the censorship. The disastrous state of the economy, the sordid struggles of the Diet of 1760–2, the unscrupulous greed of the ruling plutocracy, had been exposed to all the world; the arguments of Nordencrantz and Rudbeck were now available to any;[1] in a simplified (and perhaps distorted) form they were in every man's mouth. For the first time, the electorate was influenced by a deliberate propaganda campaign; most remarkably reflected, perhaps, in the instruction drawn up by the clergy of Västergötland to their new representatives: an instruction which commanded them to ensure that the Bank's loans were strictly controlled and forbade them to agree to any grant unless preceded by satisfactory explanations from those who managed the country's finances.[2] An *instruction*! What was this, if not the imperative mandate? The advocates of greater liberty of printing might protest that they had no intention of edging towards the doctrine of principalship, but this suggested that they were doing just that, whatever might be their intention.

The everyday experiences of the man in the street made him the more accessible to such influences. The big merchants, the exporters, had grown rich from the sale of their goods abroad at a time when Swedish currency, in international terms, had depreciated to as little as a third of its nominal value. But importers and small traders had been forced to raise domestic prices to offset the increased cost of goods as measured in Swedish money. The result was a rise in the cost of living which the ordinary man felt to be intolerable; and Nordencrantz taught them whom

---

[1] Sven LagerBring was subsequently to remark that Nordencrantz's book 'instructed the Estates in a great deal more than they needed to know': LagerBring, *Sammandrag of Swea-Rikes Historia*, v, p. 19.

[2] Malmström, *Sveriges politiska historia*, v, p. 251.

they had to thank for it. It was this, as much as anything, that produced the electoral earthquake which shook the country at the end of 1764.

The earthquake was first, and most sensationally, felt in Stockholm, a majority of whose ten seats were normally securely in Hat hands. But now, the Caps won every single seat; and among the defeated – to the stupefaction of his party – was Gustaf Kierman, former Speaker of the Burghers, and a central pillar of the Hat plutocracy. And Stockholm's lead was followed in many other towns. Unknown faces appeared at the Diet. Whether these new members already thought of themselves as Caps may be open to question: they owed their election to their hostility to the Hats, and when the Diet met became Caps almost of necessity, even though they may not have been so before. Certainly their success was much more than a party victory. It was linked to factors which were essentially social. Nearly forty years later, the poet G. F. Gyllenborg looked back at the Diet of 1765, and saw it as a portentous event. It signalised, he thought, the triumph of frantic democracy, the victory of men of a levelling spirit; it was 'distinguished by characteristics similar to those in evidence at the start of the French Revolution'.[3] Gyllenborg's judgment was no doubt distorted by the events of the period when his autobiography was written; but it is certainly true that the Diet of 1765 showed perceptible social shifts. We can discern the emergence of new, self-confident, aspiring middle classes, able to make an impact on parliamentary politics.[4] The election was in part a revolt against the municipal magistracies, the expression of resentment at the curbs which the Hats in 1752 had imposed upon the holding of public meetings in towns: it was the outcome of a long-standing struggle for municipal self-government, uncontrolled by the state and its agents. In the Estate of Burghers the new members were of distinctly lower social standing than of old: the municipal Establishment was no longer in control.[5] Whereas in the 1740s and 1750s the Burghers had been led by the wealthy Stockholm financiers Thomas Plomgren and Gustaf Kierman, in 1765 they were led by the tanner John Westin. There was a geographical shift also: the provinces grew in influence at Stockholm's expense, and the new members brought with them demands, soon to be successful, for the modification or abolition of the long-standing privileges of the staple towns, of which Stockholm was the chief. Already in 1763 the remarkable

---

[3] Gustaf Fredrik Gyllenborg, *Mitt lefverne 1731–1775. Själfbiografiska anteckningar* (Stockholm 1885), pp. 59–60. So too in our own day Per-Erik Brolin, who wrote of the Young Caps as 'a political party that propagated the ideas of the Enlightenment . . . a local manifestation of those popular forces and those political ideas which made the great American and French Revolutions': Brolin, *Hatter och mössor* p. 422.

[4] Tom Söderberg, *Den namnlösa medelklassen. Socialgrupp två i det gamla svenska samhället* (Stockholm 1956), pp. 169–72, 232.

[5] Sten Carlsson, *Byråkrati och Borgarstånd under Frihetstiden* (Stockholm 1963), p. 147.

meeting at Gamla Karleby[6] of representatives of seven towns in
Österbotten had given clear warning of the readiness of a provincial
pressure-group to cooperate in fighting for the concessions they desired.
And as the new Diet would see a new middle class in action, so even in the
socially stable Estate of Clergy the unbeneficed curates became un-
wontedly vocal – the most notable example being Anders Chydenius
from Finland, a major economic theorist who in many ways was the
forerunner of Adam Smith.[7] The Peasants were less illiterate than of old;
and they seem somehow to have imbibed physiocratic notions about the
primacy of agriculture in any social system, the necessity for an abundant
rural population, and consequently their own importance in the general
scheme of things. For almost a decade before the Young Caps came to
power the desirability of less restrictive economic policies had been urged
by men of both parties: by Anders Nordencrantz for the Caps, by A. J.
von Höpken and C. F. Scheffer for the Hats.[8] Some of the new ways of
thought which have been identified as typical of the pre-revolutionary
situations of the age made themselves felt, as new arguments in old
controversies, even in Sweden. It is perhaps understandable that the
existence of such impulses, and the reforming measures of the Diet of
1765–6, should have led such historians as Fredrik Lagerroth to think of
the rule of the Young Caps as a springtime of promise, brutally and
unnecessarily blighted by the *coup d'état* of 19 August 1772.[9]

Such were some of the feelings and purposes which animated the
electorate, and swept the Hats from power. But one factor, at all events,
was of subordinate importance: the election of 1764 was not won by
foreign corruption. The crucial Stockholm election came at a moment
when the British and Russian ministers had very few resources at their
disposal to influence the voting;[10] nor is there much sign that their money
had any effect on the other towns, or upon the Clergy. By Christmas Sir
John Goodricke and Count Osterman were no doubt well supplied; but
their money went to the buying of noble proxies, or the support of clubs
for members who had already arrived. And in any case, as Michael
Metcalf has shown, the French spent considerably more on losing this
election than their adversaries did upon winning it.[11]

[6] See above, p. 109.

[7] For Chydenius see Heckscher, *Sveriges ekonomiska historia fran Gustav Vasa* II, 2, pp. 862–8;
Karl Petander, *De nationalekonomiska åskådningarna i Sverige sådana de framträda i litteraturen*
(Stockholm 1912), pp. 236–80. For examples of championship of the unbeneficed in the Estate of
Clergy, see Bexell, pp. 113, 165.

[8] For the controversy about Swedish physiocracy, see Bo Gustafsson, 'Hur fysiokratiskt var
den svenska fysiokratismen?', and Lars Herlitz, 'Härtappad fysiokratism', both in *Scandia*
(1976).

[9] E.g. Fredrik Lagerroth, 'Det frihetstida statsskickets utvecklingsmöjligheter', *Scandia*
(1966).

[10] Roberts, *British Diplomacy and Swedish Politics*, pp. 83–4, 94, 433 *n*. 118.

[11] Metcalf, *Russia, England and Swedish Party Politics 1762–1766*, pp. 140–1.

When the Diet met in January 1765 the full extent of the Caps' victory was revealed. They carried their candidates for the Speakership of the Burghers and Peasants with ease; the Archbishop – *ex officio* Speaker of the Clergy – happened to be a Cap; and in the Nobility, Rudbeck was elected Marshal by a majority which was certainly handsome, though it owed a good deal to the help of the Court party and the defection of sixty members of the Gyllenborg clan. As was to be expected, they dominated all the major committees, and the Secret Committee in particular. The day of the Young Caps had arrived: a day of popular rejoicing, a day of hope, but also a day of vengeance.[12]

(ii)

The Hats had expected that citizens be useful; the Young Caps demanded that they also be honest. They pitched the claims of the state no lower than the Hats had done; but they insisted that those claims be not manipulated to further the private advantage of individuals. On occasion the application of this principle might mean that the state's right would entail the individual's wrong. It was a risk that they did not shrink from taking, especially if the individual was in other respects odious to them. In the name of state necessity they did not hesitate to abrogate legally binding agreements, or to ignore acquittances given by previous governments. In such instances they could be ruthless – as ruthless as Charles XI (in many respects their spiritual ancestor) in the matter of the *reduktion*: not altogether without cause did those that suffered call the Diet of 1765 a '*reduktion*-Diet'.[13] Compassion for old age, impoverished nobility, minor civil servants who had been living beyond their means, the claims of long

[12] 'It was indeed most moving to see the rejoicings of the populace at the election [of Rudbeck as Marshal of the Diet] . . . and as it grew dark to see the common people and the lesser *bourgeoisie* and so on stand apart with clasped hands upraised in thanks to God for the news; and when next day the Marshal led a deputation from the Nobility to the king, unusual crowds collected, and an unceasing sound of blessings was heard from the commonalty, as though they had obtained a man who had liberated them from the yoke of slavery': Daniel Tilas, *Anteckningar och brev från riksdagen 1765–1766* (Stockholm 1974), p. 15; or in the words of a contemporary rhymester:

God send our new administration
May prove a pattern to the nation,
Nor spew dishonour on the state
    As once in 1738,
Nor headlong rush into a fix,
    As that of 1756;
But crass self-interest now may rue
    The work of 1762,
And Order reign, and Justice thrive
    Again, in 1765.

The Swedish original quoted in Ingemar Carlsson, *Olof Dalin* (1966), p. 231.
[13] Tilas, *Anteckningar och brev från riksdagen 1765–1766*, p. 15.

service of the state, moved them as little as it had moved Charles XI: in their eyes Tessin had no more title to consideration than his great predecessor Magnus Gabriel de la Gardie had had, eighty years earlier; and when they drastically cut the pensions of former members of the Council they did not spare their old champion, the now rehabilitated Åkerhielm. When the bitter medicines which they administered in order to bring the nation's finances into something approaching solvency turned the tide of popularity against them, they did not flinch – knowing, as governments in our time have found, that austerity can neither expect nor afford to be popular; and being stiffened by a desire for 'a just retribution' at least as strong as that of their predecessors in 1743. That desire too often degenerated into a vindictive temper, especially noticeable in the Clergy and Peasants, among whom it was reinforced by a general hostility to luxury, wealth, noble privilege and French manners. It was a feeling that had long been growing among them, and its expression of 1765–6 was a presage of the social struggle, the 'strife of Estates', which was to dominate the last two years of the Age of Liberty, and was at last to transcend party differences altogether.

It was the duty of the Council to lay before the Estates at the beginning of each Diet what was termed the Secret Proposition. This was in fact not a proposition in any real sense: it was rather a review of the state of the nation, presented to the Diet for its consideration and action. On this occasion the Council had entrusted the drafting of the Proposition to Löwenhielm, and that draft they had all approved. It was an act of self-flagellation by a party which had already lost hope. For Löwenhielm was by this time undoubtedly a Cap; and the document he produced amounted to an indictment of his colleagues on the Council so comprehensive as to satisfy even their enemies.[14] The immediate question which confronted the Diet was therefore this: how was it possible that the state of affairs which the Proposition revealed could have come about? Of the excellence of the constitution it was almost blasphemy to entertain a doubt; the laws of Sweden were admitted to be good laws; and the received opinion was that good laws made good citizens and a contented people. Why, then, had Sweden's good laws produced such obviously disastrous effects?

The Diet of 1765–6 was dominated by the attempt to answer this question, and to expose and punish any who might be responsible for this subversion of the normal process of cause and effect. One of their first measures was to instruct the Secret Committee that henceforward 'all alterations in the budget, all decisions about the Bank's raising loans, or the payment of loans already incurred, and *all* other economic matters,

---

[14] RA Sekreta Propositionen, Inrikes, 1765.

are to be determined not otherwise than in the *plena*'.[15] The Estates were
no longer content to leave finance to the Secret Committee: they wanted
to know the facts for themselves, and they were determined that those
facts should be made public. The Secret Committee's effective control of
finance was ended at a stroke. The Bank Committee, appointed to look
into the affairs of the Estates' Bank, and into the actions of the Board of
Governors whom the Estates appointed, found in the course of their
investigations defalcations, embezzlements and malversations by the
Bank's personnel: some officials prudently decamped to Norway; some
were dismissed; and in May 1766 a thorough reform was completed by
the dismissal of the entire Board of Governors – a dismissal which
included some who were themselves Caps.[16] Having thus cleansed one
section of the financial Augean stables, they turned to what they supposed
to be another: the Iron Office. It was subjected to a very hostile
inquisition, and narrowly escaped abolition; but it had to suffer salutary
reforms, and was henceforth more stringently regulated:[17] the old days of
easy loans and long credit for friends would now, it was hoped, come to
an end.

These measures were of course an aspect of the Caps' diagnosis of the
root cause of the prevailing inflation. They had come to believe that it was
a consequence of the reckless issue of paper money, the laxness of the
Bank and the Iron Office in making loans, and (Nordencrantz would have
added) the unscrupulous manipulation of the exchanges by a small ring of
speculating financiers, all of them Hat. The Cap policy sought to correct
these evils in various ways: they decided to call in, within the next ten
years, a sizeable proportion of the paper money in circulation; they
increased the Bank's holdings of metallic currency by enacting that
henceforth all import duties be paid in silver; and they embarked upon a
heroic attempt to revalue the silver *daler*, which was first pegged at
seventy marks to the *riksdaler Hamburger banco*, and was subsequently to
appreciate by a fixed amount every year, until after eight years it had attained parity, at thirty-six. It was the failure of this last measure to work as
they hoped it would work that was the main cause of the collapse of the
Cap régime at the end of 1768.[18] Meanwhile these measures were to be
reinforced by rigid economy: Sweden was to be made to realise that a
country that is struggling to recover a healthy financial position must live
within its income. Their drastic reduction in expenditure on fortifications

---

[15] Brusewitz, *Frihetstidens Grundlagar*, pp. 268–70. The Hats found it expedient to give a
similar instruction in 1769.

[16] This was a violation of the privileges of the Nobility, for each Estate appointed its own
members to the Board, and it alone was entitled to dismiss them.

[17] Bertil Boëthius and Åke Kromnow, *Jernkontorets historia*, I (Stockholm 1947), pp. 588, 595,
600–1.

[18] See below, pp. 170–1.

in Finland was perhaps logical in the light of their belief in the possibility of good-neighbourly relations with Russia, though they were certainly influenced also by their dislike of that prominent Hat, Augustin Ehrensvärd, who was responsible for the great works at Sveaborg. It was reasonable also to dock the salaries of diplomats who contrived to spend much of their time at home. Their *Ordinance against Superfluous Luxuries* was the last, and certainly the most stringent, of a long series issued by successive governments, and represents a conscious reaction against that school of thought which was represented outside Sweden by Mandeville, Bayle, Montesquieu and Voltaire, and inside it by A. J. von Höpken's famous lecture (1740) 'On the usefulness of luxury'. The Caps now not only prohibited the importation of goods which they considered to be wasteful of the national resources, and prejudicial to the balance of trade; they went further, and interfered with the individual's liberty of choice by forbidding the *use* of a long list of commodities and by attempting to regulate dress. The use of all jams except those made from Swedish fruit was to be illegal; so too was the use of tobacco by anyone under the age of twenty-one (with an annual licence-fee from smokers of riper years); lace must not be deeper than one inch; silk and satin upholstery was forbidden; and the amount permitted to be expended on weddings, christenings and coffins was strictly limited. It was, indeed, not only an economic but a moral measure, an expression of a puritanical strain which was noticeable in the Caps; and though one of its objects was to prevent men from wasting money in aping their aristocratic betters, and so blurring the natural distinction between different orders of society, the fact that most of its provisions were relevant only to the nobility and the wealthy was also an expression of the growing antagonism between the middling and lower ranks of society and those above them – as for instance the prohibition of hairdressers, French governesses, running footmen, and the ownership of carriages by those under the age of twenty-one. As with previous ordinances of the same kind it proved unenforceable in practice, despite its promise of reward for delations; and the moral element in it was undeniably a little weakened when the rule against long trains to women's dresses had to be abandoned in the face of the urgent protests (delivered through the Speaker of the Peasants) of Stockholm's prostitutes.[19] The economies effected by all these measures (except in regard to defence) were insignificant, and in some cases – cuts in pensions, reduction of civil service salaries – revealed a persecuting and vengeful

[19] Nils Erdmann, *Carl Michael Bellman. En kultur- och karaktärsbild från 1700-talet* (Stockholm 1899), p. 337. For the hilarious debate in the House of Nobility on some of these prohibitions, see *SRARP*, xxv, pp. 82–99; and for the whole question Bo Peterson, '"Yppighets Nytta och Torftighets Fägnad". Pamflettsdebatten om 1766 års överflöds-ordning', *Historisk tidskrift* (1984).

temper which grew more pronounced the longer the Diet lasted. Nor was the situation much improved by the very moderate additional taxation to which the Estates – at the last minute – were persuaded to agree. And when, after the Anglo-Swedish treaty of 1766, Choiseul stopped the payment of arrears of subsidy which the Hat Council had accepted in the autumn of 1764, and when it gradually became clear that no compensating subsidy was to be expected from England, the budgetary prospects remained as bleak as ever.

Meanwhile the Estates gave their attention to other reforms. On 29 March 1765 the Secret Committee decided upon the appointment of a Grand Committee of 250 members, drawn from all four Estates, to consider three questions:[20] the accounts of the successive *consortia* to whom had been entrusted the operation of the Exchange Office; the freedom of the press; and the bad effect of Sweden's good laws. As to the Exchange Office, it was their belief that those who managed it – and particularly that *consortium* of which Gustaf Kierman had been the leading spirit – had in fact cheated the state of enormous sums. They had, no doubt, been given full discharge from responsibility by the Hat Council when they terminated their operations; but the instruction given to the Grand Committee ordered it to take no notice of that fact, since the discharge had never obtained the approval of the *plena*. Kierman was by now a highly unpopular figure. The Burghers disliked him because he had made his money by financial operations rather than by trade; the mob of Stockholm saw in him the personification of those greedy speculators who had thriven at their expense, and expressed their feelings by breaking his windows. He was taken into custody, and his assets sequestered pending the result of the Grand Committee's investigations. In reality, Kierman does not seem to have defrauded the state; but undeniably he had used his business ability to make very good bargains for himself and his colleagues: seven years later, responsible Cap leaders would frankly admit that this was the truth of the matter.[21] The Grand Committee had other views. Kierman was not given a fair trial; indeed, he was given no trial at all. The resolutions of the Grand Committee were not a judgment, they had not the force of law; but the Diet by accepting them gave them a simulacrum of legality. And they were savage: Kierman was condemned to live on bread and water for a month, to be imprisoned for life in the fortress of Marstrand (where he very soon died), and to repay to the state the impossible sum of six million silver *daler*. His colleagues in the *consortium* received lighter sentences, though they were still severe enough; and Claes Wittfoth, who had been the principal member of a later *consortium* (and the only one that the Grand Committee could get their

---

[20] Brusewitz, *Frihetstidens Grundlagar*, p. 286.
[21] *SRARP* XXXI, 191–204, 255–60, 263–82.

hands on) was given a sentence almost as severe as Kierman's.[22] The whole affair was a prime example of the intermixture of bad and good elements in the Cap régime: on the one hand the determination to root out corruption and abuses, and the full publicity given to all the proceedings; on the other, a rancorous partisan spirit and an indifference to legality which alienated the more moderate members of the party, and began a process which before the Diet ended would split it into bitterly recriminating factions.

Among the members of the former Hat Council who had been especially responsible for the arrangements with Kierman and Wittfoth were the Chancery-President, Claes Ekeblad, and C. F. Scheffer; and it was not surprising that they should be the next objects of attack. Indeed it was almost inevitable that the Caps should attempt to change a situation in which the Secret Committee was dominated by one party and the Council by another. The Hats had felt this in 1746, and as we have seen had taken steps of dubious propriety to ensure that the political views of the two bodies should be aligned. In 1765 this was the more necessary because the advent of the Caps meant a decisive reorientation of foreign policy – the substitution of an English for a French system – and it was impossible to go on for long with a Chancery-President who was 'French'. In this situation the Caps remembered – though indeed they had never forgotten – the events of 1739; and they determined on the *licentiering* of at least sufficient members of the Council to ensure that it fell under their own control. No doubt it was with malicious satisfaction that they followed the precedent to the letter.[23] After the normal scrutiny of the minutes of the Council since the end of the last Diet, the Secret Committee was ready with its recommendations. Ekeblad and Scheffer, terrified at the prospect of interrogation by the Committee, had already resigned; but the Committee resolved that four other members of the Council had merited dismissal (mainly on the ground of their acceptance of the French proposal about the arrears of subsidy, in the autumn of 1764), and that the case of three others be referred to the Estates for their consideration. But in regard to the four the Secret Committee pronounced what was in fact a verdict and a sentence; for since the matter concerned foreign policy it was contended – as in 1739 – that no debate in the *plena* was permissible. On this point there were long and bitter debates in August 1765; but in the end the three lower Estates followed the precedent of 1739, and the four members would certainly have suffered

---

[22] For the Kierman affair, Roberts, *British Diplomacy and Swedish Politics*, pp. 151–2. For the differing views about the causes of the inflation, Robert V. Eagly, 'Monetary Policy and Politics in Mid-eighteenth Century Sweden', *Journal of Economic History*, XXIX (1969), pp. 751–4; Boëthius and Kromnow, *Jernkontorets historia*, I, pp. 505–8.

[23] For the *licentieringar* of 1765–66, see Linnarsson, *Riksrådens licentiering*, pp. 187, 209–10, 220, 233, 262–5.

licentiering, had they not at the last minute submitted their resignations, and so avoided what otherwise would have been penal measures. The three for the moment escaped with censure; but in the following year an opportunity was taken to carry the *licentiering* of one of them. And so was established a precedent which would be followed in 1769 and 1772: henceforward a party's victory at the polls would be followed, almost as a matter of course, by *licentieringar* which would bring the Council into political harmony with the victors.

There had been some question, when the investigation into the affairs of the Exchange Office came under consideration, of recurring to the Hats' favourite device of a commission, despite the fact that for nearly thirty years the Caps had denounced all extraordinary tribunals and insisted on the law of the land. Rudbeck, as Marshal, did in fact exert his influence to quash the idea, and protested that he would resign his office rather than agree to any such proposal. But the trivial revolt in Västergötland in May 1766, and the ludicrous panic which it produced in Stockholm, proved sufficient to remove such scruples.[24] The three lower Estates demanded the appointment not of one commission but two: one to sit at Borås to conduct investigations on the spot, and the other to sit in Stockholm to investigate how far the events in Västergötland were 'connected' (ominous word) with sinister forces in the capital. And Rudbeck, despite his solemn protestation, supported the proposal. The Hats assumed with relish the role of Satan rebuking sin, and their opposition was so far successful that a compromise was reached by which it was agreed that the investigations of the commissions should be restricted to the events of the rising, and that matters conceivably 'connected' with it should be excluded. The most telling denunciation of the cynicism thus displayed by both parties came from the Cap side, by the mouth of that erratic and sardonic individual Baron Josias Cederhielm;[25] and it was answered, as we have seen,[26] by his expulsion from the House of Nobility for life.

Yet though a majority of the Caps might thus apparently abjure one of the great principles which had held them together in opposition, they handsomely fulfilled some of the expectations which had induced the electorate to put them into power. This was truly a reforming Diet; not merely in virtue of its correction of old and new abuses, but by its progressive measures. No Diet during the Age of Liberty could show a record of legislation as rich and as beneficial as this. Their reforms were both administrative and social. They swept away some of the Diet's superfluous standing committees; they rationalised and simplified

[24] For the background to the rebellion, see Malmström, *Sveriges politiska historia*, v, pp. 364–5.
[25] For Cederhielm's speech, *SRARP*, xxv, 394–8.
[26] See above, p. 99.

administrative machinery. The Manufactures Office was absorbed into the College of Commerce – though, with that ruthlessness which was typical of them, its staff after having its wages reduced by a third was ultimately dismissed without compensation. The management of the national debt was simplified by incorporating the old office which had been responsible for dealing with the debts left behind by Charles XII into a new institution, the National Debt Office. And they put an end to various funds which had from time to time been established for specific purposes: henceforward there was to be a Consolidated Fund into which all revenues were to be paid.

Their social and economic legislation was a clear reflection of a new state of affairs; for it was the response to demands which emanated from below. Progress towards real municipal self-government was made by the revocation of the circular of 1752, which had prohibited meetings in towns without the sanction of the magistracy. The interests of the provincial towns in the northern provinces were served by the abolition of the requirement that their exports must go through Stockholm: the special privileges of the staple towns, which had stood for a century and a half, now came to an end.[27] Equally significant were two other reforms: one was the Statute which permitted peasants to send their produce in their own schooners to whatever market they preferred; the other was the Fisheries Statute of 1766, which gave a greater liberty of fishing to outports and riparian dwellers than they had ever enjoyed before.[28] Until 1763 peasants who were tenants of the Crown had enjoyed a monopoly of the right to purchase the farms they rented (the so-called *skatteköp*); but the Hat Council had then revoked that right, on the ground that it prejudiced the Crown's interests since peasants could buy at as little as six years' purchase; but really because it prevented speculating ironmasters from acquiring Crown land by bidding for it at prices the peasants could not afford to pay. The Estate of Peasants had bitterly resented the change; and the Caps lost little time in restoring *skatteköp* as it had existed before 1763. In general, the Caps were as convinced mercantilists as were most of their opponents: they had no intention of dismantling protective tariffs, and they favoured premiums on exports. But they were not prepared to suffer that the benefits and inducements of the Hats' industrial policies should be restricted to a narrow ring of wealthy capitalists and political friends, to the exclusion of almost all others. In this, as in so much else, they were the party of the little man. And it was in line with this approach that cottage industry (*hemslöjd*) which the Hats had

[27] Gunnar Sundberg, *Partipolitik och regionala intressen 1755–1766. Studier kring det bottniska handelstvångets hävande* (Uppsala 1978).

[28] Sigbrit Plaenge Jacobson, *1766 års allmänna fiskestadga. Dess uppkomst och innebörd med hänsyn till Bottenhavsfiskets rättsfrågor* (Uppsala 1978).

discouraged as competing with their favoured 'factories', was now legitimised, in that the textiles it produced might now be sent to the Cloth Halls for inspection and approval on the same footing as the others. Hitherto, the supply of cloth to the army had been confined to certain privileged manufacturers, from one of whom every regiment was forced to order its requirements: henceforward they would be free to buy where they would. The Hats' legislation of 1748, which in effect restricted to wealthy entrepreneurs the right to set up new 'factories' (with the privileges attaching to them) was likewise rescinded, and the way opened to the establishment of businesses by lesser masters. And the exemption of 'factory'-owners from taxes, and from municipal rates (this last a source of bitter complaint, especially from the burghers of Stockholm) was abolished also.[29] Most important of all, the Diet swept away the ban upon the free movement of labour from one province to another: a ban which had driven many of those who could not find work in their own province to seek it in Norway or Denmark, to the prejudice of the principle that the wealth of a state consists in an abundant population.[30]

Lastly, the Caps in 1766 carried their *Ordinance for the Liberty of Printing*.[31] It was, no doubt, a measure which had support in both parties; the way for it had been prepared for some time, as we have seen, by the laxness of the censorship; but still it was one of the great legislative achievements of the Age of Liberty. It abolished preliminary censorship altogether except for religious books, which were still to be subject to ecclesiastical approval; and it laid down the same principles as had obtained in England since the lapsing of the Licensing Act. In many respects the transformation which it effected was truly remarkable: the debates of the Estates, the deliberations of committees, the judgments of the courts, the proceedings of government offices, and even (with certain exceptions) the discussions in the Council of State – not excluding the king's *dictamina* – might now be published, and any member of the public might require copies to be provided for him. Among other benefits, the *Ordinance* was something of a historians' charter: it opened the archives to researchers, and explicitly encouraged historians to use them. The effects of this emancipation became very evident at the election of 1769: a really lively newspaper press sprang into life, political pamphlets abounded, and Esbjörn Reuterholm's *Uplysning för det svenska folket* (*Information for*

---

[29] For all these reforms, see Per Nyström, *Stadsindustriens arbetare före 1800-talet* (Stockholm 1955), pp. 201, 211, 247–9.

[30] For the significance of these reforms, see Sten Carlsson, 'Sverige under 1760-talet', in *Från fattigdom till överflöd*, ed. Steven Koblik (Stockholm 1973).

[31] Brusewitz, *Frihetstidens Grundlagar*, pp. 541–2; and for the party background Olle Stridsberg, 'Hattarnas och mössornas ställningstaganden till tryckfrihetsfrågan på riksdagarna 1760–2 och 1765–66', *Historisk tidskrift*, 1953. For liberty of the press in general, Hilding Eek, *Om tryckfriheten* (Uppsala 1942).

the Swedish people) is said to have sold the then extraordinary number of four thousand copies.[32]

(iii)

When Lovisa Ulrika's Composition was shattered by Adolf Frederick's vote against the French offer of arrears of subsidy, the breach with the Hats which was its consequence left her – for the moment – with no alternative but to throw in her lot with the Caps; and since the Court could reckon as many as seventy adherents in the House of Nobility, the Cap leaders found it expedient to conclude a bargain. A statement of objectives to which both parties subscribed has survived in versions which differ significantly from one another;[33] but they have in common an imprecise programme of moderate reform designed to put some check on the Diet's usurpation of executive powers, and (so the Court hoped, at least) to restore to the monarchy some of the prerogatives which it had lost since 1720, and especially in 1756. It seems probable that Rudbeck – who after all had been close to the Court in 1756 – was ready to contemplate limited alterations in the constitution, and this may be true also of other Cap leaders who were concerned in the compact. But the event would show that the mass of the party, who had no knowledge of the agreement, were of a very different mind. Their interest was in financial and social reform, the exposure of the Exchange Office, and the castigation of their predecessors; and they had no idea of changes which might infringe the virtual sovereignty which the electorate had now conferred upon them. The Grand Committee was indeed charged with the task of investigating why the country's good laws had had such ill consequences, but it soon became apparent that they were in no hurry to enquire whether the constitution itself was the real culprit. This became apparent to Lovisa Ulrika very soon; and when the Committee postponed consideration of the question to measures of party persecution – in violation, as she complained, of the letter and spirit of the Composition – she renewed negotiations with the Hats. In June 1765 she made it known that she would have her own party in the Diet, led by F. C. Sinclair: ostensibly it would be neutral but in fact it would collaborate with Fersen.[34] There was indeed a moment, in July, when it seemed possible that Rudbeck might direct the Grand Committee's attention to

---

[32] Henrik Schück and Karl Warburg, *Illustrerad svensk litteraturhistoria*, II (Stockholm 1897), p. 193.

[33] For a close analysis of the various versions, and their provenance, see Metcalf, *Russia, England and Swedish Party Politics*, pp. 108–9, 150–2, supplementing Brolin, *Hattar och mössor*, pp. 335–7.

[34] Jägerskiöld, *Hovet och författningsfrågan*, pp. 293–5; Metcalf, *Russia, England and Swedish Party Politics*, pp. 145–7; Roberts, *British Diplomacy and Swedish Politics*, pp. 162–4.

the amending of the constitution;[35] but the bitter struggles over *licentiering* ensured that the moment passed without result. It was not until the summer of 1766 that the issue was raised again. That it was raised at all was largely owing to the determination of Russia and Denmark to take advantage of a friendly Diet to press for constitutional changes suitable to their own ideas of what a Swedish constitution should be.[36] The result of their discussions with the Cap leaders was the *Ordinance for the Better Execution of the Laws*: the last major legislative achievement of the Cap Diet. Despite Russian and Danish pressure, this was not a statute prescribed by the Caps' paymasters: except for a few points it was the Caps' own answer to the question which they had put to themselves when the Diet began, and to which the Grand Committee now belatedly replied.[37]

It was, in fact, the expression of one of the strongest feelings of the mass of the party: their anger at the negligence, inefficiency and petty oppressions of office-holders, to which so many of them had been subjected. Almost the whole of the *Ordinance* was concerned with such matters: in the minds of the three lower Estates the basic reason why good laws had such ill effects lay in the fact that officials did not apply the law, or misinterpreted it, or were not properly qualified to administer it. This was true even of the Estate of Clergy, which took advantage of the opportunity to insert clauses requiring strict observance of religious duties by all officials. As the future was to show, the *Ordinance* did not – perhaps could not – provide an effective remedy; and distrust of officialdom therefore remained a main preoccupation of the party until the Age of Liberty came to an end. Officialdom, they felt, was a new and sinister 'aristocracy'; and one expression of that feeling was the inclusion of a clause abolishing that Table of Ranks which had first been established in the time of Charles XI.[38] But as for any change in the constitution along the lines which Lovisa Ulrika desired, there was none: indeed, the changes, such as they were, were all the other way. Though most of the *Memorandum on the Services* of 1756 was now repealed, the Estates took care to keep in their hands the nomination of the Governor of Stockholm, and of the three most important military commands: control of the capital had been of crucial importance in 1756, and they were determined to retain it. The *Ordinance* stripped the king of his right to appoint the Chancellor of Justice. The Chancellor of Justice was a kind of cross between an Attorney-General and an ombudsman; in the latter capacity he offered at any rate some protection against official malpractices, and to

---

[35] Roberts, *British Diplomacy and Swedish Politics*, p. 165.
[36] Metcalf, *Russia, England and Swedish Party Politics*, pp. 181, 192–5.
[37] Text in Brusewitz, *Frihetstidens Grundlagar*, pp. 213–24.
[38] With the exception of service about the Court.

the lower Estates it was important that he should be chosen by themselves: henceforth he was to be nominated afresh by each succeeding Diet. An extension of existing regulations deprived the king of the ability to block the entry into the Council of a man whom he disliked: by persistent nomination, four times repeated, the Estates might now force into the Council a candidate of their own choice, let the king's feelings be what they might.

One provision of the *Ordinance*, and one only, seemed to set limits to the reinforcement of the legislature at the expense of the executive. This was the provision which purported to restrain the right of the Diet to 'interpret and improve' the constitution. It enacted that all such proposals must be submitted to two successive Diets, with a general election in between, and must finally receive the unanimous consent of all four Estates. It was an idea which Panin had put forward as early as December 1764,[39] and it reflected the anxiety of Catherine II to establish a constitutional situation which should be immune to casual alterations by a party which might be French in sympathy and willing to cooperate with the Court. But though the idea might be Russian in origin, it was very much in line with Cap principles. Any possible amendment or improvement would depend wholly on the Estates; neither the king nor the Council would have any say in the matter. It was in line with another strain in their thinking also; for the provision requiring a general election before the Diet could take a decision, reinforced by the new freedom of the press, implied a further step towards the acknowledgment of a representative's responsibility to his constituents: Panin recognised this when he wrote that after the election 'the nation' would be able 'to give strict instructions' to accept or reject what was proposed.[40] But if he – or the Caps – believed that this quasi-referendum would bind a Diet in which their opponents had a majority, or that the *Ordinance* had entrenched the doctrine of the imperative mandate in the constitution, both he and they would find themselves mistaken.

On 15 October 1766 the Cap Diet – the longest of all Diets during the Age of Liberty – at last came to an end, to the great relief of all the foreign powers who had lavished money on it, and to the equally great relief of the Cap leaders. For indeed it was high time. Rudbeck had proved but an indifferent Marshal of the Diet. He had the distinction – rare among the politicians of the age – of being absolutely incorruptible; he had considerable insight into financial questions; he was essentially a

---

[39] Metcalf, *Russia, England and Swedish Party Politics*, p. 193. Panin for a time abandoned the idea in favour of a requirement that all changes in the constitution should require the unanimous consent of king, Council and Estates; but the Caps would not accept a provision that would have given the executive a share in legislation, and in the end Panin reverted to his original suggestion: Metcalf, pp. 181, 194, 200.

[40] *Ibid.*, p. 201.

moderate. It was his misfortune that he had to try to hold together a party which almost from the beginning of the Diet was divided, and which in the end came near to tearing itself asunder; and he lacked the commanding authority which Fersen enjoyed among the Hats. Factions within the leadership, factions within the Estates, bitter quarrels between the Nobility and the Clergy on points of privilege, irreconcilable differences between moderates with some grasp of reality and extremists rampant under the influence of party animosity: all this produced a chaos which Rudbeck proved wholly unable to control.[41] To call the extremists 'radicals' can be misleading: on essential constitutional issues they were rigidly conservative, determined to maintain unimpaired – indeed, to extend – the authority of the Estates; in a better balance of the constitution they had no interest at all. But they can perhaps be called radical in another sense – that is, in their strident hostility to many features of the established social order: to aristocracy of birth, to the authority of bishops, to control of municipalities by magistrates, to restrictions upon the mobility of labour, to privileges of staple towns, fishing privileges, and limitations upon marketing. Already by 1766 we can see the emergence of some of the forces which would dominate the political scene after 1770.

(iv)

The Cap Council had now no easy task on its hands. It was highly desirable that they should be able before the next election to exhibit something to offset the loss of the French subsidies – and that meant, in effect, that they should somehow persuade the British government to come forward with subsidies in return for an alliance. Even more important, they had to make their plan for a revaluation work. In neither respects were they successful. All British administrations now subscribed to the doctrine of 'no subsidies in peacetime', and no arguments by Sir John Goodricke could move them from that position – not even the argument that the price was worth paying since a Swedish alliance was the surest, perhaps the only, road to that alliance with Russia which was now the prime objective of British foreign policy.[42]

As to revaluation, the Caps' calculation had been that it would be possible to carry through a gradual, and therefore painless, deflation. Their economic expert Chydenius had already denounced the idea as chimerical, and had been summarily expelled from the Estate of Clergy for doing so.[43] He turned out to be right as to the result, whatever the

---

[41] For a vivid picture, by a disillusioned and disgusted Cap, of the near-anarchy within the party, see Tilas, *Anteckningaroch brev från riksdagen 1765–1766*, *passim*.

[42] Roberts, *British Diplomacy and Swedish Politics*, pp. 233–50.

[43] Georg Schaumann, *Biografiska Anteckningar om Anders Chydenius* (Skrifter utgifna af

merits of his arguments. For the strategy, to be successful, must be kept secret; and secrecy proved impossible. As the prospect of a progressively appreciating *daler* became known, men began to hoard their money against the day when it would be worth more. Moreover, the *daler* appreciated at a rate which had never been intended, and could not be controlled. In July 1767 the Council, in desperation, tried to overtrump the speculators by pegging the rate at forty-two marks; a measure which proved disastrous. Most serious were the effects upon the all-important iron industry. Contracts between iron producers and British importers were made in sterling, and the appreciation of the *daler* against the pound soon produced a situation in which the ironmasters were getting for their product a price that scarcely covered the cost of production. Iron exports dropped dramatically; there was something like a strike of buyers, and an acute shortage of cash. The copper industry suffered equally badly: shortage of circulating medium meant that the Copper Office could not pay for the raw copper that was brought to the official weighbridges; its domestic price slumped; by January 1768 104 copper workshops were out of production. The general public was hard hit likewise, for those who had borrowed heavily during the inflation could not now pay their debts. Between 1766 and 1768 bankruptcies reached a peak for the century: prominent Hats and Caps failed for large sums; all the de la Gardies were said to be ruined; and even a wealthy man such as Fersen was driven to borrow 150 000 silver *daler* from the French ambassador to keep himself afloat.[44] By the autumn of 1768 it did indeed seem that the tide had begun to turn: exports of iron showed a marked improvement, for the price of iron in Great Britain, and the demand for it, were both rising. But the upturn came too late to save the Caps and their policies.[45] The Hats naturally made political capital of the widespread suffering and discontent: they began to win municipal elections; and by mid-1767 the Caps were losing control of the towns which had gone over to them in 1764.

In these circumstances it was natural that there should be a demand from the opponents of the government for the summoning of an Extraordinary Diet to deal with the economic crisis. For the Hats, an Extraordinary Diet offered a good prospect of ousting their adversaries; for the Court, the hope of using the discontent in the country to resume the attempt to secure constitutional reform under better auspices than at any time since 1764. Adolf Frederick delivered successive *dictamina* to the

Svenska Litteratursällskapet i Finland, 34) (Helsingfors 1908), pp. 227–8. There was talk of having him tried by a commission, or of sending him to a madhouse.

[44] Roberts, *British Diplomacy and Swedish Politics*, pp. 250–7, and references there cited.

[45] Recovery was helped by the fact that for three years from 1767 Sweden had unusually good harvests: Samuelsson considered that the Caps were in fact right thinking that by the autumn of 1768 the worst was over: Kurt Samuelsson, *Från stormakt till välfärdsstat* (Stockholm 1969), p. 120.

Council, demanding that it be summoned; Prince Gustav toured the mining areas to rally popular sympathy and to collect evidence of their distress. In vain: the Cap Council gritted its teeth and stuck grimly to its policies. In the face of their obduracy Hats and Court began to negotiate for common action; and at last, after many drafts and much discussion, they reached an agreement which settled the tactics to be pursued, and went much further in promises of concession to the Court than the Hat leaders had ever hitherto been ready to contemplate. For them, indeed, it represented a capitulation: a capitulation under duress.[46]

What ultimately drove them to it was the attack of the Cap Council upon the central bureaucracy. The officials of the *Collegia*, irremovable except upon legal conviction, were still predominantly Hats, survivors from the era of the Hat ascendancy. They executed the Caps' decisions reluctantly; they subjected them to acrid criticism. The Exchequer and the College of Mines, in particular, made devastating comments on the economic situation and the Cap policies which (they said) had produced it; and these comments they took care to disseminate. Already in April 1768 the Council had been goaded into addressing to the Exchequer a thundering rebuke which charged its members collectively with mendacity, partiality, and 'a presumptuous and indecent departure from the respectful submission which is at all times due to us as your superiors'. The only notice which the bureaucrats took of this *mercuriale* was to repeat their offence in aggravated form. On 8 December 1768, therefore, the Council took the extreme step of resolving to prosecute the Exchequer College before a specially constituted (and hand-picked) court: a court which would in fact be one of those extraordinary tribunals which they had so loudly denounced in the past.[47] To the Hats it seemed that a political witch-hunt was imminent. In defence of their household troops they had no option but to stand and fight: hence the constitutional capitulation implicit in their bargain with the Court. But it was a bargain on which they would certainly renege if they came into power again.

On 12 December, accordingly, Adolf Frederick presented the Council with an ultimatum: either they must forthwith agree to an Extraordinary Diet, or he would cease to exercise his royal functions until such time as they might do so. In the meantime he formally forbade the use of his name in official business, and he gave them three days to make up their minds.

[46] Hennings, *Gustav III som kronprins* (Stockholm 1935), pp. 324, 331–2, 334–5, 342; Jonas Nordensson, 'Kronprins Gustavs författningsprojekt 1768', *Statsvetenskapliga studier till statsvetenskapliga föreningens i Uppsala tjugofemårsdag* (Uppsala 1944), pp. 493–7; Roberts, *British Diplomacy and Swedish Politics*, pp. 258–62, 267–8. For royalist plans in 1768 see below, pp. 183–4.
[47] Roberts, *British Diplomacy and Swedish Politics*, pp. 269–71. They had very nearly fallen into this trap in 1765, when some of the more extreme Caps wished to indict the members of the Chancery College for their share in advising the acceptance of the French offer of arrears in 1764: Malmström, *Sveriges politiska historia*, v, p. 346; Roberts, p. 196.

The Council was taken completely by surprise. There had been moments in the last two years when it had seemed to them that Adolf Frederick might be considering abdication – a prospect which they viewed with alarm: better a dove than a hawk. But this was not abdication: the king was king still, giving orders and expecting them to be obeyed, but ceasing altogether to participate in the ordinary business of government. The word for the situation was not 'abdication', but 'Inactivity'. For a week the Council struggled with the problem. Some of them were for calling Adolf Frederick's bluff and ruling until the next meeting of the Diet by the use of the name-stamp. But the crown prince had at once gone the rounds of the central government offices, and to them had conveyed the king's orders that they take no action without his express command. All now depended upon the attitude of the bureaucracy – that bureaucracy whose perquisites the Caps had cut off, whom their economic policies had driven to the verge of bankruptcy, and who were now threatened with quasi-judicial proscription. Their opportunity for revenge had now arrived. The Exchequer, the War Office, the Audit Office, the College of Mines, the College of Commerce, the Chancery, and even the Supreme Court one after the other declared that they refused to recognise the Council's authority to issue orders. The final blow came from the Estimates Office, which declined to pay the troops whom the Council had ordered up to the capital. It was, in fact, a general strike of the civil service, such as Sweden would not see again for two centuries. After a week of vacillation the government was forced to surrender: they agreed to summon an Extraordinary Diet; and Adolf Frederick blandly resumed his regal functions. The 'Inactivity' was at an end.[48]

At an end too, for all practical purposes, was the rule of the Caps. As in 1764 the Hats had been swept aside by a tide of popular resentment, so in the election of 1769 the Caps fell victims to the widespread suffering which their economic policies had entailed. The Diet which met – first at Norrköping,[49] and very soon in Stockholm – gave the Hats their last taste of the sweets of office. But their victory could not stifle shifts of thought, political and social, which had begun to find expression in the Diet of 1765-6, and which were to be central to the complex crisis which was to dominate politics until some at least of the issues were resolved by the revolution of 19 August 1772.

<hr/>

[48] Malmström, *Sveriges politiska historia*, VI, pp. 60–80; for a contemporary account by a minor civil servant, J. G. Oxenstierna, *Ljuva ungdomstid*, pp. 172–3; for the Cap interpretation of what happened, [Esbjörn Christian Reuterholm], *Uplysning för svenska folket* (Stockholm 1769), pp. 35–40.

[49] The Caps in 1766 had decided on Norrköping in the delusive hope that a meeting away from Stockholm would relieve them of the presence of Hat bureaucrats whose duties (presumably) would keep them in the capital.

(v)

The years after 1765 saw the party system more firmly entrenched than ever before. Even in the 1740s there had been many who had felt uncomfortable with it, as a deplorable and unnecessary innovation which had never been contemplated by the constitution, and was in some sort a reflection upon it. Moderate men, forced to accept party as a fact, were repelled by the violence of party feeling, and refused to impute evil motives on the basis of a mere difference of opinion.[50] As late as 1765 Dean Forssenius informed his colleages in the Estate of Clergy that 'St Paul accounts Party as among the works of the flesh'.[51] But by the late sixties party had become not merely respectable, but a very necessary element in the polity. In 1766 that moderate and sensible Cap, Claes Frietzcky, denounced any posture of neutrality as a dereliction of the duties of a good citizen, and presumptive evidence of sinister intentions;[52] and four years later he justified party manoeuvres on the ground that since bad men use bad means, a useful association must be allowed to use them too, at any rate against any threat from the Crown.[53] The parallel with Burke is obvious. And Jakob Wallenberg, in the account of his voyage to the East Indies, went out of his way; to insert the oft-quoted lines:

> Once Romans ceased to wrangle, they saw their power declining;
> And England rules the world, 'mid parliamentary strife.
> Party, indeed, is Freedom's life.[54]

It was ironic that it was just at this moment that party began to be supplanted as the central concern of politics, and that in so far as it

[50] See, e.g. Lagerberg s powertui *votum* in the Springer case, 19 Nov. 1747: Malmström, *Sveriges politiska historia*, III, pp. 492–3; or Gustav Bonde's memorial of 1744: Remgård, *Carl Gustaf Tessin*, pp. 29n., 112; or Fersen himself in November 1761: Malmström, *Sveriges politiska historia*, V, p. 113.
[51] Bexell, *Riksdags-historiska anteckningar*, p. 66.
[52] *SRARP* XXV, Appendix pp. 159–60: this was Frietzcky's counterblast to Cederhielm's attack on the cynicism of both parties. Isak Faggott likewise believed that parties must inevitably exist, and that the only problem about them was which to choose: Faggott, p. 188.
[53] Quoted in Anders Werner, *Studier till frågan om europeiska idéer i svensk politik under den senare frihetstiden* (licentiat dissertation, Stockholm 1969), p. 51.
[54] Jakob Wallenberg, *Min son på galejan* (new edn. Stockholm 1928) p. 18.
> När Rom ej trätte mer, begynte det att falla;
> Och England når sin höjd mitt under split och kiv.
> Parti är fria staters liv.
Ingemar Carlsson, however, considers that Wallenberg is rather an exception to, than typical of, the general opinion: Carlsson, *Parti – partiväsen – partipolitiker*, p. 67. Michael Metcalf's exhaustive analysis of over 750 (mostly anonymous) publications between 1755 and 1772, which reached me only when this book was in press, suggests that Ingemar Carlsson may well have been right: Michael Metcalf, 'Unmitigated Evil, Necessary Evil in Free States, or Constructive Force? Swedish Attitudes towards Party, 1755–1772', *Consortium on Revolutionary Europe: Proceedings 1982* (Athens, Georgia, 1983).

continued to be relevant it contributed to the extinction of that Liberty of which it was now taken to be a constituent part.

Certainly the Hat Diet of 1769–70 gives an impression that an age is approaching its end. There is a depressing feeling of *déjà vu*. With unexampled expedition ten Caps were evicted from the Council. Pechlin, back again from the parliamentary exile imposed on him in 1761, once again betrayed his party; this time in return for massive financial support from England and Russia, which enabled him to ensure (among other things) that the Hats' financial proposals were irretrievably wrecked. The bargain with the Court which the Hats had made before the election hung like a dead weight about their necks. Fruitless proposals for a Composition were indicative of Fersen's desire somehow to escape from his commitments. Choiseul would pay no subsidies until he had got his revolution; Fersen had no intention of giving it to him. The party's only concession to the Court was the setting up of another Grand Committee on the model of 1765, this time the so-called United Deputations; and Fersen cozened Gustav into believing that real benefits to the Crown would emerge from its deliberations. It is more than doubtful whether he intended anything of the sort. The report of the United Deputations, in the form in which it reached the Diet (though not, apparently, in the form it was originally drafted) was a bitter disappointment. It was the basis of a proposed *Act of Security*, which embodied reforms of real importance;[55] but for the Court it did nothing. Or for the nation either; for it failed to secure the assent of the Estates. When the Diet ended in January 1770 it left behind it not only a record of unrelieved sterility,[56] but also a profound disillusionment which would soon conduce to its destruction. The unexpected death of Adolf Frederick, a year later, entailed another general election; and at this time the Hats lost it. And they lost it because the Caps now seemed, to the electorate of the three lower Estates, more accessible to new currents of thought, new social considerations, new aspirations, than their rivals. Throughout the Cap Diet of 1771–2 party warfare continued in the Estates with unabated virulence, and by 1772 the Caps had effected the *licentiering* of most of the Hat Council; but these things had become of subordinate importance, or at least only aspects of much more significant controversies. From 1770 onwards the real issues before the country were not Hat *versus* Cap, but constitutional intransigence *versus* constitutional reform, vested interests and privilege *versus* equality of opportunity; in the final analysis, the sovereignty of the Estates *versus* constitutional monarchy.

[55] For the provisions of the *Act of Security*, and its significance, see above, pp. 107–8.
[56] Unless, that is, we are prepared to account it as a merit that they ennobled Kierman's family as a reward for his services, provided Wittfoth with money to set him up in business again, and cancelled his indebtedness to the state.

V

The end of an age

In 1770 Sweden entered upon a period of crisis: a crisis which was not resolved until Gustav III's *coup d'état* of 19 August 1772. That event represented, in one aspect, the triumph of a royalist tradition whose origins reached back to the sixteenth century. But it represented also a success for those who from the 1740's onwards had seen the need for constitutional reform. And lastly it involved the abrupt termination of a movement by the non-noble Estates for self-determination, equality, and the curtailment or abolition of the privileges of the nobility: a movement which had first been apparent in 1650, again in 1723, which had been gathering strength since 1765, and which in 1772 seemed on the point of attaining its objectives. In 1772 there was not one revolution but two – a political revolution which succeeded; and a social revolution which was (temporarily) aborted, but of which also Gustav III would make himself the patron and beneficiary in 1789.

(i)

In the half-century between 1720 and 1770 royalism might at times seem dormant; and when it was active its objectives might have a narrower or more extended scope; but it was always there. For it was in fact implicit in the Constitution of 1720: one does not build defences against non-existent dangers; and no eighteenth-century monarch – save perhaps a King of Poland – was likely to be content to live under the restraints which the constitution imposed upon him.

Frederick I, translated from a successful military career in which he had especially distinguished himself at Blenheim and Malplaquet, could certainly not be expected to take kindly to the insignificance which was the destiny of a King of Sweden. He lost little time in trying to improve his position. At the Diet of 1723 his agents incited the Estate of Peasants – resentful of a new order which conferred fresh privileges upon every Estate but their own, and always mindful of the fact that it had been the

Crown which in the past had been their best protector against aristocratic exploitation – to put forward the demand that the king, though he should not be absolute, should have the powers enjoyed by earlier monarchs 'according to the ancient laws of Sweden'. It was the first expression of an idea which was to find advocates later on, when men began to talk of a return to the constitutional arrangements as they had stood in the time of Gustav Adolf; but in 1723, with the ink scarcely dry on the new constitution, it came far too early. The Peasants were sternly rebuked and quickly silenced.[1] And Frederick, realising that his gambit had failed, prudently dissociated himself from it, and never attempted anything of the sort again. He found a measure of consolation in hunting bears (of which he slew a prodigious number) and chasing pretty girls (of whom he seduced a few), and settled down to enjoy himself as best he might. His influence on appointments was not negligible, and often not salutary, and to some extent he suffered himself to take sides in the struggles for power between Horn and his opponents; but he liked his comfort and his mistress too well to venture again upon serious political enterprises. When in 1743 the latent royalism of the peasants manifested itself in the revolt in Dalarna, it was not of Frederick that the rebels were thinking – indeed, he showed characteristic courage in personally confronting them – but of the rival candidates for the succession. On occasion he came near to involving himself in constitutional difficulties in consequence of his succeeding his father as Landgrave of Hesse-Cassel (1730), and even before then the existence of a Hessian chancery in Stockholm, which meddled in politics much as the Hanoverians did in the time of George I, could have embarrassing consequences. Frederick left the conduct of Hessian affairs to his brother William – taking care, however, to retain a substantial slice of the Hessian revenues for himself; but this arrangement, in other respects highly satisfactory, was disturbed by the fact that William consistently pursued an anglophile foreign policy which conflicted sharply with the French alignment of the Hats. Yet though there were one or two awkward moments, Frederick as king followed the policy of his advisers, though as Landgrave he made no great efforts to deflect his brother from the course he preferred; and the contradiction did not seriously compromise his position in Stockholm: no Swedish Pitt found it necessary to allude to a 'despicable Landgraviate'.[2]

Adolf Frederick's private diversions were of a more domestic and respectable sort than those of Frederick I, and his previous career had not equipped him to bore his companions with old stories of Marlborough

[1] Walfrid Holst, *Fredrik I* (Stockholm 1953), pp. 149–50; and see Birger Sallnäs, 'En kraftmätning mellan konung och råd 1723. Ett bidrag till Fredrik I:s karakteristik', *Historisk tidskrift* 1950.
[2] Holst, *Fredrik I*, pp. 171–85, 204.

and Eugene; but, as with Frederick, he would have been a success as a private gentleman if Destiny had not cast him for the part of a *roi fainéant*, and on occasion he bitterly complained of the need to be involved in politics.[3] But he could not escape it; for Destiny had also provided him, in Lovisa Ulrika, with a wife of masterful temper, an unflagging interest in politics, and abilities greatly superior to his own. Lovisa Ulrika was indeed a remarkable woman: ambitious, fiercely proud of her Hohenzollern birth, devious, incorrigibly intriguing, a bad judge of what was practicable, prone to mistakes arising from wishful thinking; but steel-hard, courageous, a dangerous partisan.[4] In private life she was a lover and connoisseur of literature and the arts such as no Swedish sovereign had been since Christina. She had an insatiable intellectual curiosity which extended to astronomy, mathematics, the sciences and the applied sciences; and even if the range of her interests meant that in regard to many topics her knowledge was superficial – a fact which she disguised by her contempt for what she termed pedantry – her charm, her brilliance, and her enthusiasm made her Court a magnet for all that was most distinguished in the arts and sciences: Tessin, Dalin, Linnaeus, Klingenstierna, all enjoyed her patronage and her friendship; the first Swedish Academy of Letters was her creation; the first good theatre company, the first Italian opera company, were her importations, and (unlike the importations of Christina) they took root. She was in her own person a link with all that was new and best in the intellectual life of Europe, and especially of France; and whatever may be said of her politics, she deserved well of the Swedish people.[5]

But she also brought from Berlin not only the cultural interests of the court of Frederick the Great, but also his constitutional principles; and she had no sooner familiarised herself with Swedish politics than she decided that what the country needed was an enlightened despotism on the Prussian model. With her begins a continuous history of royalism. Already in 1747 she was stirring up trouble in the Estate of Peasants.[6] In

---

[3] See the report of his pathetic conversation with Gustaf Rålamb on 7–8 June 1765, in Sigrid Leijonhufvud, *Ur svenska herrgårdsarkiv. Bilder från karolinska tiden och frihetstiden* (Stockholm 1902), pp. 224–7. He is said to have possessed the enviable quality of looking gracious even when viewed from behind.

[4] There is an excellent, if possibly unduly sympathetic, biography of her: Olof Jägerskiöld, *Lovisa Ulrika* (Stockholm 1945). A. L. Hamilton was later to give a succinct and memorable sketch of her character: 'Too impetuous not to be sincere, she for that reason often revealed projects about which she had better have kept silent. Magnanimous, open-handed, a lover of splendour, witty, a good friend to her friends, seemly in her private life, her society was pleasant, her knowledge extensive but ill-ordered, her ambition limitless': A. L. Hamilton, *Anekdoter till svenska historien under Gustaf III:s regering* (Stockholm 1901), p. 11.

[5] For Lovisa Ulrika as 'Faustrix Musarum', see Jägerskiöld, *Lovisa Ulrika*, pp. 86–103.

[6] Jägerskiöld, p. 124; Fritz Arnheim, *Luise Ulrike die schwedische Schwester Friedrichs des Grossen* (Gotha 1910) II. 37.

1748, when Frederick I's too self-indulgent life seemed to be near its end after two strokes in close succession, she was engaged – with the eager encouragement of Frederick the Great – in plans for a *coup d'état*;[7] and when three years later Frederick I lay on his deathbed she hoped that Adolf Frederick might be able to restore absolutism without bloodshed by a simple announcement that he had assumed sovereign power. Tessin and the Council aborted this scheme by confronting the new king with a hastily-drawn Accession Charter which he lacked the nerve to decline.[8] But though the Diet of 1751 passed off without any major confrontation, in the years between 1752 and 1755 (when the next Diet met) relations between the king and the Council quickly became seriously strained.

The wrangling between them arose out of two issues, both of crucial importance. The first concerned the king's rights in regard to appointments. Clause 40 of the Constitution of 1720 had laid it down that all appointments over the rank of colonel (or their civil equivalents) must be made in Council from a short-list of three: the king was free to select one of the three; but if his selection was deemed to be possibly prejudicial to others, or contrary to law, the Council proceeded to vote, and the will of the majority prevailed. As to all other appointments, civil or military, a short-list was drawn up by the appropriate authority – by the colonel of the regiment in which the vacancy occured, by the *Collegium* or the provincial Governor under which (or whom) the office resorted, – and the king might choose at will from the three names put forward. It has been said that the control of appointments is indicative of the centre of power in the state.[9] Frederick I's Accession Charter had clearly recognised this – 'And as an unlimited power and authority in the giving of offices is by many seen as a means to the introduction of sovereignty . . .'[10] – and very careful provision had been made in the Constitutions of 1719 and 1720 for dealing with the question. Nevertheless it was not quite a simple matter to decide who did have the power; for it was evidently fairly widely distributed. Moreover, the Constitution of 1720 left a 'grey area' within which, if circumstances were favourable, the king might contrive to operate. He could sometimes pick a candidate who was not on the short-list at all: Frederick I had done so on occasion, and had had his way

---

[7] Jägerskiöld, pp. 133–4; Fritz Arnheim, *op. cit.*, II. 112–17; Gunnar Olsson, 'Fredrik den Store och Sveriges författning; *Scandia* (1961), pp. 345–6; *Politisches Correspondenz Friedrichs des Grossen*, VI. 147ff.

[8] Jägerskiöld, p. 147; Lovisa Ulrika's view of the situation in Arnheim, II, 262, 266, 271. Fersen when he came to write his Memoirs considered that a *coup* in 1751 might well have succeeded: Fersen, *Historiska skrifter*, II, p. 26.

[9] Göran Rystad, 'The King, the Nobility, and the Growth of Bureaucracy in 17th Century Sweden', in *Europe and Scandinavia. Aspects of the Process of Integration in the 17th Century*, ed. Göran Rystad, (Lund 1983), p. 70.

[10] Brusewitz, *Frihetstidens Grundlagar*, p. 62.

even though the Council had made remonstrances.[11] But what had been occasional in his time began to be claimed as a right by Adolf Frederick; and after 1752, when men were beginning to discern a division between 'royalists' and 'patriots',[12] this was a right which the Council was bound to deny.

The second issue was even more fundamental: Adolf Frederick's claim to test the Council's decisions against his own idea of the constitution, or of the welfare of the country. By 1755 he was contending that it was his duty to do this in virtue of clause 6 in his Accession Charter, which bound him to use his power to 'forward the welfare of the country in general, and that of every man in particular'. And this was a fundamental issue because if the king had had his way he would have destroyed the basic principle of the responsibility of the Council to the Estates; and, as Faggott put it, 'that balance in the constitution which our legislators have so happily achieved, and our *aequilibrium regiminis*, would be totally lost'.[13] On this question there could be no compromise; and when the Diet met in 1755 it was plain that there must be a head-on collision. It was in an effort to split the 'republican' front that royalist agents once again provoked a tumult in the Estate of Peasants; and that incident in turn led to the appointment of a commission of enquiry which in the following months would reveal with increasing clarity the plans of the queen and her agents to upset the constitution.[14]

It was not these fundamentals, however, but a relatively minor question, which precipitated the final crisis. If Lovisa Ulrika may be believed, what decided her to risk a violent revolution was the question of the education of the Crown Prince Gustav.[15] His governor had been selected by Adolf Frederick personally;[16] his tutors and entourage were men suspect to the Estates as royalists. The Estates now resolved to remove them, and to replace them with men who could be trusted to instil approved constitutional principles into the prince's mind. They based their action on a clause in the Constitution of 1720 which did indeed give them the right to do just that – though it added that they might do so 'with H.M.'s gracious good pleasure' – a phrase which may, or may not, have

---

[11] Holst, *Fredrik I*, pp. 171, 187; Birger Sallnäs, 'En kraftmätning mellan konung och råd . . .', pp. 118–125.

[12] Arnheim, *Luise Ulrike*, II, p. 338: Lovisa Ulrika to her brother August Wilhelm, 3(?) December 1753.

[13] Faggott, *Swea Rikes Styrelse efter Grundlagarne*, p. 134.

[14] For the tumult in the Estate of Peasants, and its consequences, see Fersen, *Historiska skrifter*, II. 70–77; Gardar Sahlberg, *Mer makt åt kungen!* (Stockholm 1976), pp. 53–4.

[15] Lovisa Ulrika's *Journal*, in Fersen, *Historiska skrifter*, II, p. 247.

[16] When Tessin resigned the position in 1754, as a consequence of his quarrel with the queen, Adolf Frederick appointed Stromfeldt: this appointment the Estates annulled in 1755, and entrusted the position to C. F. Scheffer.

been intended as mere formality.[17] However that might be, to Adolf Frederick and Lovisa Ulrika the action of the Estates appeared, understandably enough, as a monstrous and indecent interference in their purely family affairs. And the offence was compounded by two pieces of legislation designed to secure the rights of the Estates in the major matters of controversy: one was the *Memorial on the Services* (1756) which settled the question of appointments by enacting that henceforth seniority should be the sole criterion, and which laid it down that a candidate who had thrice been on a short-list and thrice rejected should automatically be entitled to appointment at the next vacancy;[18] the other was the provision that if the king refused his signature to a decision of the Council, the want should be supplied by the use of a name-stamp. After all, the Constitution had laid it down that the king shall govern 'with, not without, still less against' the Council's counsel, and it was a logical corollary to ensure that he should not be able to block their decisions. For the first time the king was explicitly denied the right of veto; and if it came to the pinch (as it nearly did in December 1768) the Council might carry on the work of the government without his participation.

These humiliations and defeats produced the attempted revolution of 1756: possibly they were designed to produce it. It had many of the approved ingredients of historical melodrama:[19] the queen's attempt to pawn the Crown Jewels, and their retrieval at the last moment when the Estates demanded to check them; reliance upon untrustworthy subordinate agents; the fatal indiscretion of one of them while in liquor; a treacherous Lady in Waiting; vacillating and contradictory plans by the conspirators; prompt action by the Council, which put Stockholm securely under military control; the royal pair trapped and virtually prisoners in their palace; continuous and ever more relentless investigation by the commission set up in 1755; the flight of some of the leaders, the heroic silence of a few of them under torture, the arrest of most of the others; and the final scene when Erik Brahe – the premier nobleman of Sweden, – his colleague G. J. Horn, and six others, were butchered by the public executioner within sight of the palace windows. Of the detailed plans of the conspirators Lovisa Ulrika herself had been ignorant; but a revolution, in some form or other, she had determined there should be, and on her lay the heaviest moral responsibility for the catastrophe. Severe penal measures against her were considered (Pechlin was for poisoning her soup);[20] but thanks to the efforts of Axel von Fersen she

[17] Brusewitz, *Frihetstidens Grundlagar*, p. 24. Faggott contended that the king's rights as a father must be considered to be subsumed into the right of the Estates: Faggott, *Swea Rikes Styrelse efter Grundlagarne*, p. 172.
[18] Text in Brusewitz, *Frihetstidens Grundlager*, pp. 191–206.
[19] The most detailed account of the royalist conspiracy is Gardar Sahlberg, *Mer makt åt kungen!*
[20] Or so Lovisa Ulrika believed: Fersen, *Historiska skrifter*, II, p. 298.

escaped with a humiliating rebuke by a delegation from the Estate of Clergy.[21] The Hats might now hope that royalism was dead without any prospect of resurrection; but they took care to arm themselves against any repetition of the events of 1756. The *Act of State* of that year provided that in the event of any further attempt of the same nature the bond which linked the king to the nation would be held to be dissolved.[22] The *Act* was kept secret, and was put on ice against the time when it might be wanted; but it was in fact a conditional deposition which would take effect without further ado, if the royal couple should misbehave.

Lovisa Ulrika never forgot the experiences of 1756. Never again would she attempt revolution by violence. Henceforward her objective would be the creation of a king's party, which might at last be strong enough to give her what she wanted by parliamentary means. She was in any case less certain that despotism on the Prussian model was what she desired: she foresaw with dread the time when she would be a widow – and a subject. And the curious love-hate relationship between herself and Prince Gustav, and the jealousy which she increasingly came to feel for him, disinclined her to put absolute power into his hands.[23] The control of foreign policy and of the army, a Council appointed by the sovereign and responsible to him, a veto on legislation: that was probably the extent of her constitutional ambitions after 1756. But even that could not yet be openly avowed. She must begin by playing on a feeling, which affected members of both parties, that the time had come to review the constitution as a whole with the object of pruning it of acknowledged anomalies and abuses; and she realised that even this more modest programme had no chance of success if it were allowed to become a party question. The desperate state of the Hats after 1761 gave her the opportunity she needed, and she used it with skill and determination to effect the Composition of 1762–4. The Composition broke down in November 1764, as we have seen; but until the last chance of restoring it was wrecked on the issue of the *licentiering* of the Hat Council in the following August she still hoped for reform by agreement between the parties; and there is no doubt that, irrespective of her constitutional plans, she genuinely desired to put a stop to party persecution, corruption of the Diet by foreign gold, and the ignominy of foreign ministers' leadership of Swedish parties.[24] In this she failed; but she was at least successful in

---

[21] Printed in *ibid.*, II, pp. 194–207.

[22] Printed in *ibid.*, II, pp. 205–14. Lovisa Ulrika, by her own account, would have been prepared to refuse to sign the *Act* and to face deposition, being sure that France would insist on a restoration: Fersen, II, pp. 303–4.

[23] Jägerskiöld, *Lovisa Ulrika*, pp. 250, 255–6.

[24] For detailed accounts of her policy, and the motives that inspired it, in the period 1760–1766, Olof Jägerskiöld, *Hovet och författningsfrågan 1760–1766* (Uppsala 1943), and Michael Metcalf, *Russia, England and Swedish Party Politics 1762–1766*. Sven Ulric Palme (rather unfairly)

recruiting a party of her own – with F. C. Sinclair as its able leader – which was sufficiently numerous to be a far from imponderable element in the House of Nobility, and even on occasion in the Burghers.

In 1766 the general review of the constitution for which Lovisa Ulrika had been working did indeed come about; but it came about under the auspices of a single party, in consultation with the Russian and Danish ministers, and its upshot – the *Ordinance for the Better Execution of the Laws* – gave the Court nothing, less than nothing. And from 1767, when Prince Gustav for the first time was allowed to be present at meetings of the Council, the leadership of the royalists slipped gradually from her hands to his. It was Gustav who composed those pungent *dictamina* against Cap policies which Adolf Frederick from time to time presented to the Council; it was Gustav who read them on his father's behalf, with an eloquence perfected by his participation in the performances of the masterpieces of the French drama which were a staple diversion of the Court, and to which he devoted himself with passionate enthusiasm. C. F. Scheffer, who had succeeded Tessin as his Governor, had carefully indoctrinated his pupil with the orthodox Hat view of the constitution;[25] but he had also made him acquainted with the writings of the physiocrats, and in the summer of 1768 he directed Gustav's attention to Mercier de la Rivière's *L'Ordre naturel et essential des sociétés politiques,* which propounded the idea of 'le despotisme personnel et légal', in contrast to 'le despotisme personnel et arbitraire'.[26] It was an idea which Gustav eagerly assimilated; and from 1768 onwards he made successive drafts of ideal constitutions which more or less conformed to Mercier's model. The difficulty, however, was to contrive the opportunity to implement these projects. As he looked at the fate of Poland, where Russian intervention was every day becoming more open and more brutal, it seemed to him to be a matter of urgency to provide Sweden with a monarchy strong enough and popular enough to safeguard her from the Polish experience.[27] He recurred again and again to the plan of a military *coup d' état* in Stockholm, either in conjunction with the Extraordinary Diet which Adolf Frederick was demanding, or as an alternative to it; but to either of these courses there were obstacles. On the one hand the royalists were not united on the tactics to be pursued, and Lovisa Ulrika

dismissed her policy of Composition as 'the vain and hopeless attempt of a politically unwise, hysterically ambitious woman to steer developments to her mind without having adequate real resources at her disposal': Sven Ulric Palme, reviewing Jägerskiöld, *Hovet och författningsfrågan,* in *Historisk tidskrift* (1944).

[25] Frederick Lagerroth, 'En frihetstidens lärobok i gällande svensk statsrätt'. *Statsvetenskaplig tidskrift* (1937).

[26] Beth Hennings, *Gustav III som kronprins* (Stockholm 1935) pp. 301–303.

[27] For Gustav's strong feelings about Poland, see Uppsala Universitets bibliotek, F478, Gustav III:s dagbok, 19 August 1767, 28 November 1768; *Gustav III:s och Lovisa Ulrikas brevvexling,* ed. Henrik Schück (Stockholm 1919), I, p. 117, 148–50.

still hankered after the old expedient of a Composition. Moreover, the Court lacked the necessary financial resources, and it was uncertain whether Choiseul would be able to provide them in time. On the other hand, a military *coup* in the capital was impossible without the cooperation of Fersen, who commanded the Life Guards; and Fersen was inflexibly opposed to revolution by non-parliamentary means. The Hats were, no doubt, desperately anxious to bring down the Cap régime; a few of them – such as C. F. Scheffer – had now become convinced royalists and were ready for a radical constitutional change; but the leaders of the party were mostly prepared to collaborate with the Court only for tactical reasons, and they shared Fersen's dislike of violence. Negotiations between the Court and the Hats, with the French minister, Modène, running back and forth between the two, came to a decisive point only when C. F. Scheffer formulated the plan for Adolf Frederick's 'Inactivity', which was accepted as an emergency measure by both parties. It was not what Gustav (or Choiseul) would have wished, but it was accompanied by written promises by some of the leading Hats that when the Extraordinary Diet should meet, they would carry significant extensions of the prerogative.[28]

The Caps, as we have seen, capitulated to the 'Inactivity'; and in January 1769 Gustav and the Hats reached an agreement which, if it had been put into effect, would have given Gustav most of what he aimed at. It provided – and this was a concession to the Hats – for a division of powers: 'the Nation' should legislate, the king should execute the laws, the Council should give counsel; but on the other hand the king was to control all appointments, he was to have a veto upon legislation, the control of foreign policy and of the armed forces was to be in his hands (though he might not begin an 'unjust' war); and though members of the Council were not to be dismissed without the consent of the Estates, their functions were to be reduced to the giving of advice: decisions would lie with the king. From Gustav's point of view it was a compromise which closely resembled a draft constitution which he had himself drawn up a few months earlier;[29] and it must have appeared to him to be at least a promising beginning. Of those who helped to formulate it – Scheffer, Hiärne, Stockenström, Hermansson – Scheffer certainly, the other three possibly, meant to honour the agreement. But the event was to show that Fersen, and the majority of those that followed him, certainly did not. It was a swindle from the beginning.

This became clear when in the autumn of 1769 the United Deputations

---

[28] For a full account of these plans and negotiations, see Beth Hennings, *Gustav III som kronprins*, pp. 309–340.

[29] Jonas Nordensson, 'Kronprins Gustavs författningsprojekt 1768' *Statsvetenskapliga studier till statsvetenskapliga föreningens i Uppsala tjugofemårsdag* (Uppsala 1944).

addressed themselves to the question of constitutional reform. By this time the political climate in the Diet had hardened against royalism. When a certain Assessor Virgin ventured in a pamphlet to adumbrate the possibility of giving the king a veto, he was fined 300 silver *daler* in terms of the *Ordinance for the Liberty of Printing*, and the Caps, led by Pechlin, tried without success to violate the terms of that *Ordinance* and bring the matter under the jurisdiction of Estates themselves.[30] Pechlin's desertion to the Caps put the Hats on the defensive; Pechlin himself was a member of the United Deputations, and was able to mobilise a body of opinion against any serious concessions to the Crown. Even royalists do not now seem to have ventured to suggest anything beyond a return to the letter of the Constitution of 1720; and when the report of the United Deputations came to the Estates it was found that that clause of the *Ordinance for the Better Execution of the Laws* (1766) which deprived the king of the right to exclude from the Council any person whose name had been four times put forward, still stood; and that was a provision which conflicted with clause 40 of the constitution in a vital point. The *Act of Security*, which was the really substantial outcome of the Deputations' deliberations, gave to the Crown nothing whatever, and in any case the Diet rejected it. Eighteen months of planning and negotiation had proved fruitless: the hopes and aspirations of Prince Gustav were scattered to the winds. For the Court it appeared to be total defeat.

(ii)

Nevertheless, the appearance was delusive. The rejection of the *Act of Security* proved to be a real turning-point. For that rejection meant much more than a defeat for the Court: it meant also a defeat for reform; and it inaugurated the end of the régime.

For thirty years discerning observers had perceived that the constitution was endangered by the interpretations which were put upon it, and by the abuses to which some of them gave rise: the self-aggrandisement of the Secret Committee; commissions and extraordinary courts; the interference of the Estates in appointments and promotions – a practice which reached notorious heights in the Diet of 1760–2, and against which the Estate of Nobility protested in vain.[31] Even in the strongholds of constitutional orthodoxy voices were to be heard lamenting that Liberty was degenerating into Licence. In 1751 Ulrik Scheffer was fearful that the excesses of the Diet would ultimately ruin the country:[32] and five years later his brother Carl Fredrik – at the very moment when he was writing

[30] [Arvid Virgin], *En patriots tankar om grundlagens nödvändiga förbättring* (Stockholm 1769).
[31] Malmström, *Sveriges politiska historia*, v, pp. 94–5, 97–8, 100, 179–80.
[32] Gunnar Olsson, *Hattar och mössor*, pp. 260–2.

his textbook on the constitution for the instruction of Prince Gustav – was privately commenting that what the country really needed was a Diet which would protect liberty against itself.[33] In 1764, when he had become persuaded that the old Hat party was dead, and that the only road to salvation was a Composition, he provided an analysis of the situation which was devastating:

> The whole country, and especially those who had no part in the work of the Diet, complained of the proceedings of the Estates in the matter of appointments to offices; of innumerable cases of 'prejudice'; of the emptying of the exchequer in favour of private persons; of irregularities which had never been seen to such an extent before . . . Circumstantial stories of corruption in the Diet were so general, that men recoiled at the idea of a new one, and even the greatest lovers of our liberty openly confessed that however great the necessity might turn out to be, the summoning of the Estates would be a greater evil.[34]

Daniel Tilas, who had greeted the triumph of the Caps in 1765 with jubilation, was saying a year later that Liberty had demoralised society; that both parties were equally culpable; and that the only law that men appeared to respect was *Lex Talionis*.[35] These were not isolated voices: they spoke for many men who were genuinely anxious to safeguard the constitution, and they were echoed in the debates of the United Deputations of 1769 and the trenchant formulations of the *Act of Security*. And when the *Act* was rejected, those who had sponsored or supported it were forced to ask themselves what road they were now to follow. Some had drawn the consequences of their opinions already, and turned royalist: C. F. Scheffer, for one; Daniel Tilas for another; but others, who hitherto had clung to the belief in the possibility of a reformed constitution, were being driven to a position in which they had no heart to resist royalist designs, and welcomed the coup of 19 August 1772 when it came: such was Schönberg, such was Chydenius. And though Claes Frietzcky remained a supporter of the constitution, by 1770 he was clear-sighted enough to foresee its probable overthrow.[36]

Though there was a large measure of agreement among the friends of reform in the matter of abuses to be eradicated, there was no solid common ground between them on the principles upon which the constitution must be re-established if such abuses were to be prevented from recurring. The view that the constitution was a contract began to be

[33] Olof Jägerskiöld, 'C. F. Scheffer och 1750-talets författningskris', *Historisk tidskrift* (1939), pp. 193–4.

[34] 'Egenhändig uppsats af . . . C. Fr. Scheffer', *Handlingar rörande Skandianviens historia*, XVI, pp. 182–4.

[35] Tilas, *Anteckningar och brev från riksdagen 1765–1766*, pp. 287–93.

[36] Anders Werner, *Studier till frågan om europeiska ideer i svensk politik under den senare frihetstiden* (Stockholm 1969) p. 53.

heard again;[37] and a perceptible shift in political theory reflected the prevailing *malaise*. Reformers who were disturbed by the consequences which had been drawn from Locke began to turn for ideas to Montesquieu. Remedies were suggested based on the theory of the separation of powers, or more often upon the division of powers, though the two ideas tended to become entangled.[38] There was growing support, both from critics and champions of 'Liberty', for the suggestion – hitherto suspect as an English heresy – that a constitution ought to embody some principle of Balance; but there was little agreement on how a balance was to be achieved, or even upon the forces which must balance one another. The 'Simplicists' insisted that the Constitution of 1720 had provided a balance already, and that all that was necessary was to strip away later accretions and revert to the situation as the founding fathers of the constitution had left it. But it needed faith – or obliquity – not to see that the Constitution of 1720 had given a great preponderance to the legislative over the executive; and that in consequence the executive was uncomfortably weak. The Hats had realised this very well in the dangerous years of the 1740s: the disaster in Finland, the revolt of the Dalesmen, the blackmail of Russian envoys, made them painfully aware of it. The point had been put with great force by one of their leaders, Henning Gyllenborg, in 1743, when he had told the Nobility that

All our troubles arise from that feebleness of government which is a consequence of our present constitution . . . We have a government which lacks the strength which it really ought to have, and I scarcely know what to call our present constitution, whether monarchy, aristocracy or anarchy. It is rather a mixture of all three; a confounding of rulers and ruled, of which the result has been that the former have no authority and the latter have neither respect for, nor fear of, the law.[39]

The Hats at that time saw the solution to the difficulty in the close cooperation of king and Council: hence Tessin's alliance with Lovisa Ulrika, which on at least one occasion tempted him to use language which she could construe as a promise of support for revolution.[40] But once the crisis of the 1740s had been weathered the Hats became less concerned on this score. Their Council had solid backing in the Estates; it certainly

[37] For instance, Jonas Linnerhielm on 29 January 1772, who argued against any change in the terms of Gustav III's Accession Charter from those used in Adolf Frederick's on the ground that Accession Charters were *contracts* between king and subjects, and that to alter them unilaterally would be to 'diminish the king's lawful hereditary right'. *SRARP*, xxx, 50.

[38] For the debate on Balance see Rudelius, pp. 340–3, 346: E. Fahlbeck, 'Studier öfver frihetstidens politiska idéer' (1916), pp. 41–50, 122; Georg Landberg in *Sveriges riksdag*, I, vii, 12–13, 17, 23; *idem*, 'En svensk författningshistoria från krisåret 1768. Bidrag till den gustavianska rojalismens idéhistoria', *Statsvetenskaplig tidskrift*, (1937); Kjellin, *Anders Schönberg*, pp. 20–1.

[39] *SRARP*, xiv, 120.

[40] In 1746 Tessin wrote to Lovisa Ulrika: 'I really believe that there is no other salvation for us but to pound the constitution in a mortar, put it in a pan, and leave it to simmer under the direction of the most enlightened of princesses': Jägerskiöld, *Lovisa Ulrika*, p. 132.

showed no weakness in dealing with the royalist plot of 1756; and, as we have seen, it risked participation in the Seven Years War without consulting the Diet. But this last instance in fact illustrated the difficulty of obtaining a strong government in terms of the constitution. It might be inconceivable in the mid-fifties to strengthen the executive by giving increased power to the king; but the onslaught on the Council at the Diet of 1760–2 made it clear that men were not willing to concede more power to the Council either. The 'anti-Senatorial' party accused them of aiming at an aristocracy. In England, aristocracy was considered as the palladium of the constitution, the ballast which gave stability to the ship of state. In Sweden (as Tessin once remarked)[41] aristocracy was a bogy: a charge men flung at their political opponents; it was an insidious threat hardly less fatal to liberty than Absolutism itself. In 1720 the powers of the Council had been curtailed lest it should become an aristocracy; in 1734 voting procedures in the Estate of Nobility had been modified so as to destroy the weight of the great families; the civil service strike of 1768 was justified – and the Cap Council later evicted – on the ground that the proposal to rule with the name-stamp, if Adolf Frederick persisted in the 'Inactivity', was a design to set up an aristocratic republic. History can show not a few instances of the willingness of peoples to sacrifice liberty for the sake of strong government: Sweden affords an example of readiness to sacrifice it in order to ensure a weak one.

By 1770 one trend in current political theory had become unmistakable: a tendency in those who sought to repair the constitution, as well as royalists who hoped to destroy it, to take England for their standard, and a desire to engraft English constitutional practice upon the ailing plant of Swedish liberty. They spoke enviously of trial by jury, primogeniture, Justices of the Peace, a landed gentry; they urged a higher property qualification for members of the Diet; they denounced placemen in the Estates, and office-holding for life; they looked for an ending of the interpenetration of the executive and legislative functions, in the mistaken belief that they were kept wholly separate in England; and some of them claimed for the king the right of appointment to offices, the right of dissolution, and a veto upon (at least) unconstitutional legislation. But even so they could not rid themselves of the fear of a strong executive, and the reformers were rather concerned to weaken the power of the Council than to increase it. Not only Anders Nordencrantz – a Harringtonian, as well as an anglophile – but even Anders Schönberg, favoured a system of rotation of office which would have made members of the Council during one Diet ineligible for office in the next. Nordencrantz would even have applied the principle of rotation to the Presidents of the *Collegia*, to

[41] *Tessin och Tessiniana*, p. 341.

provincial Governors, and to committees of the Diet, thus ensuring the minimum of continuity and administrative experience in the maximum number of places.[42]

(iii)

Amid this confusion of tongues, growing swiftly in the shadow cast by the disheartening defeat of reform, there emerged controversies which had their roots in material interests, no less than in abstract political theory, and were more important than all the rest in precipitating the overthrow of the constitution. Here too the rejection of the *Act of Security* marks the beginning of a crisis, a renewal of that 'strife of Estates' which had reached its first climax in 1650. When the Nobility and the Burghers rejected the *Act*, they did so – party passion and foreign corruption apart – because they were determined not to surrender one iota of those rights, or assumed rights, which they had come to consider as indispensable bulwarks against the return of Absolutism, or because they scented in the report of the United Deputations a plan which by enlarging the powers of the Council might threaten 'aristocracy'.[43] Some of these considerations may have influenced the Estate of Peasants also; but if so, they do not emerge from their debates. In 1769, as in previous years,[44] the Peasants saw the main threat to their liberties as coming from the arbitrary and high-handed proceedings of local government officials: in their debate on the *Act* this was the *only* point to be discussed.[45] Since 1756 Nordencrantz had been waging a truceless war against officials; the *Ordinance for the Better Execution of the Laws* of 1766 had made them one of its main targets; Esbjörn Reuterholm in 1769 had denounced them as the latest and most

---

[42] Nordencrantz, *Undersökning* . . ., pp. 70, 86; *idem, Anmärkning*, pp. 53–4 (on King Alfred as the inventor of juries); Daniel Helsingius, *En Chinesisk Philosophs Egna Tankar om Engelska Friheten* (Stockholm 1771), pp. 3–5; Höpken, 'Äreminne öfver . . . Claes Ekeblad', in Höpken, *Skrifter*, I, 272; Birger Sallnäs, 'England i den svenska författningsdiskussionen', *Vetenskaps-Societeten i Lund. Årsbok 1958–9* (Lund 1959). Even Tessin, the representative of an older generation, conceded that the English constitution was admirable – but not exportable: *Tessin och Tessiniana*, p. 341. English examples could be used with other ends in view also: in 1769 translations of Wilkes and Junius appeared, and were used by the Caps against the king and the Hats: Werner, *Studier till frågan om europeiska ideer i svensk politik under den senare frihetstiden*. pp. 70–4.

[43] As Ridderstolpe observed, if the Estates were to be debarred from considering appeals to them, the country might easily fall into the hands of an 'aristocratic power': what remedy then would the subject have against 'an audacious Council'?: *SRARP*, XXVIII, 73–4.

[44] So in 1755, when the Peasants complained that officials did not apply the law, and were slack and insolent. The matter was referred to the Diet's Judicial Deputation, who agreed that many were slothful, ignorant, careless and corrupt; but no action was taken. Malmström, *Sveriges politiska historia*, IV, p. 447; and cf. ibid., pp. 207–8, 443.

[45] *Bondeståndets riksdagsprotokoll*, 11, pp. 258–73. Of the 189 petitions (or grievances) put forward by the Peasants at the Diet of 1769, 22 were directed against maladministration and oppression by officials: *ibid.*, pp. 636–711.

dangerous form of aristocracy. It was not just a question of political theory: as Fredrik Lagerroth, the great champion of the Age of Liberty, ruefully confessed, the constitution was 'in many respects a disguise under which the bureaucracy could swindle the state and harry the people, unmolested'.[46] The Peasants did not believe that they could rely upon the ordinary courts for the redress of illegalities and oppressions received at the officials' hands. And if they carried their case on appeal to the final instance, which was the Judicial Division of the Council of State, the decision there would be made by a body composed exclusively of nobles, who were (moreover) themselves officials. Some control of officials was indeed provided for in the constitution: inferior officers were responsible to the *Collegium* under whose province they fell; the *Collegia* were held responsible by the Diet; but, as Nordencrantz was never tired of pointing out, the Diet was full of men who held official posts: the same men were both accountable and entrusted with the duty of enforcing accountability. The position of the Diet in this matter was thus paradoxical and self-contradictory. But if not to the Diet, to whom else could the oppressed citizen turn for redress? What other body was in a position to override, if need be, the verdict of the Council's Judicial Division? Had not the *riksdagsordning* of 1723 – which was reckoned as a fundamental law – laid it down (clause 13) that 'private persons shall be free to complain to the Estates in cases where no other redress is possible?' Was this last resort now to be taken away by 'Simplicists' who appealed to one part of the fundamental laws as a pretext for destroying another? No doubt it could be argued that interference by the Estates in judicial proceedings was objectionable in all sorts of ways, both in principle and in practice; but for the Peasants any objection was outweighed by the fact that it provided the only hope of an equitable – as against a strictly legal – decision, and (even more important) the prospect of redress which should be effective because backed by the Diet's absolute authority.

The attack upon officialdom went hand in hand with a growing hostility to privilege, and especially to the privileges of the nobility. The privileges of the Swedish nobility had been most recently defined in 1723, in terms which represented a sharp curtailment of the extravagant demands they had put forward in 1719.[47] They bestowed many of the same advantages as were usually enjoyed by the continental nobilities; though seigneurial rights were in Sweden comparatively moderate. The nobility had indeed hunting and fishing rights reserved to them (though the former not in all provinces, and though the latter had been considerably modified by the Fisheries Statute of 1766); they were entitled to labour services from their peasants, and did on occasion abuse them, as

---

[46] Lagerroth, *Frihetstidens författning*, p. 498.
[47] Brusewitz, *Frihetstidens Grundlagar*, pp. 107–123.

a revolt in Halland in 1773 was to show;[48] and they had what was the potentially very dangerous right to 'make their land and property as profitable as they can': a right which in Denmark had proved disastrous to the peasantry, but was apparently less so in Sweden.[49] But none of these things was at issue in the attack on the nobility which developed in the 1760s. For the grievances to which they gave rise, and the oppressions which they made possible, scarcely concerned the Burghers or the Peasants at all. They affected, almost exclusively, the peasants of the nobility; and these peasants had no representation in the Diet. As to whether they fared well or ill the Estate of Peasants seems only rarely to have enquired. Nor was the attack directed against the nobility's fiscal exemptions, and its freedom from other burdens such as *corvées*. For tax-exemptions applied only to the standing revenues of the Crown; and throughout the period those revenues had to be supplemented, at Diet after Diet, by parliamentary grants. The Estate of Nobility voted and paid such grants, just as the other Estates did.[50] As to the Nobility's double representation on the Secret Committee and other committees of the Diet, that was accepted without question. No: the kernel of noble privilege, the issue over which battle came to be joined, was the reservation to them, by clause 2 of their privileges, of all higher grades in the civil and armed services. It was a reservation which they felt to be vital. Charles XI's *reduktion* had so diminished the estates in noble hands that after 1720 there was not enough land available to them to provide for their greatly swollen numbers, and too few of those that had it could make a decent living out of it.[51] They were therefore driven to seek a living in the state's employ. As their numbers increased, as their ability to make ends meet was buffeted first by inflation and then by deflation, as the competition for jobs grew more intense, office became an indispensable resource; and they clung to their privilege not so much on grounds of dignity or family pride as because in regard to office it had become a necessity if they were to survive.

The origins of the attack upon the Estate of Nobility date back to the very beginning of the Age of Liberty: it had been especially vigorous in the period 1719–23. Then and afterwards it had usually been led by the Estate of Burghers; and from the beginning it had been directed against the Nobility's most sensitive point, for from the beginning it took the

---

[48] Staffan Smedberg, *Frälsebönderörelser i Halland och Skåne 1772–1776* (Uppsala 1972).

[49] Thomas Munch, *The Peasantry and the Early Absolute Monarchy in Denmark* (Copenhagen 1979).

[50] Though Ridderstolpe in 1772 explained the Peasants' hatred of the Nobility on the ground that they paid only a fifth of such grants: *SRARP*, XXXI, 16.

[51] In 1760 those classified as nobility numbered around 10 000, or about 0.5% of the total population: Eli F. Heckscher, *Sveriges ekonomiska historia från Gustav Vasa* (Stockholm 1949), II, 1, p. 130.

form of a demand that office should be open equally to all. In 1723 the Burghers, with the support (for a time) of the Clergy, demanded that commoners should be guaranteed one half of all appointments, including the higher civil service, and that three out of every four new appointments should go to them until the existing imbalance had been corrected.[52] In 1756 the Burghers renewed the claim of 1723; in 1761 they talked for a moment of putting forward a commoner as candidate for a vacancy on the Council of State, though by the privileges of 1723 membership was expressly reserved to the Nobility. By the beginning of the sixties men were seeing society as being made up of 'workers and wasters' (*närande och tärande*), and were disposed with Dean Hjortsberg in 1761 to lump all the nobility into the latter category.[53]

For the Peasants, however, the demand for equality had a significance which was not confined to the competition for office, that being an issue which was of less practical importance to them than to the Burghers. It was based rather on their sense that despite the constitution's assumption that all Estates were equal, theirs was in fact inferior, and was considered to be so. The sign of this inferiority was their exclusion from the Secret Committee: an exclusion which meant – particularly during the long ascendancy of the Hats – that they were kept in ignorance of much important business, and especially of finance and foreign policy. At Diet after Diet they put forward demands to be admitted; but when Gustav III's revolution came along – though by then the prospects were beginning to look promising – they had still not succeeded in carrying their point.

The Estate of Nobility viewed the pretensions of the Peasants with especial disquiet. For the Peasants were traditionally royalist in sympathy: 'better one king than many!' The events of 1743 haunted the memories of noble statesmen: the rising of the Dalesmen had been concerned not only to force a speedy peace but also to import Danish Absolutism in the person of a Danish successor; and it had been a protest against what they considered to be the misgovernment of the upper classes: they marched to Stockholm proclaiming that they would 'dust the wigs' of those responsible. There had been something of a panic among the nobility; and Tessin, among others, had found it prudent to leave Stockholm for his country estate. The disturbances in Västergöt-land in 1766 revived these alarms: 'We tremble before an unbridled

---

[52] *Borgarståndets riksdagsprotokoll*, 2 (Stockholm 1951), pp. 183, 347, 363, 415–9 *etc.*; *Prästeståndets riksdagsprotokoll*, 6 (Stockholm 1982), p. 6; Walfrid Enblom, *Privilegiestriderna vid frihetstidens början 1719–1723. Ett bidrag till ståndsutjämningens historia* (Uppsala 1925).

[53] He remarked also that if their number increased much more, none but nobles would get state employment, and all the rest must sink to the level of peasants: P. J. Edler, *Om börd och befordran under frihetstiden* (Stockholm 1916), pp. 95, 115.

commonalty', cried Axel von Fersen; 'so it was in 1743, and so it is now'.[54]
They had some cause to tremble. Forty years of 'Liberty' had done a good
deal to erode the old habits of deference. More and more noble land was
passing into peasant hands, by pawning or collusive arrangements,
whatever the law might say: by 1771 the Speaker of the Estate of Peasants
would be the well-to-do owner of a couple of noble manors, though such
a thing was expressly forbidden by the privileges of 1723. Over wide
bands of the social spectrum a levelling process seemed to be gathering
strength. More and more commoners were getting into the civil service
(though not into the officer class in the army), *mésalliances* by
impoverished members of the nobility were steadily on the increase.[55]
Commoners were now tending to be better educated, in schools and at
the universities, than the privately-tutored offspring of the peerage. And
outside the Estate structure, in the middle and upper ranks of that
miscellaneous population which contemporary parlance denominated as
'persons of standing' (*ståndspersoner*) the legitimacy of noble privilege was
beginning to be questioned.

   Though statistics indicate fairly clearly that commoners were much
less seriously disadvantaged by noble privilege than they believed
themselves to be, what mattered was not the objective facts, but how men
felt about them. An instance of this was provided by an event in 1762
which seemed to bring to a point these discontents and these aspirations.
In that year the Estate of Nobility resolved, unanimously, that henceforth
no newly-made peer should be permitted to take his seat until the total
number entitled to sit in the House had fallen to 800: a somewhat distant
prospect, since over 1100 attended in 1765, and the annual loss by death
was around nine.[56] No doubt it was possible to regard this as a purely
practical matter: orderly debate became difficult when more than a
thousand members in a high state of political excitement were crowded
into a chamber which had never been designed to hold so many. But this
argument does not appear at all in the report of the debate, which turned
entirely on the point that in a situation where so many nobles were driven
to seek employment in the state's service any increase in their number
would make the struggle for jobs reserved to them still fiercer.[57] This was
precisely how the other three Estates saw it – as a device to frustrate the
aspiring commoner's hope of attaining to such offices after ennoblement.
But in reality the bar upon introduction of newly-made peers had in
practice almost ceased for some years back, and experience in the years
after 1762 showed that the resolution in no way prejudiced the career

---

[54] *SRARP*, xxv, 386.
[55] Sten Carlsson, *Ståndssamhälle och ståndspersoner* (2nd edn. Lund 1973), pp. 55–8, 119–45,
185.
[56] Hugo Valentin, *Frihetstidens riddarhus*, p. 279.   [57] *SRARP*, xxiii, 499–501.

prospects of such persons.[58] Nevertheless, when men looked back with hindsight ten years later, they were inclined to see in the resolution of 1762 the spark which fired the train that led to the detonations which became so audible after 1770.[59]

The assault on the Nobility followed several lines. One of them lay in attempts to force through the congruent decisions of the three lower Estates without waiting for the Nobility to vote upon the question: this was a direct violation of clause 20 of the *riksdagsordning* of 1723, which laid it down that nothing might be promulgated as a decision of the Diet until the minute of the resolution had been properly scrutinised and accepted by each Estate.[60] In 1766 the lower Estates forced through a tax on carriages and riding-horses against the opposition of the Nobility, in defiance of the well-established convention that no Estate was to be liable to a tax which particularly concerned it unless it had given its assent.[61] They trespassed hardily upon territory which was peculiarly the Nobility's domestic preserve: they unseated the Nobility's representatives on the Bank Committee, which they had no right to do; they even voted Cederhielm's exclusion for life, though every Estate had sole jurisdiction over the behaviour of its own members; and to this outrage the Nobility could make no other reply than feebly to appeal to the king for protection.[62] But the privileges of the Nobility – and indeed the privileges of the other Estates also – had been repeatedly and explicitly guaranteed in various acts of state: by the Constitution of 1720, by the *riksdagsordning* of 1723, by Adolf Frederick's Accession Charter of 1751; and there can be little doubt that the Burghers or Clergy would have hotly resented any attempt by a majority of the Estates to override *their* privileges. Whether one liked it or not, privileges were a part of the constitution – of that same constitution that all the Estates were so passionately determined to defend. They were *law*: though whether they were to be considered as *fundamental* law was a matter upon which it was possible to hold more than one opinion.[63] Certainly the Nobility,

---

[58] As a member of the Estate of Nobility pointed out in 1772: *SRARP*, xxx. 128. It is worth remembering that in Sweden, far more than in England, peerages were bestowed upon persons distinguished in literature, the arts, science and technology: for this aspect of the matter see Michael Roberts, 'The Swedish Aristocracy in the Eighteenth Century', in *Essays in Swedish History* (1967).

[59] Valentin, *Frihetstidens riddarhus*, pp. 269–83; Per-Erik Brolin, 'Ståndsutjämning som historiskt problem', pp. 72ff.; Ingvar Elmroth, *Nyrekryteringen till de högre ämbetena* (Lund 1962), pp. 56–76; *SRARP*, xxx, 125.

[60] E.g. *SRARP*, xxiv, 138–40; xxv, 411; *cf.* Brusewitz, *Frihetstidens Grundlagar*, p. 246.

[61] Fredrik Lagerroth [*et al.*], *Sveriges riksdag*, vi, pp. 300–12.

[62] *SRARP*, xxvi, 326, 368, 376, 398.

[63] In 1751 the Secret Committee laid it down that the fundamental law of the land implied a reciprocal guarantee of each Estate's privileges: Malmström, iv. 82, and Isak Faggott thought so too: Faggott, *Swea Rikes Styrelse efter Grundlagarne*, p. 9. And see Edler, *Om börd och befordran under frihetstiden* pp. 131–44, 220, 245–6, for a discussion of this point.

confronted with the attack upon them, saw themselves as defenders of the law, and hence of the constitution also.

In 1769 the tension between noble and non-noble Estates had become acute: already Carl Sparre could see the situation as 'two nations confronting one another'.[64] Enterprising publishers availed themselves of the new freedom of the press to issue reprints of pamphlets from the great 'strife of Estates' of the mid seventeenth century.[65] An incident at the beginning of 1770 deeply embittered the controversy. In that year the Council passed over a well-qualified commoner for the post of Vice-President of the Supreme Court in Åbo, on the ground that this office had been moved up into the category of those reserved to the nobility. For this the Estate of Nobility had not the sole responsibility: the Council had acted on a recommendation from the Diet. Nevertheless, it was felt to be a wanton provocation: commoners had filled the office before; the Nobility had not hitherto pleaded their privilege as a bar to such an appointment. The reaction seems to have been immediate: Admiral Carl Tersmeden – a Hat who would soon turn royalist, and who was destined to play a not unimportant part on 19 August 1772 – in January 1770 found himself in company with some members of the lower Estates, and was plainly shaken at the frank expression of their resentment: they told him that the decline of the Hats at the Diet which was now near its end was to be attributed to the social grievances of the commoners; to the Nobility's resolution of 1762; to the reservation of higher administrative posts to the nobility; to the case of the Vice-Presidency at Åbo; and they warned him that the effect of their resentment would be felt at the next Diet.[66] The event would verify that prediction: all over the country, the Åbo case seems to have become an issue at the general election of 1771.[67]

The attack on the Nobility, however, was only one aspect of a much broader movement of ideas. The campaign against officials, for instance, was not only a demand for the proper observation of the law by the government and its agents; it was, more positively, a struggle for liberation from constraint, for self-government unpatrolled and undragooned by magistrates in the towns, or by foresters, game-wardens and petty justices in the countryside. At the beginning of 1770 an attempt was made to gather these different strands into a common programme. In January of that year Alexander Kepplerus (if indeed it was he: the point has been disputed) drew up and presented to the Estate of Burghers a

[64] SRARP, xxviii, 57.
[65] Edvard Philipsson Ehrensten's Oförgripliga Bewis emot Adelens Rättighet öfwer Skatte-Gods (1649), on the one hand, and Schering Rosenhane's Samtaal emellan Juncker Päär, Mäster Hans, Niels Andersson Borhgare och Joen i Bergha Danneman (1650), on the other.
[66] Amiral Carl Tersmedens Memoarer, ed. Nils Erdmann, v (Stockholm 1918), pp. 33–4.
[67] En Stockholmskrönika ur C. G. Gjörwells brev, ed. Otto Sylwan (Stockholm 1920), p. 34.

Memorial, in which he proposed a code of privileges which should be common to all the non-noble Estates.[68] The interests of the three lower Estates unfortunately happened to be far from coincident, and Clergy and Burghers had their privileges already, last defined in 1723; but Kepplerus sought to disguise these difficulties by availing himself of a collective noun revived (from seventeenth-century usage) by Anders Nordencrantz a few years earlier: he called them all *Odalståndet*, which meant, more or less, 'the Estate of Yeomen'. The Peasants, no doubt, might pass for yeomen; but the Clergy and the Burghers did not fit the term by any stretch of imagination. But if the name was nonsense, it was nonsense in a good cause. The privileges which he formulated in his *Memorial*, at all events, had no nonsense about them. They blended a demand for the Rule of Law on the lines of the abortive *Act of Security* of 1769 with the current cry for appointments solely on merit, and a selection of the more conspicuous grievances of the Burghers and Peasants, tactfully avoiding points of difference between them.

The Peasants had, in fact, anticipated Kepplerus. Their first move for privileges had come in 1766; and the question was raised again almost simultaneously with Kepplerus, though it was not until 1771 that they were ready with a draft.[69] In one important respect it was the expression of their long-standing desire for some sort of codification of existing rights and liberties, and of former resolutions of the Diet in their favour:[70] for lack of any such convenient handbook the law had been forgotten, or had been flouted, and was always 'subject to many arbitrary interpretations by officials'. This useful compendium they thought of as their privileges, no doubt from a feeling that since other Estates had privileges, it was only reasonable that they should have theirs also. But the draft of 1771 went much further than this. Its opening paragraphs proclaimed that this was to be a charter of liberties, not for the Estate of Peasants only, but for the whole people: for everyone, cleric or lay, landed or landless, who was not a noble. Their fundamental demand, which echoed Kepplerus and really comprehended most of the others, was for 'full right to their bodies and persons, their property and their means of livelihood': 'industry, application and constant care to provide honestly for one's self shall be the right of every subject, who shall also have the right to seek a livelihood, and to improve his circumstances, in all possible ways and by all

---

[68] For Kepplerus, see Göran von Bonsdorff, 'En finländsk insats i frihetstidens statsrättsliga diskussion', *Svenska litteratursällskapet i Finland: historiska och litteraturhistoriska studier*, 27–28 (Helsingfors 1952); Gunnar Kjellin, 'Kring Alexander Kepplerus' memorial', *Historisk tidskrift* (1955), pp. 276ff. For the suggestion that the real author was Edvard Runeberg, Beth Hennings, *Fyra gustavianska studier* (Stockholm 1967), p. 48.

[69] *Bondeståndets riksdagsprotokoll*, 10, p. 706; 11, pp. 473–4, 561–2, 753–4; 12, Appendix 30, pp. 592–603.

[70] See, e.g., *ibid.*, 11, pp. 753–6.

permissible means, to the best of his ability'. This meant, in fact, the right
to exploit their land to the best advantage, the right to alienate it freely,
free bargaining for their produce and their labour, freedom of association
within the parish, control of their own commonages and woods,[71] the
restoration to Crown peasants of the sole right to buy the land on which
they sat (*skatteköp*: the Hats in 1769 had revoked the Caps' concession on
this point), and not least a relaxation of the *Statute of Servants*
(*tjänstehjonsstadgan*). That Statute had restricted the number of sons a
farmer might keep on his farm, insisted that his household's 'superfluous'
labour-force should take service as hired labourers elsewhere, and
branded those who did not comply with the opprobrious names of
'vagabond, tramp and sturdy beggar'. Attempts to amend the Statute in
1766 had given the Peasants no satisfaction: the least they wanted was a
proclamation that no one was to be deemed a vagabond until he was
actually convicted of begging.[72] And, finally, there was a demand for the
immediate abolition of royal foresters and gamekeepers, except in the
Crown's own parks. A year later, as a kind of corollary to the draft
privileges, the Estate of Peasants was to produce a draft election
ordinance: it was provoked by some bad cases of interference by local
officials in the election of 1771; and it would have put the control of the
conduct of elections – and the decision in cases of disputed returns –
wholly into the hands of the constituencies.[73] Taken together, the two
drafts amounted to a far-reaching claim to liberty, equality of opportunity and self-government. Here, it might seem, were all the elements of a
social revolution.

Some of those elements were present also among the objectives of the
Burghers. They shared the general desire for a guarantee of the Rule of
Law, and they had throughout been the leaders in the struggle for
acceptance of the principle of appointment by merit only: they would win
their first triumph when in 1771 Burgomaster Sebaldt was chosen for the
post of Chancellor of Justice, hitherto strictly reserved to the Nobility.[74]
But their concern was also to secure that the control of the municipalities
should be in the hands of the municipal aristocracy, and should be free

[71] For an example of how the differing rights of farmers to various types of commonage might
be threatened by (e.g.) mining and industrial interests, see Birgitta Ericsson, 'Central Power and
the Local Right to dispose over the Forest Common in eighteenth-century Sweden', *Scandinavian
Journal of History*, 5 (1980), pp. 75–92.
[72] *Bondeståndets riksdagsprotokoll*, 10, pp. 968–74. Chydenius wrote in indignation: 'If it has
been a man's lot to be born the child of a farm-hand, a cottager, or a farm-servant, or to have had
the ill-fortune to be the third, fourth or fifth child of a peasant, then they are born to slavery, as
knights are born with noble blood': Heckscher, *Sveriges ekonomiska historia*, II, 2, p. 865. For the
Statute of Servants see Arthur Montgomery, 'Tjänstehjonsstadgan och äldre svensk arbetarpoli-
tik', *Historisk tidskrift* (1933), pp. 263ff.
[73] *Bondeståndets riksdagsprotokoll*, 12, Appendix 67, pp. 608ff.
[74] In the event, he declined the appointment.

from the influence of provincial Governors or Crown-appointed magistrates. The emancipation of the municipalities from such control had in fact been proceeding fairly steadily for the last two decades:[75] it was now to be completed; elections – municipal and parliamentary – were to be conducted upon such basis as the Estate might determine. In much of this the Estate of Peasants had little interest – as little as the Burghers had in the broad formulations of equality enunciated in the draft privileges of the Peasants. Kepplerus's idea of an *Odalstånd* proved in practice impossible to realise. The Estate of Clergy had their own privileges already, some of them vexatious; and though they might be concerned to end the abuses of officialdom, that was probably the limit of their interest, and they were soon quietly dropped from the negotiations for a common front of the non-noble Estates. There was much discussion and much drafting, but when the revolution of 19 August occurred the whole question of privileges for the non-noble Estates was still unresolved.

But though Burghers and Peasants might be unable to agree among themselves, against the Estate of Nobility they remained solidly united. The matter of the Vice-Presidency of the Supreme Court at Åbo, the Nobility's resolution of 1762, bound them together for the final assault on noble privilege which would develop at the Diet of 1771–2.

(iv)

Such was the prospect that confronted Gustav III upon his accession: on the one hand the hope of reform by peaceful means defeated; on the other, a movement of social unrest which was growing stronger every day, and could be expected to be formidable when the Diet should meet. What hopes for royalism from such a situation?

At the time of Adolf Frederick's death Prince Gustav was in Paris. He had gone there, accompanied by C. F. Scheffer, to solicit French assistance in carrying through a revolution, and he had every reason to expect that from Choiseul such assistance would be forthcoming. But he had got no further on his journey than Brunswick when, on 5 January 1771, he was met with the shattering news that Choiseul had been dismissed from office on Christmas Eve; and it was only Scheffer's persuasions that induced him to go on. Personally and socially his stay in Paris was a brilliant success; and though he privately confessed that he found the *philosophes* more agreeable in print than in person, he undoubtedly dazzled, and was dazzled by, the literary *salons* which he frequented.[76] But it was only the news of his father's death that put him in a position to reap substantial benefits from his visit. That news touched

---

[75] Sten Carlsson, *Byråkrati och borgarstånd under frihetstiden, passim.*
[76] Beth Hennings, *Gustav III. En biografi* (Stockholm 1957), pp. 385–8.

the good-natured sensibility of Louis XV, who with spontaneous generosity provided him with the commodity without which no revolution could hope to succeed: 750 000 *livres* immediately, a promise of up to three million for the Diet, and not least an agreement to resume the payment of those arrears of subsidy which Choiseul had interrupted in 1766. But this open-handedness went hand in hand with a revision of French policy. Vergennes, who was to be the new ambassador to Stockholm, received instructions enjoining prudence: there must be no fomenting of a royalist *coup d'état*; he was to work for a reconciliation of parties; and a reversion to the pure word of the Constitution of 1720 was to be the limit of permissible constitutional change. The money was destined, it appeared, for parliamentary corruption, for the support of the Hats no less than of the Court – for precisely those objects which Choiseul in 1766 had declared to be inadmissible. Choiseul's remedy for the Swedish situation – a *coup d'état* – was explicitly ruled out.[77]

Gustav had really no option but to accept this revision of his plans; but there is in fact good reason to think that he accepted it willingly. He had not frequented the 'republican' *salons* without receiving an impression from the tone of political conversation there; and Mme d'Egmont, who had considerable influence on him, had adjured him 'Contentez-vous, Sire, d' être absolut par la seduction, ne le reclamez jamais comme un droit'.[78] For the moment his role must be that of 'the Patriot King'. And whatever may have been the case with George III, Gustav had certainly read his Bolingbroke. Whether he would be able to extirpate 'the Hydra Faction', and to rally round the throne a ministry of All Good Men (which C. F. Scheffer had propounded as long ago as 1764) remained to be seen. Certainly he was not unaware that it might be possible to put an end to party only by becoming a party leader himself. But the part of the Patriot King cost him no effort to assume, for it corresponded in fact with his profoundest convictions.[79] He saw himself as the man destined to save his country and restore it to its former glory; and his incorrigible propensity to self-dramatisation made it easy for him to identify himself with such patriot rebels against their lawful sovereigns as Paoli, or Engelbrekt, or – above all – Gustav Vasa. His patriotism was neither affected nor superficial: it was his response to what he felt to be his country's rottenness at home and degradation abroad; and it was given a sharper edge by fear: fear of the fate of Poland for his country, fear of the humiliations of Stanislaw Augustus for himself. The fear may have been exaggerated, or even altogether illusory; but it was a fact.

[77] Roberts, *British Diplomacy and Swedish Politics*, pp. 340–1.
[78] A. Geoffroy, *Gustave III et la Cour de France*, 1 (Paris 1867), p. 124.
[79] Gunnar Kjellin, 'Gustaf III, Den Patriotiske Konungen', in *Gottfried Carlsson, 18. 12. 1952* (Lund 1952).

Within a few days of his return to Stockholm Gustav proceeded along
the new line of action which had been determined on in Paris. His
initiative took the familiar form of a Composition, and the leaders of both
parties, for their own reasons, were cajoled into agreeing that the
constitution should be unaltered; that the new Accession Charter should
be a literal copy of that given by Adolf Frederick in 1751; that two Caps
should be admitted to the Council immediately, with others to follow
later; and that one-third of the places on the Diet's committees should be
reserved for whichever party should prove to be in the minority when the
Diet met.[80] As a damper on the rage of party, as the basis for a consensus
for national ends, the Composition was no small achievement. Gustav
followed it up by a direct appeal. On 25 June he addressed the assembled
Estates – the first Speech from the Throne that they had heard for over a
century – in words which have a familiar ring to an English ear, and which
awoke echoes in Sweden which were slow to die away:

Born and educated among you, I have from my earliest youth learned to love my
country . . . If by your resolutions the happiness, the independence and the honour of
this country be but hastened, stablished and consolidated, I have no more to ask. My
utmost wish is to rule over a happy people; the height of my ambition, to guide the
steps of a free nation . . . You have it in your power to be the most fortunate people in
the world.[81]

The appeal was already too late. After some days of uncertainty it
became clear that this was to be a Diet dominated by the Caps. They
carried their candidates for Speaker in the three lower Estates; they packed
the Diet's committees – and especially the Secret Committee – with their
partisans. This was a direct violation of the terms of the Composition.
But for the Composition the mass of the party cared less than nothing: it
was a pact between aristocrats; not a single non-noble had been a party to
it. The enemies of noble privilege, and of officialdom, were now in power
in three Estates, their social programme reinforced by party fanaticism,
and they had the bit between their teeth. Their aggressive temper was
immediately manifested. In their draft instruction to the Despatching
Committee the three lower Estates formalised the usurpations of power
of 1765–6 by the insertion of a provision that a decision of three Estates
(even if it infringed the privileges of a fourth) must not be blocked by it for
more than a limited time. To this the only reply which the Nobility could
make was not to give the Committee any instructions at all – which meant
that it could not function, since the instructions of all four Estates were
necessary before it could proceed to business. But this was no more than a
preliminary skirmish. The real struggle came over the terms of the

[80] [S. Piper], 'Pro Memoria 1771', fos. 67–70; Roberts, *British Diplomacy and Swedish Politics*,
pp. 349–50.
[81] *SRARP*, xxix, 25–6.

Accession Charter.[82] The makers of the Composition might have agreed that it should conform to that of 1751; but the three lower Estates had other views. The draft which the Secret Committee drew up embodied 'republican' intransigence, party vindictiveness, and a social programme. It bound the king to reign continuously – and thus made abdication or 'Inactivity' illegal; it prohibited civil service strikes for the future; it laid it down that the king was always to agree with the Estates of the Realm – and not, as hitherto, with *all* the Estates of the Realm, – with the consequence that he must concur with the decision of a majority, even if that should entail the infringement of the privileges of one of them; and it stated unambiguously that all appointments, even to the highest offices (including, presumably, the Council itself) must be made 'only' – and not, as hitherto, 'principally' – on grounds of merit and ability. Equality was now to be entrenched in the law.

For six months, from September 1771 to March 1772, the Diet's time was occupied by a bitter strife of Estates on this issue. The nobility, as was to be expected, took their stand upon Law: 'By our fundamental law', cried Axel von Fersen, 'privileges can never be removed or altered without the unanimous consent of all four Estates . . . As long as fundamental law remains fundamental law, and our blessed constitution continues to exist, no one can advance one step along that road without our consent'. Or as C. M. Sparrschöld put it: 'We shall stand like rocks immovable among the ocean's raging billows, as long as we take our stand upon the law.[83] As rhetoric, it was splendid; as argument, it cut no ice. The lower Estates retorted simply that equity was above the law.

In vain the signatories to the Composition, from both parties, appealed for moderation and sought an acceptable compromise. The Caps in the lower Estates defied the counsels of their Russian and English paymasters, and refused to budge; the Nobility was split from top to bottom between moderates and extremists, a split which obliterated party differences: that old Cap Josias Cederhielm cried 'When it is a matter of our preservation, why should party differences divide us? We are all in the same boat.'[84] The moderates in each party saw clearly that the strife of Estates, which was tearing the political nation apart, must offer opportunities to an ambitious monarch, and must at last disgust the nation; but the language that caught the votes was that of those like Liljehorn, who shouted that they would defend their rights to the death, 'sword in hand', and that one must *vincere aut mori*.[85]

By the end of November the deadlock seemed absolute: the lower Estates brusquely informed the Nobility that they would not discuss the

[82] The text as finally agreed is in Brusewitz, *Frihetstidens Grundlagar*, pp. 83–90.
[83] SRARP, xxx, 274, 411.
[84] SRARP, xxix, 351; cf. ibid., 425, 452–3.   [85] SRARP, xxix, 463, 650.

matter further; and Gustav III was faced with the possibility that he might be presented with an Accession Charter drafted by three Estates, and another version drafted by one. In this situation he made his last effort in the spirit of the Composition. Summoning the four Speakers to meet him, he asked them to convey to their Estates an offer of his mediation; and he added a significant warning: 'If I did not regard it as the greatest of honours to reign over a free and independent people, I should remain a tranquil spectator of the course of events, or would assure myself, in the future, of a more brilliant situation at the expense of your liberty.'[86] It was a warning thrown away. The three non-noble Speakers refused to transmit the message; the Nobility, after debates, resolved that it should not be communicated to them.

Thereby they lost the last chance of saving the constitution. For at the beginning of December French policy shifted again, and this time back to the policy of Choiseul. Gustav was now exhorted by d'Aiguillon, on the express command of Louis XV, to attempt a *'coup de force'*.[87] From 1 January 1772 French financial support for the Hat club was cut off, and for lack of it the club was forced to close its doors. The effect was not perhaps what d'Aiguillon had expected. Those members of the Nobility who were most clamorous in defence of their privileges – the violent, the young, the junior officers for whom the maintenance of their privileges was of especial importance – decided to start a new club which should finance itself without French support; and in sign of their claim to 'stand on their own bottom', took the name *Svenska Botten*. Within a fortnight the club had over 200 members; and behind the rank and file were men with plenty of ability and few scruples: F. C. Sinclair was one of them, Jacob Magnus Sprengtporten, who was destined to play a leading part in the preparations for revolution, was another. For this was emphatically a club of royalists. In *Svenska Botten* the cause of privilege was transformed into the cause of the king.

The signatories of the Composition saw the danger, and realised that they could not push resistance any further. Prudence, despair or concern for the preservation of the constitution in the face of the threat from the Crown carried the day. They surrendered; and in return for face-saving assurances they accepted the Charter which the lower Estates had drawn up. The ban on civil service strikes was deleted in return for an undertaking that it would be the subject of separate legislation; and a memorial was to be appended to the Charter, signed by all four Speakers, to the effect that nothing in it was to be interpreted as infringing the privileges of any Estate: a formula which was obviously valueless. In this form the Charter was at last pushed through the Estate of Nobility, with

---

[86] *Collection des écrits politiques et littéraires de Gustave III* (Stockholm 1803), I, 90.
[87] Roberts, *British Diplomacy and Swedish Politics*, pp. 371–3.

the solid support of the moderate leaders of both parties, on the express grounds that the situation was now so serious that the interests of a single Estate must not be allowed to stand in the way of reconciliation. The Nobility had lost hope. Time and again, in the two-day debate which preceded the Charter's acceptance, members alluded to 'the universal hatred' with which they were now regarded: a hatred most notably expressed in a publication entitled *Den ofrälse soldaten* (*The Common Soldier*) (1771), which was a devastating attack upon the arrogance and brutality of the officer-class.[88] In the face of it they confessed their helplessness. That indiscreet and fractious Cap, Fredrik Gyllensvan, summed up this feeling when he said:

It is true that if the Nobility had now the same influence upon the other Estates as formerly, when we were able to do good turns to our fellow-citizens – to provide a living for this man, commercial advantages for that, a farm and tillage for a third – then our Yea or Nay might still have some effect. But now, when every section of them is in possession of the country's wealth, they feel their strength, and we stand here powerless.[89]

The final blow, the final shattering of the Composition, came with the ruthless *licentiering* of seven Hat members of the Council, voted in the three lower Estates by large majorities in defiance of the pleading of the Russian minister. The Caps' foreign patrons could no longer control them. By the summer of 1772 it seemed only a question of time before the Peasants secured representation in the Secret Committee; Nordencrantz, with senile malignity, was demanding the reopening of the case against the managers of the Exchange Control Office and the Hat financiers; the Caps were preparing cuts in the army establishment; and they were proposing an extraordinary commission reminiscent of the worst days of Hat rule. Small wonder if moderate men saw anarchy ahead, if sections of the army were discontented, if Grills' Bank and other financial interests were willing to help to provide facilities to a king who would restore order. The years 1771–2 were years of real famine, and the disgraceful failure of the Diet to take any effective ameliorative measures – their time was fully occupied with the Charter and the *licentieringar* – deeply angered Gustav III, and made many men regard the Diet's fate with indifference. By 1772 Sweden seems to have been experiencing the same feeling of distrust of parliamentary institutions as had been manifested in England three years earlier. There was, indeed, no petitioning movement to match that in England, for petitions signed by more than one person were illegal except in certain cases; but if they had been permitted, the feeling to inspire them was probably there: a broadsheet which appeared in July, entitled *The Dominion of the Kingdom of Darkness*, charged the Diet in

[88] *Cf. SRARP*, xxix, 348–58.
[89] *SRARP*, xxx, 274.

inflammatory language with indifference to the sufferings of a starving people.[90] If the Estates had set themselves to provide a climate congenial to revolution, they could hardly have done better. It was now more than half a century since Sweden had undergone the experience of Charles XII and Görtz; it was almost a generation since the royalist plot of 1756. The old constitutional spectres had lost some of their ability to make men's flesh creep; Browallius and *En Ärlig Swensk* were falling out of fashion; old loyalties could revive. If an attempt at revolution should be made, the king would not this time lack for supporters. The question now was rather how many would be ready to die in defence of the constitution. And on 19 August 1772 came the answer: not one.

By June the plans for a revolution had been made, and Gustav, with the aid of C. F. Scheffer, was drafting the constitution which he would impose if it were successful. There was to be a rising in Finland: J. M. Sprengtporten, with the regiment of light dragoons under his command, was to seize the fortress of Sveaborg, sail over to Sweden, and in Stockholm carry out a *coup d' état*.[91] At the same time a subsidiary rising at Kristianstad, in the far south, was to distract and confuse the government. The plan miscarried: Sveaborg was indeed taken, but adverse winds delayed Sprengtporten's arrival in Stockholm for so long that he did not reach the capital until eleven days after the revolution had been completed. The rising in Kristianstad, on the other hand, took place with fatal punctuality. The news of it alerted the Caps to their situation, and the king was in imminent danger of arrest. He found himself in a position which had never been contemplated: he must make the revolution immediately, and he must make it alone. His closest friends and collaborators were away at their country houses; his only hope was in the officers of the Guards who were stationed in Stockholm, and in the willingness of their men to follow them. He addressed them in the orderly room in the courtyard of the Castle, told them of the danger which threatened himself, denounced the 'aristocratic' rule of the Estates, gave them a written assurance that he had no intention of making himself absolute, and invited them to renounce their allegiance to the Estates and take an oath of loyalty to himself. The gamble succeeded; and in less than an hour the revolution was over. What followed was in the nature of a triumphal procession, as Gustav rode through wildly cheering crowds to secure one key position after another. The Council was arrested as it sat in debate; the Secret Committee slunk away, unbidden and unlamented; the city was filled with a tumult of rejoicing. Pechlin and Rudbeck alone

[90] [Johan Gestrin], *Mörksens Rike och Wäldigheter, tecknad till Åminnelse af warande hunger och dyr tid* (Stockholm 1772).
[91] For an account of the revolution, see Roberts, *British Diplomacy and Swedish Politics*, pp. 397–401.

attempted to organize opposition; but they found no one to follow them. Not a blow was struck in defence of 'liberty': to all appearance there was no will to resist. And as the revolution had been bloodless, so in the sequel it proved marvellously clement: Pechlin was indeed put in prison, but once the new régime was established he was quickly released. The contrast with the savage vengeance of 1756 could not have been more pointed. And the revolution, there can be no doubt, was instantaneously and generally popular. To dismiss it as a military *coup d'état* and nothing more is to be misled by superficial appearances.[92] The troops involved were really only a handful of Guards officers and subalterns in Stockholm; the preliminary risings in Finland and Kristianstad proved irrelevant to the issue; and the actual amount of physical force available on 19 August would hardly have been able to carry through a revolution against even moderate opposition. It succeeded because the population of Stockholm – including, it seems, the Burgher cavalry – either wanted it to succeed, or had no great objection to its succeeding. It was not the show of military force that brought out the white armbands and the cheering crowds. From the arbitrariness and vices of parliamentary rule men were prepared to turn to what promised for a time to be enlightened constitutional monarchy. For, as Anders Nordencrantz once remarked, the excellence of a form of government is to be judged by its practical effects, 'and not by verbiage and popular clamour'[93] – nor by the monotonous incantations of its hierophants. The nature of the failure of 'Liberty', and its consequences, had been spelt out twenty years before by – of all people – that fanatical champion of the constitution, Bishop Browallius; who in his famous *Memorial on False and Erroneous Ideas* had written:

When once the legislative power in the nation has come to be considered as corrupted and aberrant, then it is in everything suspect, and in nothing relied on . . . when the legislative power has become unserviceable, and as it were is got into a blind alley, then the ruler must for his own preservation assume that power, as a *res derelicta*; and appropriate it, as being lost property and treasure-trove.[94]

Whether Gustav III had Browallius' prophetic dictum in mind on 19 August 1772 may perhaps be doubted; but if so, he was not slow to apply it, nor the nation behindhand in endorsing his action.

(v)

Thus one of the two revolutionary movements in 1772 ended in

[92] So Birger Sallnäs, 'Det ofrälse inslaget i 1772 års revolution', *Historisk tidskrift* (1954), pp. 129–45; and especially Gunnar Artéus, *Krigsmakt och samhälle i frihetstidens Sverige* (Stockholm 1982), pp. 351–60.
[93] Anders Nordencrantz, *Undersökning . . .*, p. 69.
[94] '. . . såsom ett fynd och hittegods': Malmström, *Sveriges politiska historia*, IV, p. 458.

unqualified triumph. And that triumph was celebrated in Paris, no less than in Stockholm. It was not merely that the revolution was seen everywhere as a French success which did something to offset France's humiliation in Poland, nor that it was in fact the severest diplomatic defeat suffered by Catherine the Great since the start of her reign. It was thought to have deeper implications of a moral nature. The same *philosophes* who had lavished superlatives on the Constitution of 1720 joined in a chorus of approval of that constitution's overthrow, and of praise for the monarch who had done the deed. Gustav III's revolution was welcomed not only as being necessary and salutary for Sweden, but as an example to all Europe, as a victory for Enlightenment, for progress, for humanity. If so, the strategy behind it was certainly not – not yet – that of Mercier de la Rivière.

The Constitution of 1772, which the Estates assembled in *plenum plenorum* accepted with acclamation, was visibly a constitution imposed: members could see outside in the courtyard canon with their muzzles trained upon the Hall of State, and Bishop Serenius, never at a loss for the appropriate acid comment, forthwith termed it a *jus canonicum*. Nevertheless, it embodied a real division of powers, it incorporated provisions which might suggest some acknowledgment of the desirability of balance, and it steered round awkward corners with some skill.[95] The king it proclaimed, 'governs; he and none other'; but by a pleasant inversion it also described him in precisely the terms which the Diet had been used to apply to itself – namely as 'vested with authority within the limits of the law'. The Council was once again to be the King's Council, responsible to him alone, and giving advice only when asked for it; but if on a question of foreign policy the Council should be unanimous in opposition to the king's opinion, the will of the Council was to prevail. The Diet was to meet only when the king saw fit to summon it. But on the other hand it retained some of its most important functions: it alone could vote new taxes; its consent was required to a declaration of war. And though the king was to have a veto on legislation proposed by the Estates, the Estates equally were to have a veto on legislation proposed by the king. As to the great question of the privileges of the nobility, that was deftly evaded, first by a general pledge to maintain all privileges, and secondly by a double-tongued formulation which left the situation discreetly ambiguous: 'ability and experience shall be the only criterion', it ran, 'without respect to favour or birth unless they are associated with ability'. And in 1786, by a similar Delphic pronouncement, Gustav III declared that the Constitution of 1772 had intended that the decision of a majority of Estates should be taken to be the decision of the Diet – except in regard to

[95] Text in *Sveriges regeringsformer 1634–1809 samt konungaförsäkringar 1611–1800*, ed. Emil Hildebrand (Stockholm 1891), pp. 119–43.

grants of money (thus conforming to the pre-1772 practice) and in regard
to privilege (thus deciding against the contention of the lower Estates in
1771–2).

The philosophers of the Enlightenment, it is to be supposed, did not
grasp the implications of these subtleties, nor did they care very much that
in the new constitution the old rule that office-holders should have
security of tenure unless convicted was reiterated. But they saw very
clearly the constitution's most positive aspects. All commissions, all
extraordinary tribunals, were henceforth to be forbidden, as leading to
'absolutism and tyranny'; no man was to be kept in arrest without fair
trial; the king's agents and fiscals were forbidden to insult and swindle his
subjects. Almost the first action of the king after the revolution was to
prohibit torture. The physiocrats would soon be gratified by the freeing
of the corn trade and a reduction in import duties, the removal of
restraints upon internal trade, the curbing of the gilds. The *philosophes*
saw with satisfaction the beginnings of religious toleration. The demand
for civil liberties was met by a vigorous attack upon oppression,
corruption and sloth in the administration. In February 1774 Gustav told
his Council that it was the want of security before the law, and the
existence of public and private oppressions, that had induced him to make
the revolution:[96] only a determined monarch, indifferent to party
considerations, and genuinely disposed to good government, could do
what the Diet had refused to do. The Constitution of 1772, and its
implementation in the early years of the reign, in fact carried out the most
important provisions of the *Act of Security* of 1769. The revolution meant
reform. If political liberty was abridged, civil liberty was the beneficiary.

For equality there was little or nothing. The Constitution's hazy and
self-contradictory provisions regarding appointments in fact registered
the defeat of the egalitarian movement which had convulsed Swedish
politics since 1770. The Peasants' ideal of a charter of liberties for the
whole nation, with all the consequences which they would have derived
from it, was consigned to oblivion; the draft privileges which the
Burghers had designed for themselves were now so much waste paper.
The social revolution had been smothered in its cradle: for the lower
Estates, it appeared, the world was to go on much as before. It was not
only political liberty that fell a victim on 19 August.

In reality, the event was much less grievous than might at first sight
appear. For the draft privileges of both Peasants and Burghers reveal them
as Orders, jealous of their rights, suspicious of encroachments upon those

---

[96] Clas Teodor Odhner, *Sveriges politiska historia under Konung Gustaf III:s regering* (Stockholm
1885), I, p. 320. It was appropriate that the minister who carried through some of these reforms
should have been none other than Joachim Wilhelm Liljeström – the man who had been
responsible for drafting the *Ordinance for the Better Execution of the Laws* in 1766.

rights by other Orders. The first two paragraphs of the Peasants' privileges might declare a noble aspiration to benefit the whole commonalty, but when it came to practical details this altruism was notably absent: all the rest of the document is concerned with the rights and claims of the Estate of Peasants, and with them only. Freedom to pursue one's own way of living turns out to be a limited freedom, and limited too is a man's right to 'improve his position by all permissible means'. It was not to mean (for instance) that 'persons of standing' might buy land in the mining areas, or that land occupied by Crown tenants should be freely available in the market to the highest bidder. There was to be no equal access to the commonages for squatters, or cottars, or other landless members of the rural community, whom respectable farmers regarded as 'a thorn in the flesh'.[97] The objection to the *Statute of Servants* was not only that farmers resented the stigmatising of their younger sons by an ugly name; it was a consequence of the perennial shortage of labour in the countryside, and their wish to keep more hands than the law allowed: it had been possible for labourers to blackmail farmers into paying what they considered to be outrageously high wages, and the Peasants had little sympathy with this particular example of a man's attempting 'to improve his circumstances . . . to the best of his ability'.[98] The draft of 1771 did not mean any of these things. But it was to mean, apparently, that peasants might infringe the long-established privileges of the Burghers, might maintain craftsmen in the villages in defiance of gild regulations, might peddle their goods or hold markets in the countryside to the prejudice of urban retailers.

As to the Burghers, they were as little interested in granting equality to the 'lower orders' as were the Peasants, and in defence of their economic interests they were unashamedly reactionary. They had declared their attitude already during the reforming Diet of 1765–6, when they had resisted the government's moves to add to the number of burghers, had successfully opposed attempts to relax the regulations for the craft-gilds, and had blocked a proposal to permit the free importation of grain.[99] The new economic theories circulating at the time seem to have passed them by. They stood firm in 1771 for the old protectionist arrangements: maintenance of the Navigation Act (*produktplakatet*), no new foreign trading companies, no new towns, no trade outside those already existing, a maintenance and stiffening of gild regulations and gild monopolies. To them, rural trading (*landsköp*) was anathema, as it had been for centuries, though all attempts to suppress it had failed: it was a

[97] Heckscher's phrase: Eli F. Heckscher, *Sveriges ekonomiska historia från Gustav Vasa*, II, 1. (Stockholm 1949), p. 244.
[98] *Ibid.*, pp. 274–82, for these rural antagonisms.
[99] Malmström, *Sveriges politiska historia*, v, p. 383ff.

convenience which the peasants could not do without. So too with the crafts: the Burghers' insistence that they be as far as possible confined to the towns, and to properly admitted members of the appropriate gilds, was unrealistic in the Swedish situation. They would have denied the most fundamental of the Peasants' demands: the right to make the best use of their land's potential, to make the best bargain for their produce and their labour, and to buy and sell at which market they would. At bottom, the objectives of the two Estates were irreconcilable. The Peasants sought – where it accorded with their interest – to liberate; the Burghers sought in great measure to restrict; and this was really why, despite a good deal of discussion and drafting, the whole question of privileges for the lower Estates was still unresolved on 19 August.

This clash of interests reveals the real nature of the demand of the lower Estates for privileges. Stripped of the rhetoric, their programmes were directed to obtaining privileges which would apply only to the Diet's constituents. 'Persons of standing', the new wealth, the unrepresented middle ranks of society, the 'lower orders' in town and countryside, the peasants of the nobility – with these the agitation for equality had little to do, except to strengthen the barriers against them. Here and there, no doubt, isolated voices pleaded for a change: Anders Nordencrantz, impressed by the stabilising effect of the weight of landed property in the English parliament, urged representation for all landowners in a unicameral assembly; Kepplerus advocated it within the existing Estate structure. In 1769 a radical newspaper, Folkets röst (The Voice of the People) went so far as to argue for universal male suffrage.[100] The Estates gave no heed to such notions. There seems, indeed, to have been little pressure for change from those most concerned – though it is a fair guess that the editor of Folkets röst was himself a 'person of quality', and though in 1771 the forge-owners showed some anxiety not to be left out in what seemed to be becoming a general scramble for privileges.[101] It was left to Gustav III, twenty years later, to toy with the idea of something like an English parliament.

In the sixties, so far from there being any disposition to expand the membership of the Estates, the tendency was rather the other way. It was not only the Nobility who wished to restrict their intake: all the other three Estates grew increasingly concerned to preserve the 'purity' of their membership. They took steps to debar any persons from sitting whose mental attitudes might have been corrupted by association – even at

---

[100] Michael Metcalf, 'Challenges to Economic Orthodoxy and Parliamentary Sovereignty in eighteenth-century Sweden', Legislative Studies Quarterly, VII, 2 (1982), p. 256: I have not myself seen a copy of Folkets röst.

[101] Bertil Boëthius and Åke Kromnow, Jernkontorets historia, II (Stockholm 1968), p. 70; and cf. L. M. Uggla's remarks in SRARP, xxx, 111.

second hand – with an Estate other than their own: bishops whose sons had been ennobled, burghers who had accepted a meaningless title (*karaktär*), shareholders in noble-controlled companies, peasants who had at any time held government jobs, or had been peasants of the nobility, or who kept an inn – all were to be kept out. The criteria for eligibility to vote were made if anything narrower rather than wider. It is true that the proportion of those excluded looks small compared – for instance – with the Natives in Geneva, or the 'virtually represented' in the British dominions; but still the temper of the Estates at the beginning of the seventies was markedly xenophobic. And just as the 'strife of Estates' made the men of *Svenska Botten* willing to sacrifice Swedish 'liberty' and rally to the Crown in the hope of safeguarding their privileges, so some of the lower Estates were tempted to play the same game. In April 1772 a group of them offered to restore to the Crown an authority so extensive as to leave the Estates nothing but the control of taxation and finance: all the executive power was to be in the king's hands, together with a veto on legislation; and in return they asked no more than royal support for their programme of social equality and a cash reward amounting to around £120 000, to be paid after this constitutional revolution should have been accomplished.[102] It was a remarkable foreshadowing of the bargain which Gustav III would make in 1789.

For all the Estates the existing parliamentary system represented an important vested interest. Membership of the Diet gave prestige, in some respects social status, and – not least – access to the apparently bottomless pockets of the ministers of Russia, France and England. This community of interest bound them all together; membership of the Diet was at least one privilege which was common to all. Gustav III, in his speech to the Estates two days after the *coup d'état*, described the régime he had overthrown as 'an intolerable aristocratic despotism in the hands of the ruling parties';[103] and though it is obvious that 'aristocracy' was a denigratory term indiscriminately employed by contemporaries to characterise social groups and policies of which they happened to disapprove, on this occasion we may think it legitimately employed. For the social struggle, the movement for equality, was at bottom no more than an internal quarrel within a ruling *élite*. No talk of civil rights for all could obscure the sharp conflict between those who had privileges (or were on the point of getting them) and those who had not: between, for instance, the landed peasants who voted in the elections and sat in the

---

[102] Stig Hallesvik, 'Partimotsättningar vid 1771–2 års riksdag som bakgrund till Gustav III:s statskupp', *Statsvetenskaplig tidskrift* (´962), pp. 395 ff.; and *cf.* RA. Stavsundsarkivet. Smärre enskilda arkiv. [S. Piper], 'Pro Merr ria 1771', fo. 70; and *Ur J. M. Sprengtportens papper*, ed. Henrik Schück (Stockholm 1904), ´ 19.

[103] *SRARP*, xxxi, 626–30.

Estate, and the growing landless proletariat.[104] If the revolution of 19 August had never happened, the real wielders of power – the *élites* of the Estates – would have emerged from the reforms they were demanding as narrow and as omnipotent as ever. The mass of the nation, who had not been drugged into insensibility by the corrupted vapours of parliamentary politics, seems to have had some inkling of the real state of affairs; and their weariness and disgust do much to explain the rejoicing with which they greeted the overthrow of the old order.

What now remained of the hopes, the principles, the ideals, of the Age of Liberty? Had half a century of striving and struggling gone for nothing? Did the age that had ended leave any sort of legacy to the ages that lay ahead? It does not take much consideration to return a positive answer to such questions. The Age of Liberty left behind it legacies political, social, intellectual and moral which had an enduring effect upon Sweden's later history.

This is immediately apparent if we look at the country's constitutional history. Since 1720 Sweden has always had a written constitution; and the Constitution of 1720 did not fail to leave significant imprints on those that succeeded it. Gustav III's constitution of 1772, for all its alteration in the balance of forces within the state, and its framer's hope of restoring something of the spirit of the constitution as it had been in Gustav Adolf's time,[105] was built upon the general pattern of its predecessor. The work of the founding fathers of the Age of Liberty was traceable in the Constitution of 1809 also.[106] The men of 1809, like the men of 1769, were concerned to secure a better balance between executive and legislature than had obtained in the Age of Liberty. With that end in view they gave to the king far more power than he had enjoyed in the time of Adolf Frederick; and though the preamble to the Constitution of 1809 annulled Gustav III's Constitution of 1772, and his *Act of Union and Security* (1789), they did not hesitate to borrow from both. But they firmly reiterated the fundamental principle that members of the Council of State were responsible and accountable for their advice; and the instrument which ensured that accountability was a Constitution Committee – directly descended, on the one hand, from the old Grand Secret Deputation, and on the other from the old Minutes Committee. The Constitution

[104] As Sten Carlsson (*Historisk tidskrift* (1984), p. 329) points out, the more middle-class younger Caps were less interested in the plight of the poor than such Hat aristocrats as Tessin and Augustin Ehrensvärd.

[105] On 26 August 1772 the Estate of Clergy described the new constitution as 'conformable with the form of government which existed until 1680 under his [*sc.* Gustav III's] glorious predecessors': Bexell, *Riksdags-historiska anteckningar*, I, p. 253.

[106] Text in Emil Hildebrand, *Sveriges regeringsformer 1634–1809 samt konungaförsäkringar 1611–1800* (Stockholm 1891), pp. 150–194.

Committee was bound to notify the Diet if Councillors' advice seemed to violate the Constitution, or did not accord with 'the true advantage of the realm' – a phrase which almost literally repeats one of the most dubious grounds for the *licentieringar* of former days. Recollection of some of the abuses of the Age of Liberty no doubt lay behind the omission to revive the old Secret Committee; but otherwise the system of committees of the Estates was retained, very much as it had been before 1772. The *Collegia* continued; the Bank remained the Estates' Bank. Taxation, as before, was strictly reserved to the Diet; and the Younger Caps' attempt to secure full publicity for the finances was now entrenched in the Constitution. The office and functions of the Chancellor of Justice (*justitiekansler*) were restored in conformity with the *Ordinance for the Better Execution of the Laws* (1766), though that official was now designated by the more appropriate title of *justitieombudsman*. Many of the most striking clauses of the Constitution of 1809, indeed, derive directly from those 'improvements' – or attempted improvements – for which the men of the Age of Liberty had been responsible: from 1766 comes the freedom of the press; from the *Ordinance for the Better Execution of the Laws* the provision that any alteration in the Constitution shall require the unanimous assent of king and Estates, and shall not be carried through by the same Diet at which it is first proposed. The guarantee of basic civil liberties, the prohibition of the traversing of judicial decisions by the Estates, and of their meddling in private litigation, are clear echoes of the proposals of the *Act of Security* of 1769, as is also the ban upon any interference by officials in elections – though that had been enunciated already in the *riksdagsordning* of 1723. The provision that appointments be made solely upon merit revives the terms of the Accession Charter of 1772. The guarantee of religious toleration, on the other hand, they owed to Gustav III; and it was from his Constitution of 1772 that they borrowed the provision that in ordinary legislation king and Estates should each have a veto upon the other. Thus the revolution of 1809 – in contrast to that of 1719–20 – was a revolution designedly conservative. The Age of Liberty had bequeathed to Sweden parliamentary procedures, parliamentary machinery, more sophisticated than were to be seen anywhere else in 1772; and the men of 1809 naturally adopted those which suited with their new Constitution, and with the existence of a four-Estate Diet: half a century of hard experience was too valuable to be thrown aside. If in 1809 the coming of a real democracy was still another century ahead, when it arrived it would inherit a course of basic training which had begun in 1720 and 1723.

The age bequeathed another legacy also, scarcely less important. This was the *Code of Law* of 1734. Swedish law had hitherto rested on Magnus Eriksson's *Land-Law* (ca. 1350), or on a revision of it from the following century. By the time of Charles IX much of it had become inapplicable, or only partly intelligible; moreover, the Reformation had had the effect of stripping the Church of much of that jurisdiction over moral offences which it had previously exercised, but had done nothing to fill the *lacuna* by other means. Charles IX's attempts to obtain the Diet's acceptance of a new code proving fruitless, no resource was left for coping with problems of this sort but a quasi-engraftment of the Mosaic law upon the *Land-Law*. The need for a new code was recognized to be urgent; but it was not until 1686 that a commission was set up under the direction of Charles XI's minister Erik Lindschöld to take the work in hand. It made slow progress, despite the exhortations of Charles XII; and it was not until the 1720s that the labours of a great jurist, Gustav Cronhielm, brought it more or less to completion: all that was now required was the approval of the Diet. In 1731, and again in 1734, the Estates gave it their attention, and they did not scamp their work. The *Code* was debated by the whole Diet, sentence by sentence, clause by clause; and the final version, though it made little change in Cronhielm's majestic draft, was clearly the Diet's responsibility: an example, worth remembering, that if the Estates seem to have squandered their time on trivial and personal matters, they could handsomely fulfil the obligation to take serious issues seriously. To this day the *Code of 1734* remains the basis of Swedish law.

The Age of Liberty had witnessed, or initiated, at least three great social changes. One was that increase in population for which the mercantilists had hoped: in 1720 Sweden–Finland may have had about 1 440 000 inhabitants; by 1760 the number had risen to 1 925 000. How far the growth was stimulated by the act permitting enclosures, how far it was the operating cause which called forth that act, is a matter of dispute; what is certain is the effects upon the rural population. The more rational arrangement of holdings, improved methods of agriculture, the reclaiming from the waste of land hitherto forest or bog, all contributed to the increase; and the belief of statesmen that Sweden could support a much larger population was proved – for the present – to be correct. It was accompanied by very significant changes in land-ownership. In 1697 31.5% of the land was in peasant hands; by 1772 the figure had risen to 46.9%; in 1815 it would be 52.6%. Most of this increase was at the expense of the Crown, whose share fell from 35.6% in 1700 to 14.5% in 1815. In 1772 the peasants had already begun to acquire land classified as 'noble': by 1803 their share of it would rise to 11%. At the same time there had been a large increase in the number of cottars, squatters, and landless labourers: between 1751 and 1815 their number more than doubled.[107] As the villages slowly disintegrated under the influence of enclosures, as

[107] Statistics from Eli F. Heckscher, *Sveriges ekonomiska historia från Gustav Vasa*, Stockholm 1949, II, I. 33, 137, 271, 273; and Sten Carlsson, *Ståndssamhälle och ståndspersoner* (2nd edn.), pp. 25–27, 55, 135ff.

more and more of the waste was taken into cultivation, the rural proletariat was moving towards the crisis which a century later would lead to the great emigrations; but in the meantime Skåne and Östergöt-land could take the place of the lost Baltic provinces as Sweden's granaries.

It was in the Age of Liberty that Sweden for the first time acquired a politically effective and socially conscious middle class. The Diet of 1765–6 had announced their arrival and their influence; in the two decades after 1772 they would surge irresistibly forward, eclipsing and transform-ing the *élitism* of the egalitarian movement of 1770–2. By 1772, over half of the higher civil servants were drawn from non-noble 'persons of standing': twenty years earlier the proportion had been just over a third. It was mostly into their hands that noble land was passing: in 1718 they had some 6.7% of it; by 1772 they had 16.36%. Gustav III, despite his nostalgic dream of appearing as 'the first nobleman of Sweden', was astute enough to appreciate what was happening, and to make political capital out of it. Already in the first months of his reign he had founded an Order – the Order of Vasa – which was the first Order of Chivalry in any country to be specifically reserved to commoners. By 1790, though 'persons of standing' might still be excluded from the Diet, that did not prevent their becoming the king's ministers or confidential servants. When in 1789, by the *Act of Union and Security*, Gustav III sacrificed the privileges of a nobility which had turned against him, he harnessed the strong current of social change to his political designs, and drove a bargain with the lower Estates which made him at last a sovereign in the style of Mercier de la Rivière. The two revolutions of 1772 – the successful and the defeated – were thus fused into one. But the *Act of Union and Security* – for which the nobility never forgave him – in fact did no more than give legislative endorsement to an existing situation; and that situation had been engendered in the Age of Liberty.

The change was reflected in literature. Before 1772 almost all the major authors except Bellman were either noble by birth, or had been ennobled, or (like Hedvig Charlotta Nordenflycht) were the offspring of noble parents: so G. F. Gyllenborg, Creutz, Dalin, Tessin, Linnaeus. In the course of nature some of these lived on into the Gustavian age, though Gyllenborg's inspiration faded, Creutz turned diplomat, and J. G. Oxenstierna provided Gustav III with the dubious consolation of having an Oxenstierna for his minister, as his grand exemplar Gustav Adolf had had in times gone by. But the great names of the Gustavian era – Kellgren, Thorild, Lidner, Anna Maria Lenngren, Leopold (though he was ennobled in the end) – were commoners: when Gustav III established the Swedish Academy in 1786, commoners provided six of the original Eighteen. Bellman, alas, was not one of them: though Gustav III presented him with a sinecure, it required the recantation of Kellgren to secure the recognition of his genius; and by then it was almost too late.

The process of European integration, which had already been operative in the seventeenth century, was vastly accelerated in the eighteenth; and in that process Sweden participated more positively than ever before. In the Age of Greatness Sweden's contacts with European cultural and intellectual trends had been on a limited, acquisitive, and on the whole on a personal, level: Queen Christina, Magnus Gabriel de la Gardie, Karl Gustaf Wrangel, enterprising generals who collected the plunder of Germany, much as Napoleon's marshals were to do later. The Rudbeckians, with their heroic fantasies about the Ancient Goths, Atlantis, and Swedish as the language in which God spoke to man, had no doubt involved themselves with antiquarians of similar tendencies in Denmark, Holland and Germany; curious foreigners had visited and described the more accessible parts of the country – and on one famous occasion Lappland also; Dutch and Flemish entrepreneurs had contributed by injections of capital and importation of technicians to lay the basis for Sweden's commanding position as the great supplier of copper and iron. But in the main, traffic with Europe, on all levels except the military, had been a one-way traffic, inwards: Sweden received impulses from Europe; only rarely did she give them. In the Age of Liberty the balance was to some extent redressed. No doubt the Swedish upper classes assimilated, more readily and more generally than ever before, European intellectual and cultural influences, European civility; but this time it was possible to speak of a measure of interplay between the periphery and the centre. This was most obvious in the world of learning. In that world Sweden had by 1772 established herself as a recognized participant on an equal footing with other lands. The foundation of the Academy of Science, and of the Academy of Literature, History and Antiquities, provided her with institutions which facilitated the making and maintenance of contacts, and the interchange of ideas, with similar academies abroad. Swedish scholars began to be elected to those academies: in the case of the Royal Society, for instance, men such as Erik Benzelius the Younger, Serenius, Linnaeus, Triewald, Klingenstierna, Solander, Torbern Bergman. In the sciences Pehr Wilhelm Wargentin (another FRS), secretary to the Academy of Science from 1749 to 1783, developed a tireless activity which kept that body in touch with research elsewhere. In certain fields, moreover, Sweden was now clearly in the lead: Linnaeus made Uppsala the botanical capital of Europe; Nils von Rosenstein may be said to have created modern paediatrics; Anders Celsius, after participating with Maupertuis in the famous expedition to the Arctic to measure a degree of the meridian, provided Europe with its first centigrade thermometer; Scheele in 1774 was one of those who independently of each other discovered oxygen; Wargentin's Office of Statistics provided Europe with its first reliable and differentiated census.[108]

So Sweden re-entered the Europe from which she had been evicted: no longer at the sword's point, but by ways more suited to her resources and to the temper of the age. And not Europe only; for if Sweden had the good luck to escape being a colonising power, her East India Company – 'by far the best regulated and prosperous in Europe'[109] – enriched her, not only with those imports of tea which when smuggled into Great Britain provided her with an export as lucrative as iron itself, but with her first experience of the art of the East – of whose impact Lovisa Ulrika's 'China' pavilion in the park of Drottningholm is the best-known example. And, not least, with a stupendous haul of scientific information. The disciples and friends of Linnaeus – Thunberg, Sparrman, Forsskål, Osbeck, Kalm – scoured the world for specimens to bring to their master, and left behind them accounts of their experiences which were celebrated in their own day, and have become classics in ours.

Lastly, there was a shift in national ideals and national myths which in the end became permanent. The enthusiasms of the Age of Greatness had been Gothic and glorious, expressed in Olof Rudbeck's *Atlantica*, on the one hand, and in Johan Adler Salvius's paean of triumph over Breitenfeld, on the other. In the eighteenth century pride in Sweden's victories was still vigorously alive – as the Hats exemplified to their cost; Rudbeckianism was not quite extinguished, despite the irony of Dalin; Lovisa Ulrika's Academy propounded, as subjects for prize poems, such topics as Charles X's crossing of the Belt, or Charles XII's crossing of the Düna, and even so unlikely a candidate as Hedvig Charlotta Nordenflycht, the portly and passionate 'Shepherdess of the North', was moved to compose an epic (unsuccessful) on the former of these heroic moments. Charles XII himself, though his absolutism was held in abhorrence, undoubtedly remained a national hero. But it was altogether significant that it was just the cynical, Voltairean Dalin who should have produced the only epic of the period which captured the imagination of the educated reader and won the applause of the critics; and that that epic should have taken as its subject *Swedish Liberty*. Before the eighteenth century the writing of an epic on such a theme would have been inconceivable in Sweden:[110] the most celebrated poem of the seventeenth century – Georg Stiernhielm's

---

[108] Sweden seems to have similarly been a pioneer in the field of industrial statistics: the Cloth-Hall Ordinance promulgated by the College of Commerce in 1739 ordered annual returns of the number of looms and the production of cloth.

[109] Opinion of the English East India Company, quoted in Kent, *War and Trade in Northern Seas*, p. 125 *n*. 2.

[110] Dalin's epic did not stand alone: the indefatigable Fru Nordenflycht, not to be outdone, responded with a *Frälste Swea* (*Svea Liberated*).

The Swedish Hercules – had been more concerned with moral than with political questions. No doubt the liberty which the Constitution of 1720 established was a negative liberty, a defensive measure against any attempt to resurrect an abhorred régime. No doubt either that as the century progressed Swedish liberty received strong reinforcing impulses from European thought, and from the American and French Revolutions. But those impulses were the more fruitful because they fell on a soil already prepared: they strengthened something which was already accepted, was already there, something which was taken for granted in a way which had no parallel elsewhere in 1720 except in Great Britain and the Dutch Republic: the principle of government by consent of the governed. 'Liberty' was in the minds and on the tongue of every active member of the political nation. For many it was no more than the common cant of the hour, or a convenient cover for sectional interests and privileges; but for many others it was a matter of passionate conviction, an indisputable truth; and for a few – as for instance for Chydenius – it went hand in hand with a social compassion which made it more than an economic or a political creed. Neither the revolution of 1772, nor the legal despotism of 1789, nor the reaction after 1793, availed to extinguish it. The ideal of government by consent which the Age of Liberty so firmly established provided a tradition, and gave a moral force to successive oppositions, until a true democracy was attained in the twentieth century.

Bibliography

Ahnlund, Nils. *Jonas Hallenberg.* Stockholm 1957.

Alexandersson, Erland. *Bondeståndet i riksdagen 1760–1772.* Lund 1975.

Almén, Folke. *Gustav III och hans rådgivare 1772–1779. Arbetssätt och meningsbrytningar i rådkammare och konseljer.* Uppsala 1940.

Amburger, Erich. *Russland und Schweden 1762–1772. Katharina II, die schwedische Verfassung und die Ruhe des Nordens.* Berlin 1934.

Anon. *Candid Thoughts on the Parallel (lately published) between the English Constitution, and the former Government of Sweden.* London 1773.

Anon. *Tankar om Alliancer, Och hwilka kunna vara för Sverige de förmånligaste.* Stockholm 1771.

Arckenholtz, J. W. *Om Sweriges nu warande intresse i anseende till andra riken och stater i Europa.* (1732). MS copy in Sjöholms samlingen, Riksarkivet, Stockholm.

Arnheim, Fritz. *Die Memoiren der Königin von Schweden, Ulrike Luise, Schwester Friedrichs des Grossen. Ein quellenkritischer Beitrag zur Geschichte Schwedens im XVIII. Jahrhundert.* Halle 1888.

'Beiträge zur Geschichte der nordischen Frage in der zweiten Hälfte des 18. Jahrhunderts', *Deutsche Zeitschrift für Geschichtswissenschaft,* II–V, VII. (1889–92).

Luise Ulrike, die schwedische Schwester Friedrichs des Grossen. Ungedruckte Briefe an Mitglieder des preussischen Königshause, II. Gotha 1910.

Artéus, Gunnar. *Krigsmakt och samhälle i frihetstidens Sverige.* Stockholm 1982.

Awebro, Kenneth. *Gustaf III:s räfst med ämbetsmännen 1772–1779: aktionerna mot landshövdingarna och Göta hovrätt.* Uppsala 1977.

Beckman, Bjarne. *Dalupproret 1743 och andra samtida rörelser inom allmogen och bondeståndet.* Göteborg 1943.

Behre, Göran. *Underrättelseväsen och diplomati. De diplomatiska förbindelserna mellan Sverige och Storbritannien 1743–1745.* Göteborg 1965.

'Ostindiska Kompaniet och hattarna. En storpolitisk episod 1742', *Historisk tidskrift* (1966).

Bergsten, Nils. *Bevillningsutskott vid frihetstidens riksdagar.* Uppsala 1906.

Bernstorff, Johan Hartvig Ernst. *Correspondance ministérielle du Comte J. H. E. Bernstorff.* Copenhagen 1882.

Bexell, S. P. ed. *Riksdags-historiska anteckningar eller bidrag till svenska kyrkans och riksdagarnes historia ur preste-ståndets archiv. Riksdagarne 1755–1778.* Christianstad 1839.

Blackstone, Sir William. *Commentaries on the Laws of England,* I. 9th edn, London 1783.

Boberg, Stig. *Gustav III och tryckfriheten 1774–1787.* Stockholm 1951.

Boëthius, Bertil. *Magistraten och borgerskapet i Stockholm 1719–1815.* Stockholm 1943.

'Swedish Iron and Steel, 1660–1955', *Scandinavian Economic History Review*, VI (1958).

and Kromnow, Åke: *Jernkontorets historia*, II. Stockholm 1968.

Bollerup, Erik. 'Om franska inflytelser på svensk historieskrivning under frihetstiden', *Scandia* (1968).

Bondeståndets riksdagsprotokoll, 10–12, ed. Sten Landahl (Stockholm 1973–78).

Bonde, Gustaf. *Historiska uplysningar om Tillståndet i Swerige under Konung Frederic den Förstes Regering* (Stockholm 1779).

Bonsdorff, Göran von. 'En finländsk insats i frihetstidens statsrättsliga diskussion. Kring Alexander Kepplerus' Memorial angående privilegier för de ofrälse stånden', *Svenska litteratursällskapet i Finland: Historiska och litteraturhistoriska studier*, 28–9 (Helsingfors 1952).

Borelius, Hilma. *Hedvig Charlotta Nordenflycht*. Uppsala 1921.

Borgarståndets riksdagsprotokoll, II, ed. Nils Staf. Uppsala 1951.

Brandt, Otto: *Caspar von Saldern und die nordeuropäische Politik im Zeitalter Katharinas II*. Erlangen-Kiel 1932.

'Das problem der "Ruhe des Nordens" im 18. Jahrhundert.', *Historische Zeitschrift* (1929).

Brolin, Per-Erik. *Hattar och mössor i Borgarståndet 1760–1766*. Uppsala 1953.

'Ståndsutjämning som historiskt problem', *Historisk tidskrift* (1951).

'Svenskt och engelskt sjuttonhundratal', *Historielärarnas föreningens tidskrift* (1971).

Brusewitz, Axel. 'Ett konstitutionsprojekt från frihetstiden med en kommentar från Gustaf III:s tid', *Statsvetenskaplig tidskrift* (1913).

ed., *Frihetstidens Grundlagar och konstitutionella stadgar*. Stockholm 1916.

Buchholz, Werner. *Staat und Ständegesellschaft in Schweden zur Zeit des Überganges vom Absolutismus zum Ständeparlamentarismus 1719–20*. Stockholm 1979.

Carlquist, Gunnar. *Carl Fredrik Scheffer och Sveriges politiska förbindelser med Danmark åren 1752–1765*. Lund 1920.

Carlsson, Gunnar. *Enköping under frihetstiden*. Uppsala 1977.

Carlsson, Ingemar. *Frihetstidens handskrivna politiska litteratur. En bibliografi*. Göteborg 1967.

Olof Dalin och den politiska propagandan inför 'lilla ofreden'. Sagan om hästen och Wår-Wisa i samtidspolitiska belysning. Lund 1966.

Parti – partiväsen – partipolitiker 1731–1743. Kring uppkomsten av våra första politiska partier. Stockholm 1981.

Carlsson, Sten. *Byråkrati och Borgarstånd under Frihetstiden* Stockholm 1963.

Grupper och gestalter. Studier om individ och kollektiv i nordisk och europeisk historia. Stockholm 1964.

Ståndssamhälle och ståndspersoner 1700–1865, Lund 1949, 2nd edn. 1973.

'Sverige under 1760-talet', in *Från fattigdom till överflöd*, ed. Steven Koblik. Stockholm 1973.

'"Många tappra drängar ha fått sitt banesår". Den svenska adelns personella förluster under stora nordiska kriget', in *Bland böcker och människor. Bok- och personhistoriska studier till Wilhelm Odelberg den 1 juli 1983*. Uddevalla 1983.

Carter, Alice C. *The Dutch Republic in Europe in the Seven Years War*. Coral Gables, Florida 1972.

Castrén, Gunnar. *Gustav Filip Creutz*. Stockholm/Borgå 1917.

Cederbom, L. A. *Jakob Serenius i opposition mot Hattpartiet 1738–1766*. Skara 1904.

Crusenstolpe, M. J. *Portfeuille*, I. Stockholm 1837.

Dahlgren, Stellan: 'Uppgörelsen med reduktionen efter enväldets fall'. *Historisk tidskrift* (1967).

Danielson, Hilding. *Sverige och Frankrike 1736-1739*. Lund 1956.

Danielsson, J. R. *Die nordische Frage in den Jahren 1746-51*. Helsingfors 1888.

Dannert, Leif. *Svensk försvarspolitik 1743-1757 i dess utrikespolitiska och inrikespolitiska sammanhang*. Uppsala 1943.

Dickinson, H. T. 'The Eighteenth-Century Debate on the Sovereignty of Parliament', *Transactions of the Royal Historical Society*, 5th Series, XXVI (1976).

Dyberg, Nils O. *Olof Dalin och tidsideerna*. Uppsala 1946.

Eagly, Robert V. 'Monetary Policy and Politics in Mid-Eighteenth Century Sweden', *Journal of Economic History* (1969).

Edler, P. J. *Om börd och befordran under frihetstiden*. Stockholm 1915.

Eek, Hilding. *Om tryckfriheten*. Uppsala 1942.

Ehrensten, Edvard Philipsson. *Oförgripliga Bewis emot Adelens Rättighet öfver Skatte-Gods*. Stockholm 1649.

Ehrensvärd, Gustaf Johan. *Dagboksanteckningar förda vid Gustaf III:s hof*, ed. E. V. Montan. Stockholm 1877.

Elmroth, Ingvar. *Nyrekryteringen till de högre ämbetena 1720-1809*. Lund 1962.

'Generationsväxlingens problematik i den svenska nyadeln under 1600- och 1700-talen', *Scandia* (1979).

Enblom, W. *Privilegiestriderna vid frihetstidens början 1718-1723. Ett bidrag till ståndsutjämningens historia*. Uppsala 1925.

Engeström, Johan von. *Historiska Anteckningar och Bref från åren 1771-1805*, ed. E. V. Montan. Stockholm 1877.

Erdmann, Nils: *Carl Michael Bellman. En kultur- och karaktärsbild från 1700-talet*. Stockholm 1899.

Ericsson, Birgitta. 'Central Power and the Local right to Dispose Over the Forest Common in Eighteenth-Century Sweden', *Scandinavian Journal of History* (1980).

Faggott. Isak. *Swea Rikes Styrelse efter Grundlagarne*. Stockholm 1768.

Fahlbeck, Erik. 'Studier öfver frihetstidens politiska ideer', I-II, *Statsvetenskaplig tidskrift* (1915, 1916).

Fahlbeck, Pontus. 'Engelsk och svensk parlamentarism', *Statsvetenskaplig tidskrift* (1904).

Fehrman, Carl. *Vin och flickor och Fredmans stråk*. Stockholm 1977.

Ferrner, Bengt. *Resa i Europa, 1758-1762*, ed. Sten G. Lindberg. Stockholm 1956.

Fersen, Fredrik Axel von. *Riksrådet och fältmarskalken Fredrik Axel von Fersens historiska skrifter*, ed. R. M. Klinckowström. Stockholm 1867-72.

Frietzcky, Claes. *Reflexioner till Riksdagen 1771*. Uppsala Universitets bibliotek, UUB 378.

Fällström, Anne-Marie. Review of Björn Ryman, *Erik Benzelius d.y.*, *Historisk tidskrift* (1979)

Geoffroy, A. *Gustave III et la Cour de France*, I. Paris 1867.

[Gestrin, Johan]. *Mörksens Rike och Wäldigheter, tecknad till Åminnelse af warande hunger och dyrtid*. Stockholm 1772.

Gill, Conrad. 'The Affair of Porto Novo: an Incident in Anglo-Swedish Relations', *English Historical Review* (1958).

Gjörwell, Carl Gustav. *En Stockholmskrönika ur C. G. Gjörwells brev*, ed., Otto Sylwan. Stockholm 1920.

Gough, J. W. *Fundamental Law in English Constitutional History*, 2nd edn. Oxford 1961.

Gustafsson, Bo. 'Hur fysiokratiskt var den svenska fysiokratismen?', *Scandia* (1976).

Gustav III. *Gustav III:s och Lovisa Ulrikas brevvexling*, I-II, ed. Henrik Schück. Stockholm 1919.

Konung Gustaf III:s efterlemnade och femtio år efter hans bortgång öppnade papper, ed. E.
    G. Geijer, I–III. Uppsala 1943.
Collection des écrits politiques et littéraires du roi Gustave III, I. Stockholm 1803.
Gyllenborg, Gustaf Fredrik. *Mitt lefverne 1731–1775. Själfbiografiska anteckningar*, ed.
    Gudmund Frunck. Stockholm 1885.
Hagberg, Lars. *Jacob Serenius' kyrkliga insats*. Lund 1952.
Hallesvik, Stig. 'Partimotsättningar vid 1771–2 års riksdag som bakgrund till Gustav
    III:s statskupp', *Statsvetenskaplig tidskrift* (1962).
Hamilton, Adam Ludvig. *Anekdoter till svenska historien under Gustaf III:s regering*.
    Stockholm 1901.
Heckscher, Eli F. *Sveriges ekonomiska historia från Gustav Vasa*, II, 1–2. Stockholm
    1949.
Helander, Abel. *Daniel Niklas von Höpken 1669–1727*. Stockholm 1927.
Helsingius, Daniel. *En Chinesisk Philosophs egna Tankar om Engelska Friheten*.
    Stockholm 1771.
Hennings, Beth. *Gustav III som kronprins*. Stockholm 1935.
Gustav III. En biografi. Stockholm 1957.
Fyra gustavianska studier. Stockholm 1967.
Herlitz, Lars, 'Härtappad fysiokratism', *Scandia* (1976).
Hessler, Carl Arvid. *Stat och religion i upplysningstidens Sverge*. Uppsala 1956.
Hildebrand, Emil. *Svenska statsförfattningens historiska utveckling, från äldsta tid till våra
    dagar*. Stockholm 1896.
    ed., *Sveriges regeringsformer 1634–1809 samt konunga-försäkringar 1611–1800*. Stock-
    holm 1891.
Hildebrand, Karl-Gustaf. 'Foreign Markets for Swedish Iron in the 18th Century'.
    Scandinavian Economic History Review VI (1958).
Hjärne, Erland. *Från Vasatiden till Frihetstiden*. Stockholm/Uppsala 1929.
'Ämbetsmannaintressen och politiska doktriner på 1719 års riksdag', *Historisk
    tidskrift* (1916).
Holmberg, Nils. 'Oderhandeln. Preussen och svenska Pommern vid mitten av
    1700-talet. Ett historiskt perspektiv', *Scandia* (1941).
Holmdahl, Otto S. *Studier öfver prästeståndets kyrkopolitik under den tidigare frihetstiden*,
    I. Lund 1912.
Holst, Walfrid. *Carl Gustaf Tessin*. Stockholm 1936.
Fredrik I. Stockholm 1953.
Högberg, Staffan. *Utrikeshandel och sjöfart på 1700-talet. Stapelvaror i svensk export och
    import 1738–1808*. Stockholm 1969.
Höjer, Torgny. 'Christopher Springer och principalatsfrågan vid 1742–43 års
    riksdag', *Studier och handlingar rörande Stockholms historia*, I, Uppsala 1938.
Höjer, Torvald T:sson. 'Frihetstiden i 1800-talets historieskrivning', *Historisk tidskrift*
    (1940).
Ingers, E. *Bonden i svensk historia*, II. Stockholm 1948.
Jacobson, Sigbrit Plaenge. *1766 års allmänna fiskestadga. Dess uppkomst och innebörd med
    hänsyn till Bottenhavsfiskets rättsfrågor*. Uppsala 1978.
Johansson, K. H. *Svensk sockensjälvstyrelse 1686–1862*. Lund 1937.
Johansson, Ulla. 'Hattar och mössor i borgarståndet 1755–1756', *Historisk tidskrift*
    (1973).
Jägerskiöld, Olof. *Hovet och författningsfrågan 1760–1766*. Uppsala 1943.
Lovisa Ulrika. Stockholm 1945.
1721–1792 (vol. II:2 of *Den svenska utrikespolitikens historia*, ed. Nils Ahnlund et al.).
    Stockholm 1956–9.

'C. F. Scheffer och 1750-talets författningskris', *Historisk tidskrift* (1939).

Kent, H. S. K. *War and Trade in Northern Seas. Anglo-Scandinavian Economic Relations in the Mid-Eighteenth Century.* Cambridge 1973.

Kjellin, Gunnar. *Rikshistoriografen Anders Schönberg. Studier i riksdagarnas och de politiska tänkesättens historia.* Lund 1952.

'Gustaf III, Den Patriotiske Konungen', in *Gottfried Carlsson, 18. 12. 1952.* Lund 1952.

'Kring Alexander Kepplerus' memorial', *Historisk tidskrift* (1955).

Kock, Wolfram. *Olof af Acrel.* Stockholm 1967.

Konopczyński, Ladislas. 'Polen och Sverige i det adertonde århundradet', *Historisk tidskrift* (1925).

Krusius-Ahrenberg, Lolo. *Tyrannmördaren C. F. Ehrensvärd. Samhällssyn och politiskt testament.* Stockholm 1947.

LagerBring, Sven. *Sammandrag af Swea-Rikes Historia,* v. Stockholm 1779.

Lagerroth, Fredrik. *Frihetstidens författning. En studie i den svenska konstitutionalismens historia.* Stockholm 1915.

Konung och adel. Ett bidrag till Sveriges författnings-historia under Gustav III. Stockholm 1917.

'Revolution eller rättskontinuitet?', *Scandia* (1936).

'En frihetstidens lärobok i gällande svensk statsrätt', *Statsvetenskaplig tidskrift* (1937).

'Det svenska statsrådets ansvarighet i rättshistorisk belysning', *Scandia* (1939).

'Det frihetstida statsskickets utvecklingsmöjligheter', *Scandia* (1966).

'Svensk konstitutionalism i komparativ belysning', *Historisk tidskrift* (1966).

'Positivrätt eller naturrätt? Ett statsrättsligt dilemma från svenska 1700-talet', *Scandia* (1967).

'Det rättsliga utgångsläget för de stora författningsförändringarna i Sveriges historia', *Scandia* (1970).

and Nilsson, J. E., Olsson, Ragnar. *Frihetstidens maktägande ständer,* I–II in *Sveriges riksdag,* I Series, vols. v–vi. Stockholm 1934.

Landberg, Georg. *Den svenska riksdagen under den gustavianska tiden,* in *Sveriges riksdag,* I Series, vol. vii, Stockholm 1932.

'En svensk författningshistoria från krisåret 1768. Bidrag till den gustavianska rojalismens idéhistoria', *Statsvetenskaplig tidskrift* (1937).

Leijonhufvud, Sigrid. *Ur svenska herrgårdsarkiv. Bilder från karolinska tiden och frihetstiden.* Stockholm 1902.

Carl Gustaf Tessin och hans Åkerökrets, I–II. Stockholm 1931, 1933.

Levertin, Oscar. 'En aristokratisk tidningsskrivare och hans familj', in *Svenska gestalter,* new edn., Stockholm 1958.

Liedgren, Jan. 'Ridderskapet och adeln vid riksdagarna 1719 och 1765–6. (Studier över den svenska riksdagens sociala sammansättning)'. *Skrifter utgivna av statsvetenskapliga föreningen i Uppsala,* vii. Uppsala 1938.

Lindblom, Andreas. *Svensk konsthistoria,* ii. Stockholm 1944.

Lindeberg, Hj. *En ränksmidare. Strödda blad ur 1700-talets partistrider.* Stockholm 1928.

Linnaeus, Carl. *Skånska resan år 1749.* new edn, Stockholm 1977.

Linnarsson, Lennart. *Riksrådens licentiering. En studie i frihetstidens parlamentarism.* Uppsala 1943.

Lolme, J. L. de. *A Parallel between the English Constitution and the Former Government of Sweden.* London 1772.

The Constitution of England. 4th edn, London 1784.

Lundquist, Carl Lennart. *Council, King and Estates in Sweden 1713–1714.* Stockholm 1975.

Malmström, Carl Gustaf. *Sveriges politiska historia från Karl XII:s död till statshvälfning-en 1772*, I–VI, 2nd edn, Stockholm 1893.
Smärre skrifter rörande sjuttonundratalets historia. Stockholm 1889.
Metcalf, Michael F. *Russia, England and Swedish Party Politics 1762–1766. The Interplay between Great Power Diplomacy and Domestic Politics during Sweden's Age of Liberty.* Stockholm and Totowa, N.J. 1977.
Russia, England and the Younger Caps on the Eve of the Riksdag of 1765–6 (Univ. of Stockholm M.A. thesis, 1972).
'The first "Modern" Party System?', *Scandinavian Journal of History* (1977).
'Structuring Party Politics: Party Organization in Eighteenth-Century Sweden', *Parliaments Estates and Representation*, I (1981).
'Challenges to Economic Orthodoxy and Parliamentary Sovereignty in Eighteenth-Century Sweden', *Legislative Studies Quarterly*, VIII, 2 (1982).
'Unmitigated Evil, Necessary Evil in Free States, or Constructive Force? Swedish Attitudes towards Party, 1755–1772', *Consortium on Revolutionary Europe: Proceedings 1982* (Athens, Georgia, 1983).
Munch, Thomas. *The Peasantry and the Early Absolute Monarchy in Denmark.* Copenhagen 1979.
Nilzén, Göran. *Studier i 1730-talets partiväsen.* TS Stockholm 1971.
Norborg, Lars-Arne. 'Universitetet som indoktrineringsinstrument. Statsmakt och studium politicum under Nils Palmstiernas kanslerstid', in *Historia och samhälle. Studier tillägnade Jerker Rosén.* Malmö 1975.
Nordencrantz, Anders. *Anmärkning wid åtskilliga utkomna Skrifter, angående Rätte-gångens förminskning och förkortande.* Stockholm 1756.
Undersökning om de rätta orsakerna til den Blandning som skedt af Lagstiftande, Redofordrande och Redoskyldige Magternas Gjöromål . . . Tillika med Förslaget om en Säkerhets-Act, såsom hjelp deremot, hwilket wid 1769 års Riksdag förorsakade så stor misshällighet emellan Riksens höglöflige Ständer. Stockholm 1770.
Nordmann, Claude. *Grandeur et liberté de la Suède (1660–1792).* Paris 1971.
Norrman, Carl-E. *Enhetskyrka och upplysningsideer. Studier i svensk religionspolitik vid 1700-talets mitt.* Lund 1963.
Nyström, Per. *Stadsindustriens arbetare före 1800-talet.* Stockholm 1955.
Odhner, Clas Teodor. *Minne af Riksrådet m.m. Grefve Ulrik Scheffer.* Stockholm, n.d.
Sveriges politiska historia under Konung Gustaf III:s regering, I. Stockholm 1885.
Olai, Birgitta. *Storskiftet i Ekebyborna. Svensk jordbruksutveckling avspeglad i en östgötasocken.* Uppsala 1983.
Olsson, Gunnar. *Hattar och mössor. Studier över partiväsendet i Sverige 1751–1762.* Göteborg 1963.
'Krisuppgörelsen mellan hattpartiet och Carl Fredrik Pechlin 1760', *Scandia* (1959).
'Fredrik den Store och Sveriges författning', *Scandia* (1961).
Olsson, Ragnar. *Riksdagsmannavalen till bondeståndet under den senare delen av frihetstiden.* Lund 1948.
Oxenstierna, Johan Gabriel. *Dagboks-Anteckningar af Johan Gabriel Oxenstierna åren 1769–1771*, ed. Gustaf Stjernström, Uppsala 1881.
Ljuva ungdomstid. Dagbok 1766–1768. Uppsala 1965.
Palme, Sven Ulric. 'Byråkratien som historiskt problem', *Scandia* (1948–9).
'Befolkningsutvecklingen som bakgrund till partiomvälvningen 1738. Ett social-historiskt försök, *Scandia* (1960).
På Karl Staafs tid. Stockholm 1964.
'Vom Absolutismus zum Parlamentarismus in Schweden', in *Ständische Vertrte-ungen in Europa im 17. und 18. Jahrhundert*, ed. Dietrich Gerhardt. Göttingen 1969.

Schematiska framställningar av några riksdagsärendes gång vid frihetstidens
    riksdagar [unpubl. collective work by members of Palme's *seminarium*]
Petander, Karl. *De nationalekonomiska åskådningarna i Sverige sådana de framträda i
    litteraturen.* Stockholm 1912.
Peterson, Bo. '"Yppighets Nytta och Torftighets Fägnad". Pamflettdebatten om
    1766 års överflödsordning', *Historisk tidskrift* (1984).
Petersson, Anne-Marie. 'Nyköping under 1700-talet', in *Nyköpings stads historia*, ed.
    Stellan Dahlgren, 2. Nyköping 1973.
[Piper, S.]. 'Pro Memoria, 1771'. (Riksarkivet, Stockholm. Stavsundsarkivet.
    Smärre enskilda arkiv).
Planting, Birger. *Baroner och patroner. Porträtt ur Sveriges jordbruks-historia. 1700-talet.*
    Stockholm 1944.
Pleijel, Hilding. *Hustavlans värld.* Stockholm 1970.
Prästeståndets riksdagsprotokoll, ed. Axel Norborg, 6. Stockholm 1982.
Recueil des instructions données aux Ambassadeurs de France: Suède. Paris 1885. *Danemark.*
    Paris 1895.
Remgård, Arne. *Carl Gustaf Tessin och 1746–7 års riksdag.* Lund 1968.
Reuterholm, Axel. *Ur Axel Reuterholms dagbok. Några kulturbilder från frihetstiden.* ed.
    Henrik Schück. Stockholm 1921.
[Reuterholm, Esbjörn Christian]. *Uplysning för Swenska Folket om Anledningen,
    Orsaken och Afsigterne med Urtima Riksdagen 1769.* Stockholm 1769.
Roberts, Michael: *Essays in Swedish History.* London 1967.
    British Diplomacy and Swedish Politics, 1758–1773. Minnesota/London 1980/1981.
Rosenhane, Schering. *Samtaal emellan Juncker Pään, Mäster Hans, Niels Andersson
    Borghare och Joen i Bergha Danneman.* Stockholm 1650.
Rudelius, Karl-Olof. 'Författningsfrågan i de förenade deputationerna 1769',
    Statsvetenskaplig tidskrift (1935).
Rydberg, Sven. *Svenska studieresorna till England under Frihetstiden.* Stockholm 1951.
Ryman, Björn. *Eric Benzelius d.y.. En frihetstida politiker.* Motala 1978.
Rystad, Göran. 'Till frågan om tjänster och löner inom kansliet under frihetstiden',
    Historisk tidskrift (1966).
    'The King, the Nobility, and the Growth of Bureaucracy in 17th Century Sweden',
    in *Europe and Scandinavia. Aspects of the Process of Integration in the 17th Century'*, ed.
    Göran Rystad. Lund 1983.
Sallnäs, Birger. *Samuel Åkerhielm d.y. En statsmannabiografi.* Lund 1947.
    'En kraftmätning mellan konung och råd 1723. Ett bidrag till Fredrik I:s
    karakteristik'. *Historisk tidskrift* (1950).
    'Det ofrälse inslaget i 1772 års revolution', *Historisk tidskrift* (1954).
    'England i den svenska författningsdiskussionen 1771–2', *Vetenskaps-Societeten i
    Lund. Årsbok 1958–9.*
Sahlberg, Gardar. *Mer makt åt kungen!* Stockholm 1976.
Samuelsson, Kurt. *De stora köpmanhusen i Stockholm 1730–1815.* Stockholm 1951.
    Från stormakt till välfärdsstat. Stockholm 1969.
[Scheffer, Carl Fredrik]. 'Egenhändig uppsats af Riksrådet Grefve C. Fr. Scheffer,
    angående tillståndet i Riket, näst före början af 1765 och 1766 års riksdag',
    Handlingar rörande Skandinaviens historia, XVI. Stockholm 1831.
Schaumann, Georg. 'Biografiska Anteckningar om Anders Chydenius'. *Skrifter
    utgifna af Svenska Litteratursällskapet i Finland*, 34. Helsingfors 1908.
Schück, Henrik, and Warburg, Karl. *Illustrerad svensk litteraturhistoria*, II. Stockholm
    1897.

Schönberg, Anders. *Anders Schönbergs bref till Bergsrådet Adlerwald*, ed. Sam Kellin. Stockholm 1920.
'Om förbund, mellan stater', *Gjörwells Statsjournal*, II. Stockholm 1768.
Sheridan, Charles F. *A History of the Late Revolution in Sweden*. London, 2nd edn, 1783.
Smedberg, Staffan. *Frälsebonderörelser i Halland och Skåne 1772–1776*. Uppsala 1972.
Sprengtporten, Jacob Magnus. *Ur J. M. Sprengtportens papper*, ed. Henrik Schück. Stockholm 1904.
Stadin, Kekke. *Småstäder, småborgare och stora samhällsförändringar. Borgarnas sociala struktur i Arboga, Enköping och Västervik*. Uppsala 1979.
Stavenow, Ludvig. *Om riksrådsvalen under Frihetstiden*. Uppsala 1890.
Frihetstiden. Dess epoker och kulturlif. Göteborg 1907.
'De politiska doktrinernas uppkomst och första utveckling under frihetstiden', in *Festskrift tillägnade Carl Gustaf Malmström*. Stockholm 1897.
'Det adertonde århundradets parlamentarism i Sverige', *Uppsala Universitets Årsskrift*, 1923.
Steckzén, Birger. 'Adolf Fredrik under kronprinstiden', *Historisk tidskrift* (1934).
Stridsberg, Olle. 'Hattarnas och mössornas ställningstaganden till tryckfrihetsfrågan på riksdagarna 1760–2 och 1765–66', *Historisk tidskrift* (1953).
Sundberg, Gunnar. *Partipolitik och regionala intressen 1755–1766. Studier kring det bottniska handelstvångets hävande*. Uppsala 1978.
'Lantpartiet vid riksdagen 1760–2', *Historisk tidskrift* (1971).
'Merkantilismens två åsikten', *Historisk tidskrift* (1980)
Suolahti, Gunnar. *Sprengtportens statskupp och andra essayer*. Stockholm/Helsingfors 1919.
Svenska Flottans Historia. Örlogsflottan i ord och bild från dess grundläggning under Gustav Vasa fram till våra dagar, ed. Otto Lybeck, II. Malmö 1942.
Sveriges riddarhus. Ridderskap och Adeln och dess Riddarhus, ed. Carl Hallendorf. Stockholm 1926.
Sveriges ridderskaps och adels riksdagsprotokoll, ed. Sten Landahl, XIV, XIX, XXIII–XXXI. Stockholm 1955–71.
Söderberg, Tom. *Den namnlösa medelklassen. Socialgrupp två i det gamla svenska samhället*. Stockholm 1956.
Tengberg, Niklas. *Frihetstiden. Några anmärkningar*. Stockholm 1867.
Om kejsarinnan Catharina II:s åsyftade stora nordiska alliance. Lund 1863.
Tersmeden, Carl. *Amiral Carl Gustaf Tersmedens Memoarer*, ed. Nils Erdmann, V. Stockholm 1918.
Tessin, Carl Gustaf. *Carl Gustaf Tessins Dagbok 1748–1752*. Stockholm 1915.
Tessin och Tessiniana, ed. F. W. Ehrenheim. Stockholm 1819.
Thanner, Lennart. *Revolutionen i Sverige efter Karl XII:s död*. Uppsala 1953.
'Frågan om ämbetstillsättningarna i belysning av Ehrencronas anteckningar 1720', *Historisk tidskrift* (1956).
Thomas, P. G. H. *The House of Commons in the Eighteenth Century*. Oxford 1971.
Tilas, Daniel. *Anteckningar och brev från riksdagen 1765–1766*, ed. Olof Jägerskiöld. Stockholm 1974.
Anteckningar och brev från riksdagen 1769–1770, ed. Olof Jägerskiöld. Stockholm 1977.
Curriculum vitae 1712–1757, I–II. (Historiska handlingar 38:1). Stockholm 1966.
Trulsson, Lars. *Ulrik Scheffer som hattpolitiker. Studier i hattregimens politiska och diplomatiska historia*, Lund 1947.

Tønnesson, Kåre. 'Tenancy, Freehold and Enclosure in Scandinavia from the Seventeenth to the Nineteenth Century', *Scandinavian Journal of History*, VI (1981).

Valentin, Hugo. *Frihetstidens riddarhus. Några bidrag till dess karakteristik.* Stockholm 1915.

'Det sociala momentet i historieskrivningen om 1772 års statsvälvning', *Scandia* (1941).

[Virgin, Arvid]. *En patriots tanker om grundlagens nödvändiga förbättring.* Stockholm 1769.

Wallenberg, Jacob. *Min son på galejan.* new edn., Stockholm 1928.

Weibull, Martin. *Lunds Universitets historia*, I. Lund 1918.

Wensheim, Göran. *Studier kring freden i Nystad.* Lund 1973.

Werner, Anders. *Studier till frågan om europeiska idéer i svensk politik under den senare frihetstiden.* (Licentiatavhandling, Stockholm 1969).

Åström, Sven-Erik. 'Studentefrekvensen vid de svenska universiteten under 1700-talet', *Historisk tidskrift* (1949).

Öberg, Anders. *De yngre mössorna och deras utländska bundsförvanter 1765–1769. Med särskild hänsyn till de kommersiella och politiska förbindelserna med Storbritannien, Danmark och Preussen.* Uppsala 1970.

Index

Entries are arranged according to the Swedish alphabet,
in which the last three letters are Å, Ä, Ö.

Printed in the United Kingdom by
Lightning Source UK Ltd., Milton Keynes
137951UK00001B/75/A